Business Boutique

A WOMAN'S GUIDE
FOR MAKING MONEY
DOING WHAT SHE LOVES

The one who calls you is faithful, and he will do it.
1 Thessalonians 5:24

Business Boutique

A WOMAN'S GUIDE
FOR MAKING MONEY
DOING WHAT SHE LOVES

CHRISTY WRIGHT

RAMSEY
P R E S S

Published by Ramsey Press, The Lampo Group, LLC
Brentwood, Tennessee 37027

This publication is designed to provide accurate and authoritative information with regard to the subject matter covered. It is sold with the understanding that the publisher is not engaged in rendering financial, accounting, or other professional advice. If financial advice or other expert assistance is required, the services of a competent professional should be sought.

Unless otherwise noted, all Scripture quotations are from the Holy Bible, New International Version®, NIV®, Copyright © 1973, 1978, 1984, 2011 by Biblica, Inc.™ Used by permission of Zondervan. All rights reserved worldwide. Scripture quotations marked ESV are taken from the ESV® Bible (The Holy Bible, English Standard Version®). Copyright © 2001 by Crossway, a publishing ministry of Good News Publishers. Used by permission. All rights reserved. Scripture quotations marked KJV are taken from the King James Version of the Bible. Scripture quotations taken from MSG are taken from The Message. Copyright © by Eugene H. Peterson 1993, 1994, 1995, 1996, 2000, 2001, 2002. Used by permission of Tyndale House Publishers, Inc.

Editors: Becky Nesbitt, Allen Harris, Natalie Hanemann, Jen Gingerich
Creative Direction and Cover Design: Luke LeFevre, Tim Newton, Brad Dennison, Chris Carrico, and Micah Kandros
Interior Design: Mandi Cofer

ISBN: 978-1-9421-2103-9

Printed in the United States of America
17 18 19 20 21 LSC 5 4 3 2 1

dedication

For my mom, Darlene.

I am who I am because of you. Thank you for fighting for me and for giving me a life full of love and laughter, of passion and adventure. Your legacy shines in all that I do and throughout the pages of this book. Your heart will go on.

acknowledgements

Pouring my heart onto these pages has been one of the most exciting and rewarding things I've ever gotten to work on in my life. The reason it's been so incredible is because of an amazing team behind the scenes that helped me every step of the way and made it all possible. I could never thank every single person that touched, inspired, and impacted this book, but I'd like to say a special thanks to:

Dave Ramsey, for believing in me and giving me so many unbelievable opportunities, including this one of writing my own book. You are generous with your wisdom, your encouragement, and your platform. Thank you for letting me live my dream every single day.

Brian Williams and Jeremy Breland, for leading me so well. You champion me in everything that I do and push me to be better. You've always been in my corner, and you make everything we do so much fun. I couldn't ask for better leaders. You really are the dream team!

Becky Nesbitt, my editor, for helping me cram hundreds of ideas, years of research, and thousands of stories into this manuscript to give women a clear plan for growing their businesses. Your patience is unending and your encouragement is what got me through it all.

Allen Harris, Preston Cannon, and Jen Gingerich, for leading the entire editorial and publishing process from start to finish. You all trusted me with the content and challenged me to make it better. You believed in me and let me try something completely new. But most of all, you showed me how much I love writing, and that's a gift I'll forever be grateful for.

Rick Prall, for your incredible developmental, organizational, and editorial support. I'll never know how you kept everything straight, but I'm so thankful you did!

Luke LeFevre and Tim Newton, for overseeing all design elements and cover art. Let's roll up our sleeves and "go to work"!

Tim Smith, for leading the research that this book and the entire Business Boutique brand is built on. This message is a home run because of your hard work in those early days.

Meg Grunke and Elizabeth Cole, my publicists and friends, for helping me get this important message out to the world. You are both incredible at what you do!

Dawn Medley and Katie Kinderknecht, for managing my schedule and keeping me sane!

Suzanne Simms, Jen Sievertsen, Andy Barton, Cory Mabry, Alena Good, Robert Bruce, George Kamel, Naomi Parton, and many others, for your countless hours of hard work, continual kind words of encouragement, and much-needed prayers!

And last, and most importantly, my family. Carter and Conley, of anything I've ever achieved in my lifetime, nothing makes me more proud than simply getting to be your mom. And to my amazing husband, Matt, thank you for your endless support and sacrifice that made this book possible. Through all of the late nights, early mornings, and nights away on the road, you not only took care of our boys and held down the fort at home, but you also never stopped encouraging me. Thank you for supporting me in my dream and loving me so well. I love you so very much.

contents

Acknowledgments   vii

Foreword   xiii

Introduction: You Are Not Alone   xvi

CHAPTER 1

It All Starts with a Story: Finding Your Motivation   I

Chapter 1 Action Items   9

CHAPTER 2

Fear Is Normal: Overcoming Doubt and Eliminating Excuses   II

Chapter 2 Action Items   26

CHAPTER 3

A Plan to Win: Building a Business to Last   29

Chapter 3 Action Items   41

Contents

Tier 1: Build Your Foundation   43

CHAPTER 4

Why Matters: Why You Do It Affects How You Do It   45

Chapter 4 Action Items   53

CHAPTER 5

Permission to Dream: Creating a Vision for Where You Want to Go   54

Chapter 5 Action Items   65

CHAPTER 6

From Dreaming to Doing: Setting Goals that Get You There   66

Chapter 6 Action Items   78

Tier 2: Make It Yours   81

CHAPTER 7

Play to Your Strengths: Building Your Business Around Your Life   83

Chapter 7 Action Items   96

CHAPTER 8

The Love-Hate Relationship with Money:
Your Guilt-Free Guide for Making More and Stressing Less   98

Chapter 8 Action Items   108

CHAPTER 9

Make the Most of Your Resources:
Planning Your Money, Time, Schedule, and Space   110

Chapter 9 Action Items   125

Tier 3: Up and Running   129

CHAPTER 10
The Follow-Through: Figuring Out the Operational Side of Things   131

Chapter 10 Action Items   149

CHAPTER 11
Best Business Practices: Running Your Business Like a Pro   151

Chapter 11 Action Items   164

CHAPTER 12
How to Make Money at This:
Understanding Profits, Pricing, and Paying Yourself   167

Chapter 12 Action Items   183

CHAPTER 13
The Business Side of Things: Breaking through the Boring Stuff   185

Chapter 13 Action Items   196

Tier 4: Put Yourself Out There   199

CHAPTER 14
Marketing Your Business:
Four Things You Need to Know to Make an Impact   201

Chapter 14 Action Items   217

CHAPTER 15
The Story You're Telling: Reaching the Right People the Right Way   221

Chapter 15 Action Items   237

CHAPTER 16

Making the Sale: How to Promote Your Business Without Being Pushy 239

Chapter 16 Action Items 253

What's Next? Chasing Your Version of Success 257

CHAPTER 17

Take It to the Next Level:
Growing, Scaling, and Expanding Your Business 259

Chapter 17 Action Items 277

CHAPTER 18

The Balancing Act: How to Build Your Business and Still Have a Life 279

Chapter 18 Action Items 296

CHAPTER 19

You've Got This! 298

Notes 303

foreword

DAVE RAMSEY

My mom got into the real estate business in Middle Tennessee in the late 1960s. At that time and in that area, women weren't *supposed* to be in real estate. Residential real estate was sold by men, and those men wore suits. But Mom didn't care. She loved the industry, she was passionate about real estate, and she had huge professional goals that knocked down just about any obstacle that got in her way.

People laughed at her, yelled at her, and talked bad about her. They told her she couldn't do it. They said she'd never succeed. They wondered why she left her two kids at home while she showed houses to strangers. They called the house and said nasty things to whoever answered the phone. They said she should just give up. People did everything they could to steal her dream—but she wouldn't let them. Instead, she proved them all wrong. Within a few years, my mother became one of the most successful residential real estate professionals in the state. She was amazing, and the good ol' boys around her just couldn't keep up!

If you've picked up this book, then you may be standing where my mom stood fifty years ago. Maybe you're wrestling with a dream that just won't let you go. Maybe you've dipped your toe into running your own business, and now you're ready to dive in headfirst. Maybe you're looking for a way to balance family obligations and professional goals. Maybe you've got the passion and the dream, but you're struggling to come up with a plan to make it all work. And maybe, like my mom, everyone around you is telling you to give up. Trust me, I've been there. *Every* business owner has stood where you're standing right now.

I know what it takes to build a business from scratch. Our company, Ramsey Solutions, has grown into a national brand that employs almost six hundred people, but it all started on a card table in my living room. I was the teacher, speaker, and writer. I was also the one making all the sales, doing the taxes, dealing with vendors, setting the prices, creating the marketing, and setting up the folding chairs for our events. I was the CEO—Chief Everything Officer—and that came with all the responsibility plus all the fear, insecurity, jubilation, and crazy thrill of owning my own business.

And, over the years, in nearly every area our company has moved into, we've been met with opposition. We've heard from "experts" who told us we'd never make it. We've had consultants, critics, and competition write us off. But I learned how to handle that by watching my mom. She refused to give up, no matter how hard things got. She took all the negativity in stride and turned everyone else's doubts into energy that moved her forward.

Sometimes, though, that's easier said than done. The truth is, building a business is hard. Doing it alone is harder. But guess what? You're *not* alone. You've got help. I am so excited to introduce you to the person who will likely do more for your business than you can imagine—Christy Wright.

When Christy started on our team in an entry-level position, it didn't take long for everyone in our organization and at every level of leadership to recognize her drive and her smarts. She quickly rose through the ranks and became one of our most popular, most trusted public personalities. She's taken the stage in front of sold-out arenas, sharing the spotlight with some of the country's best speakers. She's become a regular on many national news shows. Hey, I even let her host my radio show when I'm not there!

As I've watched her grow as an author, speaker, and teacher, I've also watched her passion grow for women in business. I've seen her neck-deep in research for months at a time, and I've spent hours talking with her as she unpacked everything she was hearing from hundreds of interviews with different business owners. I don't think I've ever seen someone attack a field of study with so much enthusiasm and energy.

But, as you'll learn by reading this book, you'll see that's how Christy approaches everything in life.

I believe in small business, and we are just now beginning to see the potential impact of women all across the country starting and running their own businesses. The economic engine that this represents is so much larger than anyone understands. Many women start out just like I did, busting their tails to get everything done and desperate for a plan to take their businesses to the next level. If that's you, I've got great news. Christy Wright has that plan.

As you get ready to take the next step in your business, I want you to hear something loud and clear: You can do this. You've got this! And Christy will lead the charge. I've seen her walk others through this process with an arm around their shoulder. I can make this promise to you: she has your back. As you read through these pages, you'll be encouraged, motivated, challenged, taught, and ultimately set loose to live out your destiny. That's what Christy does, and that's what *Business Boutique* is all about.

introduction

YOU ARE NOT ALONE

I have always loved horses. It started when I was in elementary school and would visit my dad. He had several horses in the pasture behind his house, and and I got to ride them whenever I was there. I remember one time my dad picked me up from school in the middle of the day and rushed me to his house because one of the horses was giving birth. As a six-year-old, it was an incredible experience to watch that baby foal stumble around with gangly legs as he took his first steps. My dad even let me name him, and he became my first horse, Bo. I loved watching Bo grow up and, even when Bo was trail-broken and safe to ride, he had something wild about him that I loved. Being around horses as a child gave me an appreciation for nature and creation, for life and adventure.

My aunt deepened my love of horses. I remember thinking she was the coolest person I'd ever known. She drove a big white SUV and had a giant Rottweiler companion dog, Tucker, that went everywhere with her. And of course, she lived on a farm and had horses. She was beautiful and independent and adventurous and everything I wanted to be. Even then, I remember thinking that I wanted to create a life like hers when I grew up.

And, about two decades later, I did just that.

When I was in my early twenties, I lived in a house with two other roommates.

I was constantly trying to keep the rooms filled as girls got married or took other jobs and moved away, and I was looking to downsize and have less responsibility and less rent. I was never home anyway since I worked eighty hours a week at my full-time job, so I started scanning the classified ads for a new place to rent—something I could live in by myself that would help me simplify my life a bit.

One day, I spotted something in the paper that I wasn't expecting. Something that struck a nerve with those memories of my aunt's farm: an ad for a forty-acre farm for rent. In that moment, I didn't think; I just jumped.

I'd always thought I wouldn't be able to have a farm until much later in life, when I could afford land. It never occurred to me that I could rent a farm and fulfill my dream at such a young age.

Looking back, it wasn't a practical decision. I wanted to downsize with *less* responsibility and *less* rent, remember? But the rent on this farm was three times the amount I was currently paying and about a thousand times more work. But sometimes life's greatest adventures aren't practical.

I wasn't focused on the rent or the fact that I'd never lived on a farm before. Instead, I focused on my dream.

When I visited the farm, I saw that it had an eleven-stall barn on the property, and that's when I knew I would be fine. I was going to use that barn to start a side business. I would pay for my rent by boarding horses. Problem solved.

During the time I lived there, I owned and cared for a menagerie of interesting and ridiculous animals including horses; a miniature donkey, Hank; a miniature mule, Jack; and two fainting goats, Willie and Waylon; not to mention a hodgepodge of other characters that would show up, like barn cats, deer, and the occasional snake.

My side business, Fields of Grace Farm, was my childhood dream fulfilled, and with it came some of the funniest—and fondest—memories of my life.

It all started because I had always loved horses.

It's incredible to see how, decades later and worlds away from my first memories of horses and my own experience with farm life, I am helping other women all over the country do the exact same thing.

They might not be starting horse-boarding businesses, but millions of women all over the world are starting side businesses, home businesses, hobby businesses, and small businesses all because of something they had always loved.

Leading up to my first *Business Boutique* event and writing this book, I immersed myself in research. I spent years interviewing, surveying, and studying women with businesses. One of the first questions I asked each of them was, "How did you get the idea to start this particular business?" And almost every single one of them answered, "I had always loved . . ."

"I had always loved sewing."
"I had always loved baking."
"I had always loved design."
"I had always loved piano."
"I had always loved gardening."
"I had always loved math and numbers."
"I had always loved kids."
"I had always loved building."
"I had always loved . . ."

This response came time and time again. Just like my story on the farm, every part of why women were doing what they were doing pointed back to that thing that they had always loved. That's when I realized what they were doing wasn't just about business. It was personal. Their business was about making money, sure. But more importantly, in many cases, their business was about doing what they loved. And I found it more than just a coincidence or trend. Entrepreneur.com reports that there are more than thirty million Americans working as freelancers or independent workers.[1] Researchers anticipate that number to grow by forty million in the next three years.[2]

There is a growing movement of women stepping into their God-given gifts to find work that matters and make money doing what they love. Between the ever-increasing popularity of sites like Etsy and Pinterest, more and more women are running a part-time business in addition to their full-time responsibilities. It may be a small hobby they occasionally charge for, or it may be something that develops into a full-time company with team members.

The fact that you're reading this book means you already are one of these women, or you're at least thinking about becoming one. I've got great news for you: there has never been a better time to do it. Between the endless free social media marketing platforms and the countless online tools, resources, and solutions, entering the marketplace is easier than ever. You don't need to pay $10,000 to have a professional programmer build a website from scratch, and you don't need to pay for advertising. You don't need to maintain a huge inventory of goods, and you definitely don't need a brick-and-mortar store. You can launch your business tomorrow with nothing more than an idea and a Facebook page.

And the best part is, you are not alone. Millions of women are on the same journey as you—the exciting, sometimes terrifying, wild and crazy ride of putting yourself and your heart on the line in business. But the truth is, most of us don't start a side business because we love business. We love our craft or skill or idea— the business part is just a way to share our passion with others and make an income in the process.

But the business side of things can be overwhelming, frustrating, and exhausting. Often the business part can even distract us from our passions and drain our energy and efforts. I say "us" because I've been there too. I've had two different side businesses in my career (in addition to my full-time job). I know the struggles firsthand.

I've got stories for days of the mistakes I've made and the lessons I've learned the hard way on my journey to doing what I love. It's exciting to dream up possibilities when you have an idea and are just getting started. I know how frustrating it is when you hit a wall and you have more questions than answers and you just want to give up. I know because I've experienced all of that and much more. That's why I want to help you.

It can be overwhelming. I get overwhelmed sometimes myself. Trust me, I am overwhelmed writing this book, and I am just one thousand words into a ninety-thousand-word goal! Putting yourself out there feels vulnerable and risky, but anything worth doing usually does.

You and I are in this together, and, just like with my farm, I didn't let the minor details (such as having no idea what I was doing!) get me down. Instead, I focused on my dream—and I want you to do the same. If you can do that, I'll help you with everything else. This book isn't just based on my own experiences of starting, running, and growing different businesses; it's also based on my years of research and coaching women who've done it. You'll hear their stories and a lot of my own throughout this book, and I bet you'll see yourself in many of them. My goal in writing this book is to make sure you have everything you need to grow your business to the level that you want. This book is written *for you.*

I don't believe your talents are an afterthought or that your desires are an accident. One of the guiding principles of my life comes from the Bible verse, "'For I know the plans I have for you,' declares the LORD, 'plans to prosper you and not to harm you, plans to give you hope and a future.'"[3] I believe God has a plan for the dreams he's given me—he has a plan for the dreams he's given you! He *wants* this plan to happen. That's why I'm writing this book. My faith is part of *my* story, but you may be coming at this from a totally different perspective. That's fine too! This book is still for you if you want to learn how to start, run, and grow your business. I will share a plan that is proven with principles that work—if you're willing to do the work. *Business Boutique* has just what you need.

Throughout each chapter, I'll help you develop your own step-by-step plan specific to whatever stage you're in with your business. This isn't a corporate business textbook or a boring manual. This is a handbook that will take the ideas in your head and the dream in your heart and put them into practice. It doesn't matter if you've never taken a business class, and it doesn't matter if you're starting out with a blank computer screen in your living room. This plan will give you everything you need to start, run, and grow your business to the level you want. I've included action items at the end of every chapter so you can apply what you've learned and start working on your business plan right away. If you would like to print a complete set of the action items, you can find a free, downloadable pdf at www.businessboutique.com. *Do not skip this step!* This is your opportunity to create a customized plan for *your* business. And I'll give you specific, easy-to-understand and easy-to-implement answers to all of the common questions about the technical side of running a business, such as taxes, insurance, and legal issues.

We're also going to talk about money—a lot! We'll go over how to make it, how to keep it, and how to stop feeling bad about that in the process. We'll also tackle the sometimes uncomfortable subject of selling. I know you don't want to be pushy. I don't either. The great news is that selling doesn't mean having to be pushy. We'll set you up with some practical tips so you can talk about your product with confidence, without feeling slimy.

We're going to talk about how to market your business so you stand out among all the Facebook rants and cat pictures in your followers' newsfeeds. We'll tackle the unending struggle of time management and how to control your schedule instead of it controlling you. You'll learn how to face your fears so they don't hold you back from chasing the dream that got you excited in the first place. Starting something new feels risky and uncomfortable, but remember, the people who win in business and in life do it in spite of this.

I am so excited for you. I am excited about everything you'll learn and the brave new things you'll try. I'm excited about the confidence you'll gain, the new skills you'll develop, and the new levels of success you'll see. But most of all, I am excited about the energy that will be injected into your life and your business because you decided to take this step.

Let's get to it!

chapter 1

IT ALL STARTS WITH A STORY
Finding Your Motivation

I don't know how she did it, really. Looking back, I can't imagine it. My mom didn't expect her life to turn out that way, of course—I don't think anyone does. She looked up one day at the age of thirty-four with a six-month-old baby to support, and she felt scared, alone, and desperate. I was oblivious to what was happening in my family during those days. I'm glad I can't remember the heartache between my parents that led to their split. My mom and my dad are both wonderful, but things just didn't work out like they hoped they would.

So when my mom found herself with just sixty-four dollars to her name and a brand-new baby, she went into survival mode. That's when it occurred to her. My mom's first job, at sixteen years old, was in a little bakery called Ozment's Bakery. There she learned how to bake and decorate cakes. So, on a cold and windy day in February of 1984 in downtown Nashville, she went back to something she had always known, something she had always loved: making cakes.

At the corner of 6th Avenue and Church Street was a candy store called Candyland. My mom noticed that they had a front showcase window that wasn't being used. She had an idea and took a leap of faith. She walked into the store and asked to speak with the owner. When he came out, she presented her business idea to him. She would rent his unused showcase window for 10 percent of all of her profits in exchange for the space to make cakes. It would be eye-catching for people walking by to watch her decorate in an area that was otherwise bare and it would draw people into his store. She convinced him—and in the process, herself—that it would work.

She used all of her sixty-four dollars to buy supplies, and on her business's opening day, she earned back exactly sixty-four dollars. She used all of that day's earnings to buy just enough supplies for the next day's cakes. It wasn't long before Candyland had a line wrapped around the block, but the customers weren't in line for candy; they were in line for my mom's cakes.

And that was the very beginning. Thirty-three years, seven moves, tons of employees, thousands of customers, and hundreds of thousands of cakes later, my mom is still in business. She works on a smaller scale now. She is semiretired and she makes cakes "just for fun and to keep my skills sharp," she says. Trust me, those skills are as sharp as ever.

Making It Work

My mom's first cake shop is the backdrop for my entire childhood. I have countless memories there. I remember when she would have to bake at two or three in the morning. She would pull me out of bed in my pajamas, wrap me in several of those bright, 1980s-style comforters with huge geometric shapes and weird colors, and carry me to the car. She'd strap me in my seat belt and drive me downtown to the shop while I slept in the back seat. When we got there, she'd make a bed for me on the pallets of powdered sugar and flour sacks. They were huge fifty-pound bags, and she'd pile blankets on them and let me keep sleeping while she worked, until it was time for me to get up for school. I would go to class with the smell of flour in my fine, white-blonde hair.

When I got a little older, she'd let me stay up late and "work" with her while we listened to the oldies blaring on the radio. My contribution usually involved organizing all of the bright and colorful icing tubes in rainbow order. I insisted that they stay that way until the next day when all of her employees came in and the orders began piling up. I was always discouraged and confused when, the next night, the tubes were again out of order.

When I was in middle school, I learned how to open the cash drawer. I didn't know a thing about working a register other than pushing the button marked NS (No Sale) opened the drawer. I would often grab some dollar bills and head next door to Subway to get a cookie and then go down the street to the arcade. No wonder the cash never balanced out at the end of the day and Mom's bookkeeper hated me!

When I was in high school, I made deliveries to downtown businesses and, as a bonus, I got to keep the tips. It makes sense why so many of the memories I cherish—moments that helped shape me—in some way involve that cake shop. But more than that, they all involved my mother.

My mom is a fighter and a survivor, a mover and a shaker. She is optimistic to a fault, persistent to no end, and has a heart that is good to the core. She is creative, resourceful, and always full of life. And now as a grown woman myself, as a mom and wife and leader, I would like to believe I have developed every one of those qualities as a result of her. Her story of struggle is my own story of struggle, but her story of victory is my own victory as well. My mom made a business and life doing what she loved. That's why this message is so important to me. And it's why I want to help equip other women to do the same.

YOUR VERSION OF SUCCESS

My story is why this matters so much to me. Seeing my mom step into her gifts and make things happen is what pushes me and challenges me and inspires me to do the same all these years later. I want to see women set free to pursue what they love and unapologetically make money doing it. I want to see women confident and happy and satisfied with the life they've created instead of just tolerating some version of life they felt pressured into or settled for. I want to see women moving and shaking up the business world by stepping into their God-given gifts to bring something amazing only they can offer. I want women to give themselves permission to take time for their skills and hobbies and interests and themselves. Ultimately, I want to see women become successful in the way Maya Angelou defines it: "Success is liking yourself, liking what you do, and liking how you do it."[4]

That's what I want you to achieve in your business. I'm not interested in pushing you to become a powerhouse entrepreneur who takes the world by storm, ends up on the cover of *Forbes* magazine, and makes millions of dollars. If you want to do that, I fully support it. But if your version of success looks more like my friend Amy, who just wants to be able to quit her full-time job and stay home with her kids, I support that too. Or if you're like my friend Hannah who just wants to be able to contribute to the family income and pay for soccer camp this summer, I am behind you on that. Or if you are like one of my clients, Nikki, who wants to ditch corporate America so she can call the shots and be her own boss while using her degree and skills in finance, I am by your side to help you do that. Your vision of success may be different than these. I want you to know, whatever your reason, it's valid and worthy and important.

A Variety of Whys

In my years of coaching women in business, I have heard some amazing, inspiring, and insightful stories of how different women got started. And when I asked women why they wanted to do their particular business, their answers were as varied as the businesses they represented.

When Your Passion Is Your Why

Tina is a travel planner for Disney. She is one of those people who loves—and I mean loves—Disney. You know people like that, don't you? It's like a club. They know all of the latest news and events, go there for every vacation, and talk about it nonstop. That's how Tina is. My memories of visiting Disney when I was ten are fantastic, but I will likely not step foot back there until I take my own children. But Tina's love of Disney is not for her family or kids. She loves it for herself.

When Tina talked about her side business of planning Disney vacations for clients, her energy shot through the phone line and I couldn't help but smile. Her enthusiasm about her business was contagious. When I asked Tina why she decided to do this particular business, I'll never forget what she said. "Oh that's easy," she answered. "I *love* Disney—really, really love it. So all day I get to talk about this thing that I love."

What an awesome story of a woman who not only knows what she loves, but also found a way to make money doing it. And *that* very thing is what I love.

When Your Story Is Your Why

I also remember meeting Angela in Phoenix during one of my coaching session meet-ups. She has an Etsy store that sells handmade jewelry for people to give as gifts. Now, I know what you're thinking. A bazillion people sell handmade jewelry on Etsy! What's the big deal? Angela's *why* is THE BIG DEAL.

When Angela was a little girl, her mom regularly gave her gifts of jewelry. They weren't fancy or expensive, but it isn't just the specific pieces of jewelry that Angela remembers. It is the significance of them.

Each time her mother would give Angela a new piece of jewelry, her mother would tell Angela that the piece of jewelry symbolized a certain quality. As we talked, Angela recalled one time when her mother said, "This bracelet represents your beauty. You are beautiful, Angela, and I want you to always remember that. Even when a boy is mean to you or a girl talks about you behind your back, look at this bracelet and remember that you are beautiful." Angela went on to recount example after example of the jewelry her mother had given her along with the significance attached to each piece. As Angela told me the story behind her why, I had to fight back tears and resist the temptation to log onto Etsy and buy something for someone in my life. That is the power of knowing your *why*.

What's your *why*? What's the reason you got started? It can be as touching and inspiring as Angela's story about her mother's gifts of jewelry, but it certainly doesn't have to be. It can also be as practical as "paying for gymnastics this fall." There is no wrong answer to the question. It's just important that you have one.

Maybe you've never thought about why you're doing this. That's okay. We'll talk about it more when we start digging into your business plan. For now, I want you to start thinking about your story and how you got the idea for your business in the first place. Start thinking about why this matters to you.

PRESSING ON AND PUSHING THROUGH

Even today, when my mom has a stressful day and vents to me about being bogged down with orders, sometimes I can't help but ask, "Mom, why do you still do it? You don't have to."

As soon as the question hits the air, Mom instantly switches gears, defending her passion. "Because it matters, Christy. It matters if I get up in the morning. It matters to the families who have gotten their cakes from me for over thirty years. It matters to that bride who will never forget her wedding day and all of the details that made it perfect—including the cake I made. I'm not just making cakes. I'm a part of some of the most special, important, and remembered moments in someone's life. That's why I still do it." Mom is in her midsixties now, but she still knows why she does it.

Your Why *Gets You Through the Hard Days*

Business can be tough. You will have hard days, days you will have questions that overwhelm you and to-do lists that seem unending. I know, because I have them too.

If I am totally honest, I have days I don't want to walk on stage. Speaking is a part of my career and I love it, but sometimes it's hard and I just don't feel up for it. This was especially true during both of my pregnancies. Many days I was tired and simply taking a few steps would knock the breath out of me. I felt big and swollen and altogether ugly, and I certainly didn't feel I could bring my A game. The last thing I wanted was to stand on a giant platform with bright lights and thousands of eyeballs on me!

But here's the thing: I'm not doing this for me. My why is not to be seen or known or heard or liked. If I was doing this just to make myself look good, do you think I would have taken the stage eight months pregnant? Heck no! I would have hidden backstage while a video played of me at my thinnest while wearing a cute outfit and having a perfect hair day. But in that moment, I had a roomful of faces representing my *why*. Women, passionate about living their dreams, who were bold and committed about changing their lives. Their excitement was contagious, and even when I was feeling my worst, they reignited my *why*. They got me through the day. And, along the way, I was able to help them too. When you remember your *why*, amazing things start to happen. That's what I want to help you discover for yourself.

Regardless of your business, some days will be hard, and you'll be discouraged and beaten down or just not in the mood and want to sit one out. But when you remember why it matters to you, you can take your eyes off of your momentary obstacle and quickly gain perspective to propel you forward. It will give you just the boost you need to keep going, even when it's hard.

THE WORLD NEEDS YOUR GIFTS, TALENT, AND PASSION

Sometimes the heaviness of everything—our roles, responsibilities, commitments, and obligations—can weigh us down and get in the way of living our dream. And, despite our best efforts, sometimes life just gets in the way. Working toward our dream feels like too much. I know how it feels to lose your identity in motherhood, to try and do a hundred different things but feel like you're doing none of them well, to feel like you're always coming from behind. I know what it's like to naturally and unconsciously put every other person on the planet before yourself. It can lead to the heavy feeling of being rushed and resentful, busy and burned-out.

But I want to encourage you. You were made for more than just getting by; fulfillment is waiting for you in work that you love. You're not a supporting character in the movie of your life; you're the lead role. You have permission, the responsibility even, to be in the driver's seat of your own life. That includes investing in things that bring you joy and make you proud. You have permission to do things that make you like yourself. It's not selfish; it's self-preservation, and it's smart.

It can feel scary. We'll deal with the fear soon enough. It can feel overwhelming. This whole book is designed to get you past that. You may feel like your gifts, talents, hobbies, and interests are just random and maybe even useless. *But they are not.* You're wired this way for a reason. You were designed for success, and, my friend, it's time to unlock all of that potential that God's put inside of you. The Bible talks about another woman, Esther, who had to face her own fear, limitations, and sense of calling. The encouragement she received from her mentor is the same encouragement I want to give you as we begin this incredible journey together: Perhaps this is the moment for which you have been created.[5]

Here's the best part: When you stop treating yourself, your gifts, and your desires like an afterthought and start chasing your dream, watch what happens. All of those roles and responsibilities and relationships will improve as the quality of your own life improves. You will actually be a better wife or mom or friend or leader when you start creating and living a life you love.

I'm proud of you for picking up this book and choosing to invest in something that's important to you. If you can commit to going on the wild ride of putting yourself and your heart and soul and dreams on the line in business, I'll promise you this: you'll not only completely change the trajectory of where your life is headed, but you'll also have a whole lot more fun getting there.

chapter 1 action items
LET'S APPLY WHAT YOU'VE LEARNED!

If you want to succeed in business, you need the right tools to get started. Use the action items at the end of every chapter as a template to begin building your customized plan for your business. When you think through the principles in each chapter and apply them to your business, you'll have a clear, actionable plan for running your business by the time you finish this book.

INSPIRATION FOR YOUR BUSINESS

What Have You Loved?
Finish the sentence below with any ideas that come to mind.

I have always loved . . .

I have always loved . . .

I have always loved . . .

Can your *why* be traced back to something you've always loved? If you're dreaming of starting a business, do any of your answers spark a business idea? For example, I had always loved horses and that inspired my first side business.

What's Your Story?

What are some puzzle pieces from your life story that might help you identify your *why*? Brainstorm key parts of your story for inspiration, times when you felt happiest or most alive. Growing up in my mom's cake shop is a part of my story and the inspiration behind Business Boutique. Write pieces of your story here:

chapter 2

FEAR IS NORMAL

Overcoming Doubt and Eliminating Excuses

I wish I could forget it. I have tried to block that speaking event from my mind since the day it happened. I would like to say I learned from the experience and shrugged off all of the emotions associated with the complete and utter failure I felt like I was, but I haven't. Even now, writing about it makes my chest tight. Some things just stick with you. Several years ago, I was booked to speak on the topic of money at one of the top business schools in the nation. Since I was just starting my speaking career with Dave Ramsey, I spoke mostly to teens and young adults at high schools and colleges. But this audience was different. This was a group of MBA students who were close to graduation, many of them in the process of signing huge contracts with Fortune 500 companies, complete with big signing bonuses and even bigger starting salaries.

Today, this kind of event wouldn't bother me because I have over a decade of experience talking to audiences of all ages and coaching business leaders all over the country. But I was years younger then and had been speaking for less than a year.

Even though I was a little intimidated by the group, the conference call with the client leading up to the event had gone so well that I wasn't too worried. I saw it as a new challenge and decided to go for it. Twenty-five men and a few women were present in the classroom that day. The first twenty minutes, everything went fine. I shared my story of getting out of debt and began to teach them Dave Ramsey's 7 Baby Steps. Baby Step 2 is to pay off all debt and only use cash for all purchases. That's when one of the men in the audience interrupted my presentation. "Why would I want to pay for a car in cash and be debt-free when I can take out a loan with 0% interest and invest that money to gain a higher rate of return during that time?"

What happened next was every speaker's worst nightmare. I froze. I froze, and then I stuttered. I mumbled something about needing to pay off all debt because then you can invest with even more money. But he continued to pour on a barrage of accusatory counterarguments, one of which included, "Do you even understand the time value of money?" I stuttered more. The audience began whispering to one another, which became so loud I couldn't hear myself think. I have never wanted to disappear more than I did in that moment, in that hot room with all of those eyes glaring at me. It wasn't that I didn't know the answer to his question. I knew the answer before I walked out the door.[6] But I had never been interrupted and asked such a pointed question before, and I was already feeling intimidated, so I panicked. The whole thing was a traumatic blur, but I think I finally said in a defeated voice, "You can. You can do that if you want."

I tried to continue my talk after that but it was pointless. The audience continued to whisper. I had lost them—as well as every bit of belief I had in myself. I wrapped it up quickly and got to my rental car as fast as I could. And then I cried. I cried the entire drive back to Nashville, sobbing and wiping away tears of humiliation and complete defeat. It was something I'll never forget, no matter how many times I have tried. And oh how I've tried!

That one event made me want to never speak publicly again. The whole drive home, I kept replaying what had happened and assuring myself that I would never put myself in that situation again. Never again would I put myself out there to be criticized or rejected. It was too embarrassing and too painful. It just wasn't worth it. But a few weeks after that terrible speaking event, and once my emotions settled down, thankfully, I changed my mind. I pushed past my fear of failing again and decided to keep going anyway. And I've been doing it ever since. Even though I was sure I'd never speak again, what a shame it would have been if I had let that happen.

I would have missed out on an incredible career—one that I believe is just getting started. I had to keep going *anyway*. Deep down I knew, whether it's bombing a speaking event or something else entirely, what happened to me would happen again. And the truth is, it will happen to you.

Bad things will happen. Someone will embarrass you, or the rug will get pulled out from under you in a way you never saw coming. You'll make a bad decision. People will reject you, or your ideas, or your product, or your dream. Those things *will* happen and they *will* hurt. There's no way around it. Those experiences may scare you from ever trying again, but you have to try again *anyway*. You have to keep going even though it hurts, even though you're scared and you've lost faith in yourself. Even if it scarred you to the core, you have to keep going *anyway*. Pushing through the failures is the only way we have a chance to reach success. I love the quote: "Success is not final; failure is not fatal: it is the courage to continue that counts."

STARTING WITH FEAR

That's right. We're going to spend this entire chapter talking about overcoming our fear. We're also going to dig into a plan for your business, but if we don't first learn to wrestle our fear to the ground, then the best-made plans will never work anyway. The Suzy Kassem quote, "Fear kills more dreams than failure ever will" rings all too true for many business owners. For some, wrestling with fear is a bigger struggle in their business than running the actual business! If you want to win with your business, you've got to get comfortable dealing with your fear.

Fear Is Normal

Say this out loud right now: fear is normal. Expect it. I've coached many women who miss out on huge opportunities not only because they get scared, but also because they think their fear means they're doing something wrong. The truth is, it can mean just the opposite.

Amy, a woman I coached a few years ago, was scared to start her graphic design business. She had a long list of fears that she would share with me in coaching sessions. Every time we talked about them, she used her fears as the reason why she shouldn't even start. She wasn't "ready." She didn't have "enough experience." Her website wasn't perfect. She'd have too much competition. And on and on. She thought if the idea was good or the business was viable, she wouldn't be so scared. She was sure that her fears were a red flag that she shouldn't do it.

I told her what is true for all of us. The reality is that fear is a normal part of the journey. Fear isn't a sign that you're doing something wrong. It's a sign that you're doing something new. It doesn't mean you're not capable, qualified, or ready. It just means you're doing something that matters to you. And fear doesn't mean you're doing something bad. It means you're doing something bold.

Fear Holds You Back

My friend Pete says, "Fear establishes the limits of your life. The bigger your fear, the smaller your life. If you're scared of heights, you'll stay low. If you're scared of the outdoors, you'll stay indoors. If you're scared of failure, you'll never try anything." Fear wants you to live a small life, but God never created us or called us to live a small life. God wants us to have life and have it "abundantly." In fact, the Bible says to "fear not" 365 times—one for every day of the year.

Before my first Business Boutique event, I was scared out of my mind. Just planning it brought to the surface countless insecurities. But after the first event, which was an amazing success by every possible measure, I wasn't scared of putting on another one. And then it was time to write this book. In all of the planning and preparing and outlining, new fears began to creep in. *What if I can't come up with enough to say? What if no one buys it? What if the writing is terrible and the reviews rip it apart?*

It's what Joyce Meyer calls, "New levels, new devils."[7] Even if you conquer your fear of doing one thing, the moment you try something new, push your limits, or take on a new challenge, you're going to have a whole new set of fears that come with it. The bad news is, you'll probably have some level of fear with you the rest of your life. But the great news is, it doesn't have to stop you from doing the things you want to do.

Who Are You to Do This?

Fear isn't just a theoretical idea we talk about, either. Being scared of putting yourself out there is actually scientific. Researchers in the 1970s coined this feeling the

"Imposter Syndrome."[8] The Imposter Syndrome is when someone feels undeserving of their achievements and is afraid of being found out. Many people with these feelings have the thought, *Who am I to do this?*

According to Margie Warrell in *Forbes* magazine, researchers believe that up to 70 percent of people suffer from Imposter Syndrome at some point in their lives.[9] She explains:

> Those who often fear being "found out" have a tendency to attribute their success to external factors—like luck or a helping hand. Unsurprisingly, women tend to do this more often than men who are more likely to attribute their successes to a combination of internal factors, such as grit, talent, brains, and sheer hard work.[10]

Ironically, those who suffer the most from Imposter Syndrome are high achievers. Someone sitting on their couch all day eating Cheetos and watching TV doesn't really wonder if they are performing up to standard. It's the people out on the front lines, the movers and shakers who are making a difference. They are the people worried about whether or not they deserve to be there.

As I studied Imposter Syndrome, I learned that even famous people suffer from it. For example, Academy Award-winning actress Kate Winslet said, "I'd wake up in the morning before going off to a shoot, and think, *I can't do this; I'm a fraud.*"[11] Also, Nobel Laureate and best-selling author Maya Angelou said, "I have written eleven books, but each time I think, *Uh oh, they're going to find out now. I've run a game on everybody, and they're going to find me out.*"[12] And that's Maya Angelou!

The truth is, everyone gets scared. We have a tendency to think that supersuccessful people aren't scared and everything is effortless for them, but that's simply not true. It's not that they've never had fears; it's just that they don't let their fears hold them back. Like I said earlier, starting something new is risky and uncomfortable. But the people who win in business and in life press on anyway. Once we realize that fear is normal, then we don't have to wait until we aren't scared to do the thing we want to do. We just do it scared.

Failure Is Good

It's common for people to have a fear of failure. Fear of failure can keep you from ever trying anything. Before you even put your toe in the water to test something out, the fear of failure is already telling you you're going to sink. And then, once you have failed in some way, those fears get even louder and stronger. The moment you have an embarrassing experience like I did speaking to that group of MBA students, you no longer need the voice of fear taunting you with hypothetical what-ifs because now you have proof. Something bad *did* happen. See? That fear was right!

The truth is, a time will come when you might not meet your goal, you might hit a roadblock, and you might disappoint someone. So what? Is that failure? Letdowns, setbacks, and shortcomings are a part of life. I've "failed." But so has every successful person on the planet, so you and I are in good company. You can't succeed unless you fail along the way. I love what Michael Jordan, arguably the greatest basketball player of all time, has to say about failure: "I've missed more than nine thousand shots in my career. I've lost almost three hundred games. Twenty-six times, I've been trusted to take the game-winning shot and missed. I've failed over and over and over again in my life. And that is why I succeed."[13] Failure isn't fun but, believe it or not, it's actually a good thing. That's because failure is a sign you're out there, you're trying, and unlike so many people, you're actually doing something.

Who Are You Fighting For?

The first time I spoke on life balance for our company, I couldn't wait to read the post-event surveys. I received dozens of positive notes—and a couple of negative ones. I bet you can guess which ones got my attention. All the nice things people had said fell by the wayside, and all I could see were the complaints.

If you've ever gotten a negative review of your product or a complaint about your service, or maybe just a hateful comment on social media, then you know what it feels like. It seems like one or two negative reviews negate the thousands of positive ones. Intellectually, I know that I can't please everyone, but that does not change the visceral pit I feel in my stomach when I read a negative comment.

As I told my husband about it over lunch, I found myself getting defensive. I ranted while smashing turkey onto two pieces of whole grain bread. My patient husband just listened. "His comment said I should practice what I teach. That guy doesn't get it. I tell stories of my failures so that everyone in the audience sees that I understand them. That's the whole point! I am not perfect, and that's where I teach from—what I've learned through my mistakes."

Then, I was silent for a minute, processing my thoughts as I sat down with my sandwich. It hit me. "You know what? I'm not fighting for the people who didn't get it, who it didn't connect with. I am fighting for everyone who *did* get it. The man who went home and took his wife on a date because of that talk. The woman who moved her office out of her bedroom so she could have a work-free space in her at-home business. The family that now eats around the dinner table instead of in front of the TV. I'm fighting for *them*." That was years ago, but before I put myself out there, I still remind myself of who I am fighting for.

We want to grow our business, increase our reach, and make more of an impact, but the reality is that, as we increase our exposure, we increase something else: the haters. With more Facebook likes and blog views come more critics and complainers.

It's not personal; it's just how things scale. More people means more supporters and more critics.

Maybe those naysayers don't understand you. Maybe they don't agree with your message. Or maybe they just don't realize how negative they sound. Even though I know that's going to happen, it still hurts. In those moments, I want you to remind yourself who you're fighting for. When someone is mean, when someone doesn't get it, and when someone tries to tear you down for no reason, remember that you're not fighting for them. You are fighting for the ones who need what you have to offer. Those are the ones who get a say and the ones you should listen to. You can listen to your critics or you can listen to your calling, but not both. The critics will distract your efforts and destroy your progress.

But the opposite is also true. The more that you listen to your calling, the more the critics will fade into the background. Whatever you focus on increases. When you listen to the right people, you're able to focus your attention on the ones you're fighting for.

The Voice of Fear

While you're out there doing something, fear will still use its arsenal of threats to taunt you, worry you, scare you, and paralyze you. Even though the threats are frightening, most often, they aren't true. Sure, you may need a better plan, more time, or a little help to accomplish what you're working on. But fear never says that, does it? That voice in your head keeping you up at night? It never says in a friendly tone, "Hey, rock star! You're doing an amazing job! Remember you need to get some professional advice before you launch that project, but it's going great so far!" Nope. It's always the voice of worst-case scenarios that, more often than not, sound ridiculous when you say them out loud.

Before planning the first Business Boutique event, I had voices in my head that said, *No one is going to show up; They're all going to leave so disappointed;* and, *Who are you to do this?* No one is going to show up, and yet they are going to leave disappointed? I'm not sure exactly how both are possible. But that's what fear does. It hits you coming and going. Fear tells you that you aren't good enough and you can't do it, but if you do it, you'll definitely fail.

Even though I'm certain I'm doing what I'm supposed to be doing, I experience what you and other women feel every day as you build, launch, and grow your businesses. But as I keep pushing forward toward my goal, I want to remind you that the only way to combat fear's lies is with truth. Those voices that scare me, tear me down, and hold me back are not true about me. And they are not true about you either. The more you remind yourself of the truth, the more you'll be able to identify and tune out the lies.

THE TRUTH ABOUT LIES

What starts as a voice of fear in our heads can eventually turn into excuses that keep us from living our dream. Sometimes, we get so used to hearing, believing, and accepting the excuses that we don't even realize they are holding us back or that we have a choice in the matter. In reality, an excuse is just a lie presented as truth. Let's take a look at some of those lies and replace them with the truth we all need to hear.

Lie: You're not good enough.
Truth: You don't have to be the best to add value.

What is "good enough" anyway? Like failure, good enough is elusive and, when we don't quantify it, we never get there. We don't know what good enough really is; all we know is that it's always more than what we currently offer. The finish line always moves and, the truth is, we'll never *feel* good enough. This is the signature trait of Imposter Syndrome and, since we can never pinpoint what good enough is, it can torment us at every level of success. Sure, you may need more experience to get better at a task, but you won't get that experience unless you start doing the task.

The good news is, you don't have to wait until you feel validated or qualified or good enough to start because that feeling may never come. You don't have to be the best in the world to add value to someone's life. You can start helping people, making a difference, and adding value on your very first day. But to do that, you have to *have* a first day. You have to start.

Lie: You're not ready.
Truth: There's no such thing as ready.

When Matt and I decided to start a family, we just knew we were ready to be parents. What a joke! People can tell you how drastically a baby will change your life, and you can read all of the parenting books in the world, but in reality you figure it out as you go, just like everyone else. And while preparation is good in parenting and in business, you learn the most while you're on the job.

When I walked on my first stage as a professional public speaker, I was in my early twenties and way out of my league. I was speaking to an audience full of people twenty to thirty years older than me. I felt unqualified, inexperienced, and scared out of my mind. But I walked out there anyway. I smiled, held my head high, and spoke with confidence as if I had been doing it my whole life. I just did it scared.

If you're waiting until you're no longer scared to put yourself out there, you'll never do it. And if you're waiting until you have a foolproof plan to launch your project, you'll never launch it. Instead of delaying until the mythical "ready" arrives, just go for it. There are people who need what you have to offer *today*. So put yourself out there and try something. See what sticks. Fall down, get back up, and do it again. You learn and grow by *doing*, so go for it—ready or not.

Lie: Someone is already doing it better.
Truth: There's room for you too.

A few years ago I was working on a large project over the span of a few months—it was important and I was excited about it. That is, until two weeks before it was going to launch when I saw a tweet by a well-known author who was sharing an almost identical project. As I read her post, I felt like the wind had been knocked out of me. *This person is a much more experienced writer than me. She has significantly more influence than me and is respected by hundreds of thousands of people (including me). She's done it. She's already done what I am trying to do.*

Everything in me wanted to give up. What would be the point in launching the project now? Someone had already done it and done it better. Maybe you've been through this same dream-shattering panic. Maybe there's a calling in your life and a passion in your heart, but you're discouraged because someone else is already doing it. And maybe, like me, you want to give up.

Here's why we can't: In the midst of my fear, doubt, and intimidation, God assured me, "There's room for you too." The world is not a place of limits and scarcity. The options and opportunities and needs in this world are infinite. And I believe there is a place for your unique voice and passion and talent. That thing you want to do—the calling on your heart and the dream that keeps nagging at you—it's a job only you can do. While there may be others offering a similar product, that doesn't take away from what you are uniquely gifted to offer. So don't give up on your calling or ignore your passions and talents just because you've been distracted by someone else's. Instead, press on and do what you've been called to do. Because I know from firsthand experience, there's room for you too.

PUSHING PAST YOUR FEAR

Fear is a reality in life and in business. So, what do we do about it? I'd love to offer you a quick fix or flip a switch so you would never be scared again, but it's not possible. Fear is new every morning. Regardless of what brings your fears to the surface, here are a few things you can do to wrestle them to the ground.

Do It Once

As we know, fear is full of hypotheticals. *If you launch that blog, everyone will make fun of you behind your back. If you put that price on your product, everyone will think you're greedy. If you start that business, no one will buy your service. If you post that update, no one is going to like it and you'll look like a fool.* And on and on and on. The best way to make those voices shut up is to just do it. I coach women to do it one time. Because once you do it, regardless of how scary that first time may be, fear can't harass you with all of the frightening possibilities of what could happen. Because you did it! And guess what? You survived!

Remember how scared I was leading up to the first Business Boutique event? Well, one day a month before the event, when I was working on my sessions, I had a complete breakdown—ugly crying face and all. I called my leader in tears (which is embarrassing in and of itself) and told him I couldn't do it. The project was so new and so big and so important, and I was so scared of not being able to pull it off. He talked me off the ledge, thank goodness, and I did pull it off. I did it once, and I survived.

Contrast that to the next event when I was as cool as a cucumber. I didn't worry, stress, or have any meltdowns. I survived it once, so I knew I could do it again. And the same is true for you. If you can just muster the courage to do something once, you'll be amazed at how much easier it is to do it again.

Give Yourself Permission to Be a Beginner

In the last five years of professional speaking, I have spoken at hundreds of events, but only a few I'd call "impressive." I've spoken in one-thousand-seat college auditoriums with only six people spread out in the seats. I learned that those poor six people only attended because they got extra credit from a finance teacher for showing up. I've spoken at a family reunion where the audience ranged from four years old to eighty-four years old. We ate refrigerated chicken fingers for lunch, and they saved me a seat at the kid's table. I've spoken in more high school cafeterias than I can count, and I've spent many Friday nights at different county libraries in Kentucky presenting for community events. I know—what's more exciting on a Friday night than a financial presentation at a county library? Nothing, I tell you. Nothing.

I've spoken to an audience of exactly three in a room set for one hundred people. The best part is, that of the three, one lady fell asleep and started snoring . . . loudly. The second one clipped her fingernails, and the last one talked on her cell phone—not texted, *talked*—while I was presenting. I couldn't make this up. Some events were so bad, I cringe just thinking about them. But I had to start somewhere, and so do you.

It's easy to look at people who are at the top of their game and assume they just woke up there one day, as if their success came overnight. But anyone who has ever accomplished anything in life knows that there's no such thing as an overnight success. No one lands on the mountaintop by accident. You have to work to get there.

The people you see on TV and in the headlines have put in years, decades even, of hard work when no one was watching. Taylor Swift, of whom I am an unabashed superfan, tweeted a picture a few years ago of one of her first concerts. She was set up on an eight-foot-wide stage near the riverfront in Nashville, just her and her guitar. Above her was a banner, the words "Taylor Swift" in red ink, which looked like it had been printed at FedEx Office. Her tweet said, "Getting ready to play five shows at Staples Center in LA this week and reminiscing about what my gigs used to be like."[14] I love that example because it's a powerful reminder that everyone starts somewhere. Dave Ramsey started his business on a card table in his living room. Oprah Winfrey was a local news reporter in Nashville. Every successful person you know started somewhere.

The late Zig Ziglar used to quote Joe Sabah's wise observation, "You don't have to be great to start, but you have to start to be great."[15] Give yourself permission to be a beginner. When you do, you allow yourself the opportunity to learn, grow, and improve. Eventually, after years of blood, sweat, and lots of tears, you become an "overnight success."

Talk to Yourself

You've probably never heard of James Gills. Until a few years ago, I hadn't either. But his story fascinated me. First of all, James Gills owns multiple businesses with over four hundred team members, has been named Florida Entrepreneur of the Year multiple times, has performed more cataract eye surgeries than anyone else in the world, and has given millions of dollars to colleges, charities, and YMCAs across the country. But that's not all. Dr. James Pitzer Gills II is the only man in the world to have completed the Double Ironman Triathlon within the thirty-six-hour maximum time frame *six times*! Just so you know, a regular Ironman includes a 2.4-mile swim, followed immediately by a 112-mile bicycle ride, followed immediately by a 26.2-mile run. A double Ironman is when you do all of that *twice*, back to back within thirty-six hours! And this man has done that not once, but six times! And I thought I was busy!

Here's what I love about James's story though. Years ago, when interviewed about how he was able to push past his fear to complete six Double Ironman Triathlons, the only person in the world to have done so, he gave a simple but profound answer:

> I've learned to *talk* to myself rather than *listen* to myself. When I listen to myself, all I hear is fear, doubt, lies, and failure. But when I talk to myself, I can tell myself anything I want to. I can feed myself good thoughts of hope, confidence, truth, and victory. I can tell myself I can do it. When I learned to talk to myself rather than listen to myself, I realized that there was nothing I couldn't do.[16]

You don't have to wait to *feel* positive, hopeful, or confident. You have the power right now to tell yourself anything you want. You can tell yourself that you *can* do it, you *will* change, you *won't* always be broke, you *will* start that business, you *can* reach that goal, you *will* chase that dream.

So the next time fears, doubts, or lies start swirling around in your head, confusing you and keeping you stuck, remember you don't have to listen to them. You can talk to yourself instead. As your words of hope and truth take hold in your heart, watch how your actions follow. You may have a breakthrough right around the corner. All you have to do is talk yourself into it.

THE OTHER SIDE OF FEAR

One year, for our big anniversary gift to each other, Matt and I decided to take a trip to Hawaii. Our first morning in paradise, while we were sitting on our balcony overlooking the beach below us, Matt surprised me with an envelope. I had no idea what he was up to, especially because we had agreed not to exchange any gifts beyond the trip itself. However, I love surprises, so I was thrilled. When I opened the envelope, my mouth dropped. I was speechless. And trust me, that never happens! I pulled out a gift certificate to North Shore Shark Adventures. We were going cage diving with sharks, something that had been on my (ever-growing) bucket list for years.

The next morning, we got up early to drive to the site. When we pulled up, I scanned the marina, looking at all of the piers, boats, and huts. And then I saw the boat. It wasn't just any boat; it was a diving boat that had a giant metal cage hanging off of the back, just like the one in the movie *Jaws*! The cage I was supposed to trust with my life had sections of rust at every crevice. Large buoys surrounded the top edge, and Plexiglas lined the rim for viewing sharks from inside. The only thing standing between me and a dozen hungry sharks was an old, rusty cage with a thin, plastic wall. In that moment, I knew I was looking at the cage I was going to die in.

We boarded the boat with two other groups and headed to open water. Less than sixty seconds after dropping anchor, the boat was surrounded by more than twenty, fifteen-foot-long Galapagos sharks. Dorsal fins darted around every edge of our boat—a boat that suddenly seemed tiny and insufficient to save us from this asinine position we actually paid to put ourselves in. My heart was beating out of my chest. I had wanted to do this for as long as I could remember, but now, in my big shining moment, I had never been more terrified in my life.

As scared as I was, my fears doubled at what happened next. After each of the swimmers in the first group got into the cage, the guide unhooked it from the boat. The cage, which was previously attached to the side of the boat, was now floating off into the ocean. It, and the swimmers inside, remained tethered to our boat only by a thin nylon rope. And that was supposed to save us if something went wrong? I had done a lot of big talking about shark diving for years, but when it came down to it, the actual experience was scarier than I ever could have imagined. I'd never been so sorry for opening my big mouth in my life.

Even though everything went fine and the first group made it back alive (a miracle!), I was terrified to get into the water myself. I put on my mask and snorkel, and, while my entire body was shaking from head to toe, I walked down the ladder and into the cage. The cold water took my breath away and I treaded franticly. If sharks used the smell of fear to find their meals, I was going to be next on the menu. Since I watched Shark Week every year religiously, I thought that if I was ever in the ocean and came across a shark, I'd know just what to do. Be cool. Don't freak out or flail. Don't act like a wounded seal. But in this moment, I was as wounded seal as they come!

Our cage floated out into the ocean and, on the count of three, my husband and I went underwater. With that flash of courage, everything changed. Immediately I was surrounded by silence. And what I saw was one of the most beautiful things I'd ever laid eyes on. Instantly, my fears were gone. My body relaxed. My heart rate slowed. I had entered another world, and it was extraordinary. The sharks swam around us, not with rage but with grace. The silence was peaceful. And despite all of my fears, the sharks didn't seem too interested in eating us. I am not kidding when I say that I could have stayed in that cage, surrounded by those amazing creatures, for hours. It was one of the most incredible experiences of my life.

Believe it or not, that's what happens when we step into our fears. As crazy as it may sound, my experience diving with sharks isn't all that different from how it feels to put yourself out there in business. It can be terrifying. But when you do it anyway, something amazing, beautiful, and extraordinary awaits you on the other side of your fear.

Whether you step into the water, walk onto the stage, launch the blog, start the business, or put yourself out there is your decision. It's up to you to get to the other side. Don't wait until you're not scared to do the thing you want to do. You'll never do it. Instead, just do it scared. There's something extraordinary waiting for you on the other side.

chapter 2 action items
LET'S APPLY WHAT YOU'VE LEARNED!

CALLING YOUR FEAR OUT

Fear has more power when it stays in the battlefield of your mind. Instead, call your fears out by listing them below.

FOCUS ON THE TRUTH

Instead of letting fear tell you lies and hold you back, focus on the truth.

Lie: You're not good enough.
Truth: You don't have to be the best to add value.
Write out all of the ways that you add value through your business.

Lie: You're not ready.
Truth: There's no such thing as ready.
Write out all of the reasons that you can start now.

Lie: Someone is already doing it better.
Truth: There's room for you too.
Write out everything that is unique and special about you that you have to offer. (Hint: It's easier than you think! Your voice, talent, story, and experiences are all great examples!)

PUSHING PAST YOUR FEAR

Do It Once
What is something you want to do that you've been avoiding because you're scared? Write out a date that you commit to do it just once.

Give Yourself Permission to Be a Beginner

This isn't the first time that you've had to start as a beginner. Write other examples in your life where you started small and were able to grow your skills, abilities, and experiences. Use this to remind yourself that you won't be a beginner forever and that everyone starts somewhere!

Talk to Yourself

You can tell yourself anything you want. Use the space below to tell yourself good things and remind yourself that you can do this.

chapter 3

A PLAN TO WIN

Building a Business to Last

When Matt and I bought our first home, I did what everyone does when they buy their first home: I immediately dreamed of all of the things I wanted to do to it. Since I had spent the past ten years renting and moving a lot, I was never able to make those homes my own. The same was true for my husband, so we couldn't wait to update and decorate the house to make it ours. During the weeks leading up to our move, we would dream for hours about all the changes we'd make.

We wanted to build a little window seat in the bay window. We were going to fence in the backyard for our dog, Jackson, and build a pergola on the patio. We dreamed of turning one of the empty bedrooms into a nursery in the future. We talked and dreamed and planned and imagined. We were overflowing with excitement at the possibilities.

The house we bought was built in the early 1980s and hadn't been updated in at least twenty years. It had dark maroon and hunter-green walls, lots of brass, and old, rickety ceiling fans. Thankfully, almost everything we wanted to change was cosmetic, easy to fix, and fairly inexpensive. A fresh coat of neutral-color paint would transform the rooms instantly and switching out doorknobs would be easy.

We planned to tackle those projects eventually, but there was one change I couldn't wait to make: the kitchen cabinets. Like most families, we spend more time in the kitchen than almost any other room. We cook there, eat there, and, when we have friends over, we all tend to gather and visit there. The kitchen was my number one priority.

The cabinets were solid oak and well made, but the dark honey-colored wood was dated and made the room seem small and dim. We certainly didn't have the budget to replace the cabinets, so I decided to paint them. It would completely change the feel of the whole downstairs if I could pull it off. The only problem was that I had absolutely no idea how to do it. I searched online for "how to paint cabinets" and found pages and pages of all the things to consider and prepare before I even picked up my paintbrush. If I wasn't intimidated about the project before, I certainly was now.

My mind was full of questions. *Do you take the cabinets off the wall? What kind of paint do you use? Do you use a clear coat to seal it afterward? How many coats would they need? Do you have to prime them first? How do you clean off the years of grease and grime so the paint will stick? Do you paint the insides of the cabinets? Where do you find new hardware that will fit thirty-year-old cabinets? How long will the whole thing take?* I'm a pretty motivated person, especially when I want something really badly, but the enormity of this project was enough to make me want to curl into the fetal position and give up.

Maybe that's you. Maybe you haven't had to deal with figuring out how to fix and update ugly cabinets, but that's how you feel about your business. What started as a fun, exciting adventure full of possibilities has now turned into something huge, daunting, and stressful. Maybe you know you want to build your business—you know you *can* build your business. You just have no idea how to do it. Maybe you're where I was: you have more questions than answers and are more overwhelmed than excited. And maybe, like me, you want to give up and just ditch the dream.

The good news is I didn't give up, and you don't have to give up either. I am happy to report that my ugly cabinets are now a beautiful shade of off-white and they are stunning, if I do say so myself. I spray-painted the old hinges and added new hardware. The end result exceeded my expectations, and I couldn't be happier. Looking back, I realize that the one thing that helped me get over the wall of being overwhelmed and make my dream a reality is the very same thing that will help you with your business: a plan.

A PLAN ON PURPOSE

Many women slide into business instead of intentionally deciding to start a business. They get busy moving, shaking, and getting things done, and I love that. But when they do this, they often miss several foundational steps to build a business that will last.

Eve, for instance, got into business because she loved quilting, and after posting a few pictures on Facebook, she began getting requests from her friends and family for her to make them one. She got continuing requests to make "just one more thing," and soon she was making quilts in her living room on a regular basis. That's when she realized she could make money at it. Suddenly, she had the beginnings of a small business.

This is true for many small businesses. Whether it's product-based or service-based, starting a business happens, for many women, accidentally and organically. But when you start your business this way, you immediately go from idea to action without doing much (if any) actual planning. You take your enthusiasm and just start doing stuff. You set up a Facebook page. You print business cards. You tell people. You come up with a name. You make up prices. You put yourself out there. It's all an exciting whirlwind of experimenting and seeing what works. I love this phase because it's energizing, hopeful, creative, and fun! There's just one problem, and it's one that can eventually wreck your business.

The problem is that, in all of your action, you forget to plan. You make it up as you go, and you forget—or don't even realize—some best practices that actually make businesses run. Without them you can quickly end up discouraged and ready to abandon your dream. It's important to note here that I'm not against a person getting up and moving. In fact, I encourage people to start *right now*! But just because you've already started doesn't mean you can't stop and take some time to plan.

It doesn't matter if you're just starting out or if you've been in business for a few years already; this plan is for you. Having a plan will reduce your stress and help you focus on the fun stuff that you love about your business. It will give you control, help guide you through all of your steps, and tell you what you need to do. It will cover everything from casting your vision to setting goals, from pricing to marketing, and even some of the boring business details most of us hate like taxes and accounting. We'll look at each step in order and answer the most common questions about starting and growing a business. And the best news is that you don't have to shut down your shop or take a break in order to plan. You can keep your day-to-day business running while you work on it.

A Plan Identifies What You Need to Know

It can be intimidating to have hundreds of questions about your business swirling around in your mind with no answers in sight. You can lose the excitement you started with and feel like you have no control over your dream. You need help but don't know where to get it. You're willing to do what you need to do, but you don't know what that is. It's a frustrating place for sure. More often than not, the problem is not that you have *too much* to do. The problem is that you don't know *what* to do. When I went online and found an exact, easy-to-understand-and-implement plan for my cabinets, I knew what I had to do. I simply had to follow those fifteen steps to get the result I wanted. The same is true in your business. Once you follow the steps, you'll get the results you want.

A Plan Identifies What You Don't Know

But sometimes you don't even know what you don't know. For example, I had no idea that I was supposed to use something called a "tack cloth" to clean my sanded cabinets. I didn't even know what one was, so I had to ask someone at the hardware store to help me find it. It is a small, sticky rag you rub across the cabinets and in all of the crevices so the dust will stick to it and give you a clean surface to work with. I never would have known about this crucial step if I hadn't found the right plan. The plan didn't just show me the steps to take, but also the tools I didn't even know I needed. The same is true of your business plan. It will help you make the most of what you already know and help you identify things you weren't even aware of.

A Plan Gets You Back on Track

Whether you're writing a book, launching a blog, building a website, setting up your systems and processes, or any one of the other endless things you have to do to build your business, sometimes you just get stuck and some days it can be hard making those dreams a reality. You don't have the energy, you can't focus, and you've lost your motivation. Other days, things go wrong, customers are hateful, and an idea doesn't work. While those days are no fun, they are a reality in business and an expected part of the journey. That's why a plan is so important. It not only gives you the steps you need to get where you want to go, but it'll also get you unstuck and back on track. A plan can help you reset and keep moving even when things go wrong. It shows you the bigger picture, which is a powerful reminder that one bad day or grumpy customer doesn't have to completely derail your efforts. When you have a plan, you'll know how to push and persist and persevere—even through the tough times.

A PLAN WITH TIERS

I've watched my mom bake, set up, and decorate countless wedding cakes over the years. Of course, with any element of a wedding day, things can go wrong. But the cake is one of the more delicate features of the day. Stacked several tiers high, it is usually cut by an enthusiastic and nervous new couple and has the potential for a variety of disasters.

That's why it's so important to set up the cake correctly. My mom taught me several ways to make sure the cake is properly supported in order to prevent any cake-toppling disasters. One way is to make sure that the bottom tiers have dowel rods in them. Then, the weight of each tier rests on the wooden dowel rods inserted into the cake tier below it. Another way is to make sure that your base layer is the largest, and every tier that stacks above it is smaller than the one below it. You never see cakes with larger toppers than bases because the physics wouldn't work. Unless you want your wedding cake-cutting moment to appear on YouTube Cake Fails, it's important that you build it with a strong foundation and each tier above it in order by size.

Since cakes have been the backdrop for my entire childhood and my mom's shop was the inspiration for me getting into business, I use a cake metaphor for the Business Boutique business plan. The importance of building both correctly is surprisingly similar. The Business Boutique business plan has four tiers. The tiers are designed in order, and each tier supports everything else above it. As you work through the tiers, you will see how each decision you make informs and supports the decisions that follow. We're going to drill deeper into each of these tiers in the coming chapters, but let's talk about them briefly so you have an idea of what to expect later.

Tier 1: Build Your Foundation

The first tier is the most important. Many people may think about this tier in passing, but few take the time to dig into it and even fewer commit to it in writing. In this tier, we are going to identify and define five elements that make up your foundation.

In Tier 1, we will cover your *why*, dreams, vision, mission statement, and goals. This is where you will think about and define your version of success so that you can reach it.

Your Why

This is your motivation for going into business in the first place. Knowing your *why* will not only keep you motivated when things get tough (because in business, things will get tough), but it will also help you communicate your brand when we get to the later stages of marketing.

Your Dream

Knowing your dream for your business is important because your dream defines your direction.

Your Vision

Your vision is the finish line you're working toward, and it's more specific than your dream. Your vision is owning your dream on a different level, and it is stating a truth about the future you.

Your Mission Statement

This is easier than you may think. Your mission is about purpose, and it should be short, simple, and concise.

Your Goals

Setting goals provides incremental steps to make everything else actually happen. We will unpack how to set effective goals that get you to where you want to be.

Tier 2: Make It Yours

In this tier, you get to put your goals into action and plan your business around your unique talents, situation, and resources. Instead of comparing yourself to others and doing things the way everyone else is doing them, you get to make the business yours. That's the best part of going into business for yourself. You get to build your business around your life versus the other way around. In this tier, we will cover six more elements: your strengths, values, money, time, schedule, and space.

Strengths

The more time you spend in your strengths, the more fun you'll have, and the more successful you'll be. This also helps you identify areas that aren't your strengths, things you *shouldn't* be spending your time on.

Values

Knowing your personal values will inform the core values of the business. Identifying your values helps you keep your business true to who you are.

Money

We will spend a lot of time covering finances in later chapters, but, starting out, you need to establish a limit so your business doesn't gradually drain your personal accounts.

Time

The goals you set in Tier 1 will help you determine how much time to spend on your business to reach your desired results.

Schedule

Where, in your crazy-busy schedule, is your business going to fit? We will talk about what to consider when scheduling your business work hours to reach your goals.

Space

This is the dedicated space where you will work on your business that you and your family honor. And to protect your sanity, your entire home can't be your space.

Tier 3: Up and Running

Tier 3 is full of practical elements. This is where we get operational. In this tier, we will cover ten basic elements: products and services, location, logistics, platform, point-of-sale, records, competition, policies, ways to protect yourself, and pricing.

Products and Services

This is where you determine the products or services your business provides. Don't get distracted by all the opportunities out there; if you want to win in business, you need to focus on doing one thing and doing it well.

Location

The place where you will operate your business. It might be a brick-and-mortar store, an office or studio, a shared location, or somewhere else entirely. You will have unique opportunities and challenges to plan for depending on your location.

Logistics

Intentionally planning your processes, shipping, and fulfillment will set your business up for growth and expansion. It also helps you cut costs by increasing efficiency.

Platform

This is where your business will live online. Maybe it's on a blog, website, or Etsy store. The platform you use will inform marketing decisions you make later.

Point-of-Sale

Where and how will you take payment? The good news is that with all the options available, invoicing and getting paid is easier than ever.

Records

Easy-to-use resources take the guesswork out of accounting and record keeping, because keeping your receipts crumpled up in a shoe box is not a good plan. And trust me, I know from experience.

Competition

Knowing your competition will help you learn from others' mistakes as well as learn best practices in your particular industry. You can also find ways to set yourself apart from everybody else.

Policies

You need policies for shipping, returns, cancellations, and other situations that will come up. Setting your policies on the front end helps ensure you aren't taken advantage of later.

Protecting Yourself

Knowing how you will handle sticky situations (such as when people try to get things for free) reduces the stress of being put on the spot and allows you to say the right thing in the moment. It also helps you avoid saying yes to something that you end up resenting and regretting later.

Pricing

Setting the right price point is critical to your profitability, marketing ability, and overall success in business. It also affects how much you get paid, which, if you haven't guessed, is really important.

Tier 4: Put Yourself Out There

You made it! Finally, you get to put the topper on your wedding cake and announce your business to the world by marketing it. This is the fun part, but that doesn't mean it doesn't take some hard work. Most people throw together a website or brochure and just put it out there. Unfortunately, ugly, confusing, or cluttered advertising will do more damage than good to your business. Not all marketing is effective marketing. That's why these five final elements of your business plan are so important: unique position, branding, target market, social media, and elevator pitch.

Unique Position

This is what sets you apart from the competition and makes people want to buy from you instead of someone else. We will talk about how to identify your unique position and how to leverage it in your marketing.

Branding

This is the look, tone, and feel that customers experience when they interact with you. Your branding decisions can and should come through in every aspect of your business.

Target Market

Your target market is a group of people who want what you have to offer and are willing to pay the price you charge. When you know who that is, you can reach the right people in the right way.

Social Media

Social media doesn't have to be a mystery. We will talk about the different options you have to reach your target customer online as well as best practices to make the most impact with the least effort.

Elevator Pitch

You want to be able to state in two sentences or fewer (the length of an elevator ride) what your business does. We will walk through how to create an elevator pitch that sparks interest and leads to more customers.

FOLLOW THE PLAN

That's the plan. At first, it might seem like a lot to keep track of, but it's completely manageable and since this is *your* business, you don't have to do it all in one day, one week, or even one year. In the coming chapters, I'll walk you through each step and give examples of how to make this plan work—for you. You'll be enjoying your business more than ever. But there's one catch: You have to follow the plan. You can't just put it together and tuck it away only to forget about it later. You actually have to use it.

I get how hard it is to follow through sometimes. I'm seriously entrepreneurial, and one signature trait of entrepreneurs is that we have one hundred new ideas every day—ideas we just know are all brilliant! We have no shortage of ideas, but the problem is that we have real shortage in follow-through. All the fun is in the creative process and idea generation, but when it comes to putting that idea into action, we fall off the wagon.

In college I had this grand plan to study abroad in Australia. I looked at my calendar, researched the steps, and even made plans with my friend Whitney. I had a timeline for each application deadline, but a little at a time, I got off track with the plan. Needless to say, Whitney studied abroad an entire semester in beautiful Australia, and I did not. It's something I regret to this day, and Australia is still on my bucket list of places to visit.

Plans are a valuable tool to get you where you want to be, but you have to actually follow through with them or they won't work. Maya Angelou said it best, "Nothing will work unless you do." Whether that's studying abroad or building your business, it's on us to follow our plans to make our dreams a reality.

The Work Behind the Scenes

I've participated in and watched many half and full marathons over the last decade. Standing at the finish line, watching the leaders fly by at five minutes per mile, is an incredible experience. Inevitably, you always hear other spectators whisper things like, "They were built to run," "Running just comes naturally to them," "They're lucky running is easy for them." I hear the same thing with people who are winning with money, in business, and in life. People observing their success say similar things. "Well, he just got lucky," "She can do that because she has a ton of help," "If I had their (job, money, time . . . fill in the blank), I could do that too." But in both situations, spectators miss the reality of the situation because they are judging a person's successes only by what they see at the finish line. They glamorize the finish line but dismiss what it took to get there. Spectators attribute that person's success as a fluke or accident, the family they were born into, or a lucky break at work.

But ask anyone who is winning in any area of life and they will tell you that it doesn't happen by luck. Winning happens in the miles logged at 4:00 a.m., the hours dedicated after the family is asleep, the money saved by eating Ramen Noodles and tuna at home instead of going out. It's the sacrifices made—the blood, sweat, and tears behind the scenes—that no one ever sees. Winning happens when you want it bad enough and are willing to work hard enough for it. The finish line is just the result. In his book *The 21 Irrefutable Laws of Leadership*, John Maxwell says, "There's an old saying, 'Champions don't *become* champions in the ring—they are merely *recognized* there.'"[17] Or as Pastor Craig Groeschel said, "It's often the small things that no one sees that result in the big things that everyone wants."[18]

Your Finish Line

I was frustrated when I wanted to paint my cabinets and didn't know how, but the moment I had a plan, I knew what I needed to do and I did it. That's what this plan will do for you and your business. I've coached women at every level of business—from those who have just a tiny dream they are scared to say out loud all the way to those running multimillion dollar companies. I've learned that regardless of the size of your business or where you are on your journey, a plan is your path to success. Maybe you're just starting out. Or maybe you've been at this a while and you just need a little boost. Don't give up. You've already come this far. If you're willing to take the steps, do the work, and follow the plan, I promise you will win.

chapter 3 action items

LET'S APPLY WHAT YOU'VE LEARNED!

THE PLAN

Before we dive into creating your business plan, look over the list of topics we will cover. You may be thinking you're great at some of these items but others may be a struggle. Put a check mark next to the items you feel are strengths of your business, and put a question mark next to the ones you have the most questions about. The great news is, we are going to cover all of it to get you to where you want to be.

Tier 1: Build Your Foundation
___ Your *Why*
___ Your Dream
___ Your Vision
___ Your Mission Statement
___ Your Goals

Tier 2: Make It Yours
___ Strengths
___ Values
___ Money
___ Time
___ Schedule
___ Space

Tier 3: Up and Running

___ Products and Services

___ Location

___ Logistics

___ Platform

___ Point-of-Sale

___ Records

___ Competition

___ Policies

___ Protecting Yourself

___ Pricing

Tier 4: Put Yourself Out There

___ Unique Position

___ Branding

___ Target Market

___ Social Media

___ Elevator Pitch

Tier One

BUILD YOUR
FOUNDATION

As I mentioned earlier, this plan is designed like a wedding cake with four tiers. The bottom tier, Tier 1, is the most important. This is where you build your foundation. In this tier, we will cover your *why*, your dream, your vision, your mission statement, and your goals. The decisions you make in this tier will inform all other decisions in your business, so it's important that you start here. You ready? Let's get to it!

chapter 4

WHY MATTERS

Why You Do It Affects How You Do It

Growing up around my mom's cake shop was crazy. It was messy, loud, chaotic, and anything but traditional. Our car constantly had icing on the cloth seats that inevitably got on our clothes every time we drove anywhere. We always smelled like freshly baked cakes (which, believe it or not, got old after a while). And, during my childhood years, I easily spent more time with Mom's employees than my own friends.

During that time, I always focused on all that I didn't have. I didn't have a typical family. I never had home-cooked meals around a dinner table, and I didn't feel what every middle school kid wants to feel more than anything: "normal." But what I see so clearly now, something I could never see as a child, is that my story wasn't a second-rate, bummer of a backup plan. The cake shop wasn't a consolation prize for a life that turned out wrong. It was the perfect setup for me to witness firsthand something powerful, beautiful, and rare: a strong and passionate woman making an impact through her God-given gifts. My story wasn't an accident or an afterthought, it was written on purpose and it is priceless. Sure, it was crazy at times, but most of the best things in life are.

I watched my mom work hard, and I saw her hard work pay off. I watched her hope when situations seemed hopeless. I watched her persevere with an absurd level of persistence. And to this day, my mom boldly embraces everything she is and everything she has to offer. She doesn't apologize for her dreams or take a back seat in her own life. And you know what? I don't either. She didn't just *teach* me work ethic, passion, values, and character; she *lived* it. And as a result, I do too. My mom showed me it was possible to use her skills, fully be herself, and bravely go after her dreams—and not apologize for it. Now I'm on a mission to do for other women what my mom did for me. As I stated in chapter 1, that's my *why*.

And now it's time to take a closer look at your *why*. Why is this important to you? Why does it matter? You may have never stopped to think about it. But taking a moment to reflect on your *why* is important. It's so important, in fact, that defining your *why* is the first step in your business plan.

MEANING MATTERS

Your *why* is what gives meaning to your work. When you know why you do it, your actions have a deeper level of satisfaction and purpose. Now more than ever, people want to feel like they are doing work that matters. The old days of working at the same company for thirty or forty years, collecting a paycheck, and retiring with a pension are long gone.

Our desires, strengths, and gifts are important. The things that bring us joy and satisfaction matter. That's what today's movers, shakers, and difference-makers have figured out. They don't just want a paycheck. They want passion and purpose and significance, and they aren't settling for anything less. The marketplace is full of creative, unconventional, outside-the-box businesses that are allowing people to work in their strengths while still making money and truly changing the world.

The idea of people wanting meaning in their work isn't new. We've always desired purpose in what we do. We just haven't always had such easy access to create it.

Meaning vs. Money

When Dave Ramsey talks about the contrast between purpose and paycheck, he often tells the story of a group of researchers who decided to do an experiment. The researchers invited participants out to a worksite where they would make five dollars per hour. The participants had to dig a ditch from 8:00 a.m. to noon. Then, after a lunch break, they had to work from one to 5:00 p.m. filling the ditch back in. At the end of the day, each participant would be paid forty dollars. Then the researchers told the participants if they came back the next day, they would be doing the exact same job but would be paid double, ten dollars per hour.

The next day, only half of the participants returned. They did the same work on the same schedule, digging the ditch for the first half of the day and filling it back in for the second half of the day. They were paid ten dollars per hour. The researchers then told participants if they came back a third day, they would be doing the same job, but they would be paid double again and would make twenty dollars per hour.

On the third day, only a quarter of the original group showed up. Those few remaining participants did the same work that day, digging the ditch and filling it back in and they earned twenty dollars per hour. Finally, the researchers told them that if they came back for a fourth day, they'd do the same job but they would earn double again and would make forty dollars an hour. On the fourth day, not a single participant showed up.

This story illustrates the importance of purpose. It shows how we are wired for meaning in our work, and it demonstrates the direct correlation between meaningful work and motivation. Without meaning, it's difficult to stay motivated. But everything—enjoyment, satisfaction, productivity, and even success—increases exponentially when there's a sense of purpose behind what we are doing. We want our work to count for something—something that makes a difference. And we don't want to do meaningless work, regardless of how much we're paid to do it. The opposite is also true. Often we are happy to work for a cause or purpose we believe in, regardless of the size of the paycheck.

The best news is, you don't have to choose between your passion and a good paycheck. You can have both. Thanks to technology and an ever-evolving marketplace, we have the ability to build businesses that combine work and play and allow us to make money doing what we love. There's never been a better time to step into your God-given gifts and make money doing what you love.

What's Your Why?

So what's your motivation? Is it the joy you get from creating or the satisfaction of planning someone's wedding? Maybe your *why* is using your education or having the flexibility to work from home and spend more time with your family. Your *why* is what moves, drives, and energizes you.

Every Why Is Unique

Over the years, I have asked hundreds of women, "Why do you do this? Why is it important to you?" Each answer is as unique as the woman and the business she represented.

Meg said, "My full-time job is incredibly boring. I'd love to do something different, but right now this pays the bills. My Etsy business selling my watercolor artwork is a creative outlet for me to use the gifts God gave me. It's one of the only things I do in my life that actually gives me energy instead of *sucking* the energy out of me. I give to my work, I give to my family and kids, I give to others, and those are all good things, but sometimes they drain me. My business allows me to be free and creative. It fills me back up!"

Abby told me, "Being a stay-at-home mom is incredibly rewarding, and I know it's right for me. But like anything, it has downsides. I have a degree in accounting, and I love numbers. Other than teaching my little ones how to count blocks and toys, I don't get to actually use my education. My freelance accounting business allows me to keep my skills sharp and do something I know and am good at. It also allows me to feel like an adult sometimes. That may sound silly, but when your days are filled with laundry and Legos, it's easy to lose sight of the skills you have as a grown, educated, and talented woman. My business is an opportunity for me to feel like I'm more than a mom."

Stacy said, "That's easy. I love it. That's why I do it. I love music and I love teaching, so my business lets me do both through music lessons. I have so much fun when

I'm teaching that it doesn't even feel like work. I can't imagine *not* doing it. I don't do it for the money, but that's the best part of having a business where you love what you do. You get to make money too!"

Maybe your motivator sounds like one of these women, or maybe it's more like my friend Cordia Harrington. Cordia is famously known as the "Bun Lady," and she is the founder, CEO, and president of the Tennessee Bun Company, the world's fastest high-speed baked goods company, producing one thousand buns per minute. She was named #16 of the 25 Top Women Business Builders by *FAST Company* in 2005, and she's received a long list of other awards and accolades over the years.[19] Cordia's motivation, she once told me, comes down to flexibility. She had been working in real estate and worked most nights and weekends. She was a single mom with three kids, and she wanted to spend more time with them while still supporting her family. That's a common theme with women business owners: they start businesses to have more time and flexibility and to earn money, but they want to do it on their own terms.

Or maybe you want to solve a problem like my friend Megan Hardwick. Megan is the owner and inventor of Wings Cosmetics, a makeup company with tools to help women achieve a cat-eye look with their eyeliner. Megan came up with the idea after having a hard time putting on her own makeup. It took too much time to get a winged look with her eyeliner, so she invented a tool out of necessity to help her achieve the look she was going for in less time and with less smudges.

Megan recalled:

I was a mom and wife who wanted to feel beautiful again, regardless of time, talent, or skill. I wanted to be able to provide that to anyone who was in the same boat as I was. Women and moms like me are my *why*. Once I made my *why* clear for myself, I felt like I had a breakthrough in my business. It was easier to market, and it was easier to answer questions and be present for those who needed my help. I knew where I was needed in the marketplace to fill a need.[20]

There's no right answer to why you're doing what you're doing. The right answer is simply *your* answer. You can do it for more time, energy, or fun. You can do it for the people you're helping, or you can do it for yourself. All that matters is that you know why you do it.

WHY AFFECTS HOW

When starting out, most people focus on *how* to run their business, not *why*. But, whether you realize it or not, *why* you do it affects *how* you do it. The tale of the three bricklayers illustrates this perfectly. Three bricklayers were working on the same building. When asked what they were doing, the first answered grumpily, "I'm laying bricks." The second replied with a bit more vision, "I'm putting up a wall." The third bricklayer's response was different. He replied enthusiastically and with pride, "I'm building a beautiful cathedral. It will be the finest building in town, and it will be a place of peace and comfort for everyone who walks by it!" What a difference knowing why makes. When you know why you do it, even the most mundane work can become meaningful.

Regardless of the type of business you run or the type of work you do, your *why* will always affect your *how*. As an example, when my first son, Carter, was born, I gave my mother-in-law and grandmother-in-law a personalized necklace I bought from an Etsy business. It had three layered charms engraved with the names of the children in each generation. When we found out that my son Conley was on the way, I reached out to the Etsy store owner asking how much she would charge me to add his name to the necklaces. I knew it would be off-center since the charms weren't designed with space for two names, but I told her that it was okay. She responded immediately, congratulating me and saying that she'd be happy to send me completely new charms with both of my sons' names centered. She was generous with the pricing, and the shipping was included. She went above and beyond what I'd asked of her. She cared about her work, her customer, and the entire experience. That's what happens when you know your *why*. You care a little deeper and it shows. It shows in how you conduct your business and how you treat your customers. They will feel your passion and purpose when they interact with you and your business.

Never forget: regardless of the work you do, why you do it will always affect how you do it.

Why Keeps You Going

Let's be honest. Business can be really hard sometimes. You will face challenges, setbacks, and, yes, even failures. You'll get knocked off your feet, feel down-and-out, and be discouraged to no end. You will want to throw up your hands and walk away. Those are the times when knowing your *why* is so important—because it keeps you going. World-renowned psychiatrist Viktor Frankl paraphrased a quote from Friedrich Nietzsche when he said, "When you know your why, you can endure any how." [21] Your *why* is what centers you—it will help you stay on track, even when things get rough.

Cordia Harrington, for example, wasn't always a success story. Her success was built on a large pile of failures. Her idea to start a bun company wasn't an overnight success. In fact, she was rejected by McDonalds not once, not twice, but thirty-one times! Thirty-one times, she "failed." But thirty-one times, she persisted. I would have given up after seven or eight at least! When I asked her why she didn't give up, she told me, "No wasn't an option." [22]

Cordia knew her *why*—she wanted to spend time with her kids—and she knew if she didn't give up, she'd eventually get to. What an incredible story of perseverance. She could continue past thirty-one setbacks to create her success story because she knew what moved and motivated her.

Our Brains Know Why

This idea of *why* has become more popular in recent years largely because of the work of Simon Sinek, the best-selling author of *Start with Why* and presenter of the popular TED Talk, "How Great Leaders Inspire Action," which has had more than 30 million views. In his talk, he shares a brilliant idea that has transformed how businesses market their products and services. He says, "People don't buy what you do. They buy why you do it." [23]

You might think that customers decide to buy from you simply based on the products and services you provide. Your customers probably think that too. But they don't. According to Sinek, people make decisions—including purchasing decisions—from the limbic center of the brain, which has no capacity for language, details, information, facts, or figures. [24] It's the part of the brain that is responsible for feelings and emotions. That's why we can have all the data we need but we still say things like, "I don't have a good feeling about that," or "My gut tells me not to do this." We can't put words to it but the decision either feels right or it doesn't. By the way, it's not until after we make a decision that we justify it with the language center of the brain, which processes details, information, facts, and figures.[25]

When you tell people *what* you do or *how* you do it, you're appealing to the language center of the brain—but that's not the part of the brain responsible for decision-making. In other words, *what* and *how* don't convince people to buy from you. But when you communicate why, you're speaking to the limbic part of the brain—the part that not only understands values and beliefs, but also makes decisions. Can you see why your *why* is so important? It's the language that our brain speaks, even if we don't realize it. That means, as Sinek argues, that if "people don't buy what you do, they buy why you do it," then you better know why you do it!

WHY MAKES A DIFFERENCE

Let's say that you have a business building custom furniture. You might think furniture is just furniture, but when you think about it in terms of why, it's no longer just a table. It's the place where a family gathers. It's the place where meals are shared, memories are made, and lives are built. My mom doesn't just bake cakes. She creates moments and memories. My friend Megan doesn't just sell cosmetics. She sells confidence. And I don't just give people business plans and tools. I empower and equip them to use their gifts to turn their dreams into reality. And the same is true for you. When you know your *why*, you see everything and everyone differently. You work differently. You become passionate about your business and the people you're impacting.

So what's the *why* behind what you do? Think about it. I guarantee if you dig deep and reflect on it, you'll realize that your passion has a greater purpose than you might realize. You are making a difference. You are changing lives. Not only your customers' lives, but yours too. Your work takes on a new level of significance when you recognize that your business is no longer about the products you're selling or the service you're providing, but about the difference you're making. And that's a *why* anyone can get behind.

LET'S APPLY WHAT YOU'VE LEARNED!

A fundamental step in your business plan is to define your *why*. Defining it can be tough at first, so start by answering a few related questions. As you write out your answers, your *why* statement will start to emerge.

Why does this matter to you?

Why this specific business?

What excites you about it?

As you look at the answers to the above three questions, your *why* will become clear.

What's your *why*? Write it here.

chapter 5

PERMISSION TO DREAM

Creating a Vision for Where You Want to Go

I was lying on the beach trying to soak up every drop of sunshine I could. It was January and it had been snowing in Nashville, so for our eighth annual girls' trip, we decided to go as far south as possible—to Miami. This group of girls and I have never all lived in the same city, but thankfully it hasn't stopped us from taking an annual trip together. We've been doing it since 2006 when we bonded over a random and completely disastrous trip to Myrtle Beach. Fortunately, our trips have only gotten better since. We've walked through exciting life changes, new jobs, weddings, and babies, yet we have never stopped finding time to meet up every year. And over the years, these girls have become my very best friends.

As we were all lying there, trying to get some glimmer of a tan on our stark-white winter skin, Jenny broke the silence. "Let's dream about what we want to do this year. What does everyone want to have done by our girls' trip next year?" We got quiet as we thought about it. Susan spoke first. She was living in New York and working a great job, but she was ready to grow, move up, and move on. Sarah, on the other hand, wanted to get back to playing music. She's an incredible singer and musician, but life had gotten busy and she hadn't played anywhere in a while.

As I listened to my friends respond, a thought instantly came to mind. I had toyed with the idea for about two years but never allowed it to come to the forefront, never acknowledged it as valid or real or possible. It was the first and only thought I had while sitting with them. I immediately knew it was my dream for the year. But I couldn't seem to say it. Even when the only people around me were my closest friends, I still couldn't muster up the courage to say the words. It felt too risky. Too vulnerable. Too silly. And if I said it out loud, I'd have to do something about it, right?

It took me a few minutes to speak up but eventually I said, "I want to be a certified business and life coach. I've thought about it for years, but I have never said it out loud until just now." Even though I was certain I wanted to do it and I was with my best friends, it still felt scary.

IT HURTS TO DREAM

I hesitated to speak up that day on the beach because sometimes it hurts to dream. It hurts to desire and want and wish and hope because we know what disappointment feels like. We've been there before, and we don't want to go back. We know all too well the pain of being let down, of getting blindsided by bad news, of ending up brokenhearted. We know what it feels like to muster up the nerve to put our heart on the line only to have it denied.

So, somewhere along the way, we become scared to dream. We shut down and give up hope that our desires will ever be fulfilled. Instead we rationalize that it's just not worth the risk of being let down. We surrender our dreams under the banner of "maturity" and decide to be practical with phrases like:

Don't get your hopes up; you will just be disappointed.
I'll believe it when I see it.
I'd rather expect the worst and be surprised.
There's no point in thinking about that because it's never going to happen.
I'm not a pessimist; I'm a realist.

Dreams sometimes feel impractical, unrealistic, and uncertain. So we keep our dreams to ourselves, tucked away and unspoken. It feels scary to acknowledge them, much less say them out loud for others to hear. Before we admit our dreams, we're safe with nothing to lose. But the moment we own our dreams, we have something on the line—something to be won or lost.

"I Want"

The reason dreams feel that way is because they are dreams. They are something beyond our current situation, skills, or abilities. Dreams are something bigger and better, and that's exactly what makes them worthwhile. Dreams represent hope, excitement, and possibility. They take our eyes off our daily struggles and invite us to look up, to see something better to come. Dreams draw out our deepest desires— desires that I believe God gave us. The signature on all of my personal emails reads, "Delight yourself in the LORD, and he will give you the desires of your heart."[26] Often we think of our heart's desires as silly or selfish things. We see them as optional ornaments to be pushed into the back corner of our lives to collect dust. But our heart's desires are not bad things; I personally believe they're God things. They are bravely owning the words, "I want." *I want* to stay home with my kids. *I want* to make more money. *I want* to quit my full-time job that I hate. *I want* to grow a national business with multiple locations. *I want* to be able to financially support my parents. *I want* something better for myself, my family, and my business. As Seth Godin says, "Own your dreams. There is no better way to make them happen."[27] But it all starts with owning them.

Dreams That Scare You

While dreams draw out our deepest desires, they can also bring to the surface our deepest buried fears. Fear doesn't want us to dream. Fear wants us to live small and safe lives, scared of the possibilities instead of excited about them. But I believe we're designed to live full lives, not small, safe lives. Some of the best success stories we read about are wild and adventurous, impractical and "impossible." That's the kind of life story I want for myself and the kind that I hope for you too.

Just like I was scared to dream out loud on the beach with my best friends, many of the women I coach have the same struggle. When I ask, "What is your big dream for your business?" they hesitate. I hear silence on the other end of the line as they wrestle with their fear of saying it out loud. Sometimes they will give me a small answer such as, "I just want to keep doing what I love," or "I just want to pay for soccer this year." But I can tell they are giving me the safe answer. I encourage them and try to get to the root of what they want.

I'll urge, "No, come on. I mean your big dream. The one that scares you. The one that doesn't consider time, money, or limitations. What's that dream?"

I can always hear an audible shift in the tone of their voices as they let go and say something like, "Oh, well, if I could dream anything (and you can by the way— that's what dreams are!), then I want to be able to quit my full-time job. I want to be able to stay home with my kids. I want to be able to do *this* big thing or *that* impossible thing." Hear the key phrase in this? "I want."

I've found that if my dream is within reach, then it's not big enough. But when I get to that terrifying place of impossible, that's where miracles happen and those crazy, impractical dreams become a reality. But I've found in my own life that in order for the miraculous to happen, I've got to first trust God with the dream he gave me.

MAKING YOUR DREAMS A REALITY

So what do you want? After identifying your *why*, defining your dream is the second step in Tier 1 of your business plan. What is your big dream for your business? In a world without fear or limitations, without considering anyone else for a moment, what do you want? As you give yourself permission to dream and answer that question, you also take a giant leap toward making that dream a reality in your life.

Speak Up

Once I told my friends I wanted to become a business and life coach—as soon as the words left my mouth—I exhaled with relief. The truth is, I had been coaching people for years. I'd helped friends get out of debt, run marathons, and find new jobs. I am a natural encourager and I love helping people put their ideas into action. And now I was ready to put my own idea into action as well. I didn't want to just coach friends using intuition alone. I wanted to become educated on actual practices and gain the tools I needed to be a successful coach to more than just my friends.

As soon as I said the words out loud, I not only had the encouragement, support, and affirmation of my friends, but I also felt a deeper level of ownership and accountability to my dream. The moment I put it out there for the world to know, I felt a responsibility to do something about it.

That's what saying your dream out loud will do for you too. When you declare your desires, amazing things happen. The ground starts to move beneath your feet and people rally around you. They'll give the encouragement and affirmation you need to keep going. They'll offer their resources and connections and voluntarily work themselves into your plans. "I have a friend who's an accountant. She can help you set up your bookkeeping." "A guy at my church does graphic design. I'm sure he'd help you with your logo and business cards for your new business." "Oh, my cousin works in marketing. She can help you with your social media."

And as you gain encouragement, you'll find yourself leaning into your dreams with a new level of enthusiasm and confidence. You'll find yourself thinking, *Maybe this dream isn't so crazy after all.*

Put It on Paper

As soon as you start to own your dreams in front of others, fear will creep up again. This time it will get really loud. It will argue with you, tell you that your dream will never happen, and assure you that you are headed for disappointment. Fear convinces you that those you shared your dream with are making fun of you behind your back. It will make you feel silly for dreaming and stupid for saying it out loud. It will wear you out until you want to take it all back and give up.

You see, as long as fear keeps your dreams locked in the secret places of your heart, they stay inactive and unrealized. That's why it's also important to write your dream down. Just like when you say it out loud, the moment you write your dream on paper, fear lessens its hold on you. When you put the dream on paper, it's no longer just living inside of you; it's now tangible in the real world. It has more power because it's a real thing that you can touch and feel and see and remind yourself of. According to Dr. Gail Matthews, psychology professor at Dominican University in California, you are 42 percent more likely to achieve it just by writing it down.[28] Maybe it's a Post-it Note on your mirror or an index card taped to your computer screen. Whatever it is, it has more power because it's physically present outside of the battleground of your thoughts. Seeing your dream in writing serves as a powerful reminder of what you want.

Years ago, my mom passed to me a brilliant Christmas tradition. Every year, when Matt and I pack up our Christmas decorations after the season is over, we each write a note and tuck it away in the box. We write about all the major things that happened that year and all we hope for in the following year. Then, when we get our ornaments out of the attic the next Christmas season, we sit down and read the letters. They're a mixture of memories, prayers, and dreams. It's incredible—and often funny—to see what we were thinking the previous year. For example, before Matt and I were married, my 2006 letter begged, "God, please let me go on at least one date next year!" Well bless my heart. I guess that had been a tough year in the love department!

Reading those letters reminds me of prayers answered, dreams fulfilled, and goals reached. Hearing from "past me" about what I was thinking, desiring, and doing helps "present me" not only celebrate where I am but also motivates me to set bigger, better goals for the coming year.

Your dreams are inspiring, energizing, and life-giving. And the potential of what they can do for you is powerful. Don't dismiss them. Instead, treat them like something of great value—because they are. Own them, say them out loud, and write them down. When you do this, you take one brave step after another toward making them a reality.

CASTING A VISION

A dream often starts out fuzzy, but as you get more intentional about making it a reality, the dream will come into focus and become your vision. Your vision is more specific—it's still your dream, but now with more clarity. Like dreaming, it may feel silly at first because it requires another level of ownership and accountability. But your vision takes you one step closer to making your dream happen.

Your Vision Is a Statement of Truth

While your dream says, "I want," your vision says, "I am." The vision you have for yourself and your business is a statement of truth about the future you. This is where you change your language from "I dream," "I hope," or "I wish" to the declarative statement: "I am." This is the third step in building the foundation of your business plan and where you begin to speak truth into being.

My dream "to become a certified business and life coach" over time became my vision for Business Boutique. Back then, my vision sounded something like this: "[In five years,] I am a relatable, trustworthy, and credible friend, guide, leader, and coach to all current and aspiring women business owners. I am a household name and trusted source for educating, empowering, and equipping women in all stages of business. I am helping women through events, products, community, and coaching. I am leading a movement of women unapologetically stepping into their God-given gifts to make money doing what they love."

Do you see how my dream was general: "to become a certified business and life coach," but my vision was specific? Your dream is a broad stroke, a first pass. Your vision is how your dream looks *for you*. Someone else might have a dream "to become a certified business and life coach," but their vision might be: "to work with Fortune 500 companies helping executive-level leaders improve their bottom line." The beauty is that your vision is specific to you. It's the ability to see and believe where you're going before you've actually gotten there. So, where are you going? What is your vision for yourself and your business? What is the statement of truth about the future you?

Seeing the Future

Vision is important for a lot of reasons. For one, it gives direction and hope. As the proverb says, "Where there is no vision, the people perish."[29] Basically, when you have no direction or hope for the future, something *dies* inside of you. Dies! This is serious! Having a vision statement is more than a nice idea or cheesy corporate company practice. It breathes life into your business.

Your vision also informs the goals you will set and plans you will make to move you toward that vision. For example, Rachel created the vision for her clothing rental business that stated, "In three years, I am working on my business full time, and it has at least one retail storefront location with a full inventory of women's clothing. It produces annual revenues of at least $500,000." When Rachel created that vision statement, her business was run from her basement and she was barely breaking even.

Some people might think Rachel's vision was too big, too far-fetched. But that's what casting a vision is all about: looking ahead. If you don't think about the future and where you want to be, you'll never get there. Jonathan Swift once said, "Vision is the art of seeing what is invisible to others." When you create a vision statement of truth about the future, you begin to actually see it. And when you can see it, that's when you can start to make it a reality.

Your vision is also important for your momentum. Having a clear vision injects excitement and energy into your efforts. In an interview, Steve Jobs once said, "If you are working on something exciting that you really care about, you don't have to be pushed. The vision pulls you." And I can certainly speak from experience; that's true for me.

Permission to Grow and Change

If you're like me and you love options, then locking yourself into a vision statement about what will be happening in the future might feel limiting. You may be thinking, *but what if I change my situation or plans or mind?* I get it. The great news is that casting a vision doesn't have to be concrete. It can evolve over time as your business grows, your plans expand, and your dreams and desires change.

I remember Diane telling me about her experience building her booming wedding planning business. She said, "I never had any intention of this business becoming full time, much less employing my husband and sixteen other people! My vision when I started out was just to be able to supplement our family income. But, as the business grew, the bigger and bigger my vision became as I realized how much I loved it! My vision for the future looks much different today than it did when I was just starting out!"

Don't feel locked into or limited by your vision. This is your business, and it can change over time as much or as little as you want it to.

UNDERSTANDING YOUR MISSION

After you've identified your *why*, owned your dream, and cast your vision, the next step in Tier 1 of your business plan is to define and write a mission statement.

Stick with me here. You may be overwhelmed by the idea and tempted to skip it altogether. But that's only because most of the mission statements you've seen were probably long run-on sentences with a bunch of words that meant nothing. What a waste of time, right?

Your Mission Should Be Simple

A mission statement doesn't need to be fancy, complicated, wordy, or long. To be effective, it actually needs to be the exact opposite: short, simple, clear, and concise. Google has a great mission statement: "Google's mission is to organize the world's information and make it universally accessible and useful." When you read that, you understand immediately what they are about. And as a powerful testimonial to Google, the world's largest search engine, they actually do that. Google stays true to their mission, and that's one of the many reasons they are so successful.

Ramsey Solutions, where I work, has had basically the same mission statement since day one: "We provide biblically based, commonsense education and empowerment that give HOPE to everyone in every walk of life." That's what we've done for twenty-five years; it was true then, and it's still true today. You see, your dreams can change, your vision can change, and the goals that drive you can certainly change, but your mission statement usually won't. At least not very often.

Your mission statement is birthed out of purpose, principles, and conviction. While your dream says, "I want," and your vision says, "I am," your mission statement says, "I exist to." It defines what you're about, and at the same time, it defines what you're not about. I love how career coach Dan Miller defines it: "A mission statement turns a light bulb into a laser."[30] It's another layer of clarity for you and your business.

Stay in Your Lane

The best part of a mission statement is that it defines your lane and helps you stay in it as you are running toward your finish line. Opportunities in business are endless, but not every opportunity is a good one. Some "opportunities" won't be right for you or your business. These are called distractions. They take your eyes off what you're trying to do. Remember, just because you *can* do something does not mean you *should*. Successful business leaders are willing to let good opportunities pass them by if they aren't the *right* opportunities for their specific businesses.

You can think of your mission statement as an out-of-bounds marker. When you know your business's boundaries, your decision-making becomes much easier. Your mission statement becomes a litmus test or filter you run all of your options and opportunities through. It helps you decide which projects, products, or people are right for your business and which ones are not. It informs when to say yes and when to say no.

When an opportunity comes your way, all you have to do is ask yourself if it lines up with your mission statement. If it doesn't, it's a clear indicator that the opportunity is not right for you or your business. I know we want to please people and be liked. We don't want to let anyone down. But as my friend Chris Hogan says, "We have to ask ourselves, *Do I want to be liked or do I want to be effective?*" They aren't always the same thing, so knowing your answer to that simple question can give you the confidence to say no to the distractions.

Listen, I know it's tough to turn down business or growth opportunities, especially when you're just starting out. You feel like saying no to an opportunity is saying no to more money. But the truth is, deciding what *not* to do is more important than deciding what *to* do. Every time we say yes to something that doesn't line up with our mission statement, it takes us further and further away from who we want to be.

When something doesn't line up with your mission statement, you can usually feel it pretty quickly. You start to feel stressed and strained. When something doesn't align with where you're going, it zaps your strength, takes a ton of energy, and frustrates you easily. That's because you're trying to be something you're not. Sure, it might feel like you're moving, but in the *wrong* direction. Anything that takes you away from your goal also takes time away from things that are more important, productive, and beneficial to you, your business, and your customers. It's just not worth it. That's why a mission statement is so valuable, because it can help you readily identify which opportunities to take on and which to let go. And most of all, it helps you stay true to you.

LIVING THE DREAM

Today, I get to coach business leaders from all over the country in all stages of business. I've worked with CEOs, Fortune 500 companies, entrepreneurs, start-ups, "mompreneurs," hobby businesses, and home-based businesses. I'm in my sweet spot doing what I love and helping others do the same. But I didn't wake up one day in this position with this opportunity, platform, and influence.

It started with a girl in her midtwenties nervously saying her dream out loud to her girlfriends on the beach. But then as I took that dream and owned it and wrote it down, things started to happen. I created a vision of where I was going and how I was going to get there. Then I put it into action, made plans, and set goals.

I registered for online classes. I did assignments and classwork after I got home from my real job and on the weekends. I read books. I listened to sample coaching calls on my headphones while walking my dog on the greenway by my house. I practiced. I highlighted pages in my textbook and filled out coaching plans and forms. I set up a website. One at a time, I got clients. With every tiny step I took, the momentum grew and with it, my confidence grew as well. And now, years later, I get to live my dream.

And if you follow these foundational steps in building your business, the same will happen for you.

chapter 5 action items
LET'S APPLY WHAT YOU'VE LEARNED!

Dream

What is your dream for your business? This is the "I want" piece of your plan. Finish the statement:

"I want _____."

Vision

What is your vision for your business? This is the "I am" part of the process. If you were to meet yourself in the future—maybe one, five, ten years down the road—what would you be doing? Write down that future-tense statement and claim it. Just fill in the blanks:

"In _____ (time frame), I am _____."

Mission Statement

What is your mission statement? This is the "I exist to" statement. Keep it simple and focus on your purpose. Finish the sentence:

"My business exists to _____."

chapter 6

FROM DREAMING TO DOING

Setting Goals That Get You There

I love running. In fact, I've run Nashville's Country Music Marathon or Half-Marathon every year since 2009, when I ran my first full marathon. I met my husband while I was training for the half-marathon in 2010, and, in 2012, we ran it together—dressed as a bride and groom a week before our wedding! I love that race for several reasons, and one big one is that the company I work for, Ramsey Solutions, donates $1,000 to each runner's favorite charity if they finish the half marathon in under two hours.

I am right on the line of being a two-hour half-marathon runner, so the opportunity to raise $1,000 for my chosen charity always motivates me to train well. In the fall of 2014, while pregnant with my first son, Carter, I registered for the upcoming half-marathon in April. I thought training for the half would be a perfect way to lose the baby weight. I was due on January 31, and the race was set for April 26—exactly twelve weeks later. Ambitious, but I like big goals. What I was not expecting, and what actually happened, was a traumatic emergency cesarean surgery on January 31. Carter was just fine, but my training schedule was pushed back for a longer recovery.

I did what I could in the weeks I had left to train, but my hopes of finishing in under two hours had started to fade. But if you've learned anything about me so far, you know I'm not a quitter. Once I was cleared for exercise by my doctor, I set the fears and frustrations aside and trained as hard as I could in the time I had left.

The morning of the race, I felt great at the starting line. The weather was mild. My nerves were high, and I was ready to go for it. The first few miles felt good, but after seven miles and two bathroom breaks, I realized I was cutting it really close on time. A two-hour finish was still possible, but only if I could hold a nine-minute-per-mile pace for the entire second half of the race. Considering the huge hills ahead, I had no idea if I would make it in time. But I wanted to hit my goal *that year* more than any other year.

The next few miles were fine, but, by mile eleven, my legs felt like concrete and I was losing steam. At mile twelve, I was barely hanging on. I had chills and felt pretty sure I was on the verge of throwing up. But with one heavy foot in front of the other, I forced myself to keep running. Then I saw it ahead in the distance: the finish line! I checked my watch again. I had less than a minute to cross. One thousand dollars for my favorite charity was on the line.

I crested the final hill and, as the seconds ticked by, I began to sprint, digging deep with everything in me. I ran as fast as I possibly could, not caring if the other runners could hear the pep talk I was giving myself: *Do not throw up. Do not throw up. There are cameras everywhere, and you are wearing a Dave Ramsey shirt. Do not embarrass your company! Do not throw up!* I held on to the sprint pace, unable to feel my legs, until I crossed the timing pad and finally, thank you, Jesus, stopped my watch: 1:59:55:42. I MADE IT! By the skin of my teeth, I made it.

I think I cried a little and probably collapsed dramatically. I looked around, ready to wave to the thousands of adoring fans no doubt stunned by the incredible feat I had just accomplished. No one noticed or cared that I had hit my goal time. More likely, anyone who watched me probably wondered why a random woman decided to sprint like a maniac and throw her entire body across the finish line like an Olympian going for the gold. I didn't care if anyone else noticed. I was ecstatic! I broke two hours and raised $1,000 for my charity. I did it!

But looking back, if I am honest, it wasn't all about the race, the time, or the money raised for charity. That accomplishment was about me. I was so proud of that particular half-marathon because I did something I didn't think I could do: I overcame some huge obstacles to achieve a difficult goal. That's the power of goals. Goals push us and stretch us. They hold us accountable and enable us to accomplish things we didn't think were possible. That's why the last step in Tier 1 of building the foundation of the business plan is to set goals.

WHAT ARE YOU GOING TO DO?

If you want to do things you never thought you could do, goals will get you there. Whether it's running a marathon or running a business, your goals are what get you to the finish line. They take the impossible and make it possible. That's why setting goals is so important. Remember what we said in the last chapter:

Your dreams say *I want*.
Your vision says *I am*.
Your mission statement says *I exist to*.

Now it's time to put these statements into action. Once you've claimed your dreams, cast your vision, and clarified your mission, goals break them into bite-sized pieces and make them possible. Or to put it another way:

Goals say, *I will*.

Goals help drive all future decisions as you build or grow your business. But like everything in your business plan, all the elements work together and build on each other for a reason. If you try to set goals first, before determining your *why*, dream, vision, or mission statement, your goals will have no soul. Sure, they will be ideas to aim at, but they won't be born out of a deep conviction and calling in your heart. However, when you know your foundation, your goals will not simply be words on paper; they will be crucial action steps—steps that help make your dream and vision happen.

How to Set a Power Goal

Goals are often used as a synonym for new resolutions, intentions, or habits. Big mistake! Goals are different. New Year's resolutions are forgotten by February, best intentions don't always happen, and new habits aren't as measurable. Goals, on the other hand, have a high follow-through rate and success—if they're set the right way. That's why I want you to set power goals. And in order for them to be power goals they need to be specific, measurable, and time-limited. Let's take a closer look at what makes a power goal.

Goals Must Be Specific

First, your power goal needs to be specific. This seems obvious, I know, but often we confuse our desires, dreams, or intentions with goals. We say things like, "My goal is to grow my business." You may have a desire to grow your business. You may *dream* of doing that. You may even have the *intention* to do so. But "My goal is to grow my business" isn't specific. A power goal needs to be more precise. For instance, "My goal is to *increase orders* for my business." See the difference? With that specific detail, "increase orders," you've specified *how* you want to grow. You've added focus and moved one step closer to creating a power goal that will work for you.

Goals Must Be Measurable

Your goals also need to be measurable. A specific target like "increase orders" isn't measurable. That's why you need to add something quantifiable to your goal. "My goal is to increase orders for my business *by 50 percent*." By adding "50 percent," you've given yourself something measurable. If you currently have one thousand orders, then your goal is to increase your orders by five hundred. Now you can track your progress simply by comparing the number you have with the number you want to reach. A measurable goal allows you to track your progress toward where you want to be.

Goals Must Have a Time Limit

Finally, your goals need to have a time limit. Without a time limit, you lose the urgency and motivation of working toward a deadline. I've often heard it said,

"There are only seven days in a week, and 'someday' isn't one of them." If we say we'll get to our goals "someday," we're guaranteeing we'll never reach them. That's why having a time limit is crucial. It further defines your goal and adds a ticking clock: "My goal is to increase orders for my business by 50 percent *by the end of this year*." Now you have a time frame to accomplish your goal. Having a time limit is important because it holds you accountable to actually do it. When December 31 rolls around, you can see if you reached your goal or not. The time limit can vary depending on what you're working on. Just don't set a goal too far into the future or you'll lose the urgency and enthusiasm to work toward it now.

When you put all the pieces together, "My goal is to grow my business" becomes, "My goal is to increase orders for my business by 50 percent by December 31." And that's how a power goal is made. You take an idea with potential and turn it into something achievable. You can see what you need to do and when you need to do it. By setting goals that are specific, measurable, and time-limited, you set yourself up to actually accomplish them.

Microgoals Move to Your To-Do List

Once you've set a power goal with a time limit, you make it even more attainable by breaking it into weekly microgoals. Microgoals are smaller tasks, set on a weekly basis, that help you accomplish your larger goal. Instead of one big project looming on the horizon, you'll have little tasks that keep you on track. To develop a microgoal, you start with your time limit (December 31) and goal (500 new orders) and begin to work backward, setting incremental progress milestones. If it's November 15, for example, then you have just over a month (5 weeks) to get 500 new orders. When you do the math, (500 orders divided by 5 weeks) you get 100. That breaks down to 100 new orders per week. Now you have a manageable number. When you break down your goal this way, you're left with weekly micro-goals that help you stay on track toward your larger goal. This is how your goals say, "I will." *I will make two new calls today. I will design eight pages today. I will assemble fifteen hair bows today.*

When you develop weekly microgoals and add those tasks to your daily or weekly to-do list, you are not only making your goals more manageable, but you're also making more progress.

Setting Yourself Up to Reach Your Goals

Turning big goals into smaller tasks is pretty rewarding. It allows you to cross items off as you make progress, which leads to more progress, and your goal starts to become a reality instead of a wish for "someday." But it's important to keep in mind that a goal is only as good as you make it. That's why I want you to take goal-setting a step further and consider three more ideas in order to set power goals that will actually work.

Goals Must Be Yours

I have a friend who has a goal to read thirty books this year. Thirty! Some quick math will tell you that's more than two books per month. I love to read, so when I heard him talking about it, I thought, *I should do that too!* Let me just tell you, that's a terrible idea. In my season of life, with two young children and lots of new, demanding work projects, I do not have the desire to dedicate that amount of time to reading. I *could* do it of course. I just don't *want* to. I could try it, but I know I would eventually get frustrated and give up. That's what happens when you take on goals that aren't yours. It feels like you are putting a lot of effort and energy (whether you actually are or not) into reaching a result you don't even care about.

A lot of people spend their lives chasing someone else's goals. Their mom wanted them to be a doctor. Their spouse wanted them to take that new job. Their friend told them they should go into business together. When you take on someone else's version of success, it's like taking on water in a boat. You're going to get weighed down and eventually sink. You're going to be burdened by pressure you don't want, stressed about a result you don't actually care about, and overwhelmed with the work required to get there. Instead, set goals *you* want to achieve. When the goal is yours, you're much more likely to actually reach it.

Goals Must Be in Writing

I've gone over the importance of writing down your dream, vision, and mission statement. Your goals are no exception. Writing down your goals makes them more effective because you state what you are going to do and commit to it. For example, I have a weekly recurring appointment on my calendar. It's an all-day "appointment" to write a chapter of this book, every week, until it's finished. And to be totally honest, as I sit here writing, I am behind! I am supposed to be on chapter 7, but a few setbacks put me a little off schedule. That is what's so great about having my big goal (writing a book) written down, and the smaller goals (chapters and word count) written down as well. My progress, good or bad, becomes instantly apparent.

Goals Must Be Realistic

At some point in your life, you've heard that you can be anything you want to be, but it's simply not true. No one loves to inspire people more than I do, but let's get real. You cannot be *anything* you want to be, and neither can I. I cannot win *American Idol*, be president of the United States, or play in the WNBA to name a few. First, I can't sing. Second, I don't care for the political rat race. And third, I have terrible depth perception and hand-eye coordination. I can set a goal to accomplish those things, but I'll just be working really hard toward an inevitable disappointment.

Being realistic with your goals also means that you take into consideration any limitations you're currently facing. During the dreaming stage, we didn't consider limitations, but as we move into action, we need to become more realistic so that we actually reach our goals. Maybe you have a limited amount of money, resources, or energy to work with, so you set a goal with a slower growth rate to account for that. You might have other priorities that are more important to you right now, inflexible commitments you have to work around, or family needs that take precedence over a particular goal. That's perfectly fine. Taking your current situation into consideration when setting your goal isn't settling, it's smart. Rather than developing unattainable goals that eventually leave you feeling discouraged and frustrated, setting realistic goals actually sets you up for success.

Progress Propels You Forward

Today, my to-do list looks like this: pick up my dry cleaning, make a bank deposit, get groceries, and pay bills, among other tasks. I live by my to-do list and I am always adding to it. It's satisfying to check things off and feel like I've made progress toward getting things done. It's so satisfying, in fact, that many times if I do something that wasn't on my list, I add it—even though I already did it—and then immediately check it off. Some people may think I'm weird, but you may do the same thing.

The reason I love checking things off my list is because it seems we humans are wired for progress. We like to see how far we've come. At the bottom of a large hill on a run, I feel nervous and overwhelmed, unsure what it will take out of me to make it to the top. And every time I get up there, I pause, look backward, and feel a sense of satisfaction at how far I've come. It's the same for all of us. No matter what we're doing, we like seeing what we've accomplished. It's natural to want to feel like you're working toward something, and it's defeating when you feel like you aren't.

That's what progress does for you. It gives you a sense of pride and satisfaction and fulfillment, which in turn propels you to keep going.

MAKE IT EASY ON YOURSELF TO WIN

Have you ever noticed that the first step of almost every diet plan on earth is the same? Step one: clean out your pantry! It's easy to understand why. If you want to lose the extra padding you picked up through the holidays, you need to throw out the junk food before you even *act* like you're starting a diet. If you don't, every time you go looking for a healthy snack, you'll end up stuffing an old Little Debbie Christmas Tree Cake in your face. Because, seriously, those things are amazing— even in January. We all have things we want to do, but following through is tough. Usually the reason we don't follow through is simply that we don't set ourselves up to win.

We can do tiny things that take almost no effort but increase the likelihood of follow-through on our well-intentioned goals and plans. I know that I'm less likely to skip an early morning workout if I set my gym clothes and sneakers out the night before. One minute of preparation goes a long way toward helping me achieve my goal. What could you do to help yourself achieve your goals? Maybe it means clearing some space for a home office or working during the kids' nap times or turning off social media during work hours. We all know that accomplishing goals takes work. But if you want to accomplish something, do everything you can ahead of time to set yourself up to follow through—and win.

Anticipate the Reward

Reaching goals requires change, and change is hard. That's because it always requires some level of sacrifice. To grow your business, you have to work on it more. To write a book, you have to commit the time to write. To sell more products, you have to make them. With every new goal and level of growth, there will always be an uncomfortable sacrifice that goes with it. But we often make change harder on ourselves because we focus only on what we have to give up. We imagine how hard it will be to dedicate those hours, wake up early, give up free time, or have the discipline to sit down behind the computer and focus. We anticipate the sacrifice and all it's going to require of us and we get discouraged before we even start.

I learned a trick that has worked for me: stop anticipating the *sacrifice* and start anticipating the *reward*. Instead of focusing on how tired I'd be in the morning when I had to wake up early to write, I imagined how proud I would feel seeing that blog post shared on social media. Instead of focusing on how early and dark and cold a morning workout would be, I started anticipating how great I would feel afterward, how much energy I would have, and how proud of myself I would be.

I have a client who did this. After years of a successful corporate career at a publishing house, Katie decided to become a freelance book editor. I remember her telling me that, even though leaving her job was a scary step, she focused on all she would gain by working for herself. Instead of worrying about losing the steady salary and benefits, she was excited about the time she would be able to spend with her kids during the summers, when she'd normally be at the office. She anticipated actually being able to talk with them when they wanted to talk, instead of when she had a few spare moments at the end of the day. She anticipated being able to work on one project at a time instead of having to juggle several projects and meetings in a single day. I remember her saying that it was so rewarding to think of all she was going to gain instead of all she was going to "lose" by leaving her job. In any situation, we can dread the sacrifice or anticipate the reward. It just turns out that anticipating the reward leads to far better results!

There's actually scientific proof to back this too. I read an article in which Dr. Paul Hokemeyer, a Manhattan psychiatrist said, "When you're looking forward to something, your brain releases feel-good hormones along your brain's reward system, the 'mesolimbic dopamine pathway,' which helps to reinforce behaviors that are beneficial."[31] In other words, when you anticipate the reward instead of the sacrifice, your brain makes you feel good about it and it sets your focus on it. You're actually changing the way your mind thinks about going after that goal, and when you change your mind, your behaviors will immediately follow. Before you know it, you're looking forward to waking up early, working out, writing that book, creating the products, or dedicating time to your business.

Dealing with Disappointment

Regardless of how ambitious, hardworking, dedicated, and occasionally crazy we can be, sometimes we just don't get there. We fall short, miss the mark, and don't reach the goal we've set. Sometimes it's a result of factors outside of our control, and other times life just gets in the way. When that happens, it can be discouraging, disappointing, and defeating. For every heroic running story in which I reached my goal, I have plenty of others where I didn't. For every great talk I've given, I also have stories of train-wreck presentations.

I know it can be hard to let go of an idea that's stuck in your head. You wanted to grow your email list to five thousand, but you only hit twenty-three hundred. You wanted to fill the conference center for your event, but it was only half full. You wanted to increase your sales to $3,000 this month, but you only earned $1,900. You wanted to get ten thousand likes on a social post, but you only got sixty-four hundred. You had a goal to do something, but you didn't quite get there.

In those moments, I want to encourage you to stop beating yourself up and instead give yourself some grace. Instead of focusing on all you didn't do, look at what you did do. You have twenty-three hundred people who asked to be on your email list! You sold $1,900 in your business this month! You reached sixty-four hundred people with a single social post! That's awesome!

Instead of giving in to the guilt and dragging around that heavy shame, remind yourself of what you have done. Best-selling author and sociologist, Brené Brown offers great advice when she says to talk to yourself the way you would talk to someone you love.[32] Would you talk down to a friend or child or spouse who fell short? No, you'd pick them up and encourage them. And that's what you need to do for yourself. Sure, there may be a long list of things you feel like you've fallen short on. In place of all things you "failed" at are shining examples of things you succeeded in. It's a matter of taking your eyes off of what you didn't get to and focusing instead on what you did do.

Don't stress if something doesn't work out as planned. Things happen and none of us, despite our best efforts, can control the universe. You can reset your goals or revisit them later. You can move on to the next thing. Falling down and getting back up is a normal part of the journey, so all you can do is get over it, get back up, and get moving.

WHAT IS SUCCESS, ANYWAY?

You already know I'm entrepreneurial by nature, and one signature quality of entrepreneurs is that we are extremists. I have been like this my entire life. I'm either all in or all out. I'm either exercising every day or sitting on the couch eating Oreos by the sleeve. I'm either hot or cold, on or off. There's no in-between.

During a recent leadership conference for small-business owners, I spoke about making small changes to how we interact with our phones and technology in order to be more present for our families. Afterward, an attendee came up to me and said, "I loved your talk. You're so right. I just want to rip out every electronic device in my house!" I laughed at his enthusiasm because I could relate. I always gravitate toward the extremes in my life—never resting in the safe middle of moderation.

The problem with this habit is that I get so fixated on the finish line that I forget to enjoy the process of getting there. It's not *just* about hitting the goal; it's about everything that happens along the way. I love Earl Nightingale's definition of success from his classic presentation *The Strangest Secret*: "Success is the *progressive realization* of a worthy ideal or goal." [33] That means you're not just a success at the finish line or end goal; you're successful every step you take toward that goal. Reaching the goal doesn't make you a success. Striving toward a goal does.

My friend Natalie describes her goals for her consulting business as experiments. I love that. If she doesn't meet a goal, she doesn't describe it as a failure because it was just an experiment. When you experiment, you can't fail because the whole point of experimenting is to try something and see what happens. She told me she has tried several new ideas to grow her business that haven't worked at all, but she doesn't mind. Those ideas were just some of the many stepping stones on her journey—not a journey *to* success but a journey *of* success.

When we realize that getting to the end goal is a journey, full of highs and lows, then we aren't a success only when we accomplish a certain goal. And we aren't a failure if we fall short. We are a success because of the work we put in, the hours we dedicate, the sacrifices we make, and the effort we invest on the way to the finish line. When we look at it this way, we don't have to wait to cross a certain finish line to feel successful. We can realize that we are already there. So set strong goals, create your to-do list, and get going. If you want it bad enough and you're willing to work hard enough, you'll eventually get to where you want to be, and, in many cases, even further!

chapter 6 action items
LET'S APPLY WHAT YOU'VE LEARNED!

Strong Goals

In this chapter we learned the importance of setting goals. Remember, in order to set strong goals, they need to be specific, measurable, and have a time limit. Use this formula to help you write out strong goals. Practice writing your goals below.

1. My goal is to _____(specific)_____ by _____(measure)_____ by _____(date)_____.
2. My goal is to _____ by _____ by _____.
3. My goal is to _____ by _____ by _____.
4. My goal is to _____ by _____ by _____.
5. My goal is to _____ by _____ by _____.

Microgoals

We also learned the importance of breaking your larger goals into weekly micro-goals to help you stay on track. Calculate your weekly microgoals by using the formula below. For example, my goal is to finish this book.

1. What is my goal? _____
   Write the measurable metric you're aiming for—clients, word count, units, sales, etc. (In my case, my goal is to write 48,000 more words.)
2. What is my deadline? _____ (July 20)
3. How many weeks do I have between when I will begin and the deadline? _____ weeks. (In my case, I have six weeks left to write the book.)

4. What is your weekly microgoal to reach in order to stay on track? Divide your answer in #1 by your answer in #3. Write that number here: _____. That tells you what you need to accomplish each week. (My weekly microgoal is to write 8,000 words.)

Use the graph below to list your goals and plug in your numbers. This will give you your weekly microgoals for each larger goal you are working toward. You will see we have the examples of gaining five hundred new orders from earlier in the chapter as well as my book goal.

Goal	No. of Units Needed	Weeks to Deadline	Weekly Microgoal (Units / Total Hours)
Ex. New orders	500	5	100
Ex. Write book	48,000	6	8,000

Congratulations! Now, not only have you set strong goals, but you also have weekly microgoals to keep you on track to get there.

Tier Two

MAKE IT
YOURS

Congratulations! You've finished the entire first tier of your business plan, and you've done a lot of the hard foundational work. In Tier 2, you'll plan out how to build your business around your life versus the other way around. In these next chapters, we'll work through six more steps so your business is developed around your strengths, values, money, time, schedule, and space. By the time you're finished with this tier, your business should look the way you want it to.

chapter 7

PLAY TO YOUR STRENGTHS

Building Your Business Around Your Life

"Dough, Ray, Meeeee, Faghhh, So, La, Tee, Daaaaoooooooo."

By the time I went for the high note, I was half squealing and half screaming—neither of which could be mistaken for actual singing. The screeching of my preteen voice could be heard echoing through the halls of McMurray Middle School. I'm sure that students and teachers wondered if the sound was someone auditioning for Select Chorus or if it was some unfortunate animal being harmed! Either way, no one suffered from my audition more than Mrs. Hastings, the chorus director, who had to sit through and evaluate my disastrous performance that day. Any student could be in the general seventh grade chorus. They took the screechers, tone-deaf, and delusionally self-confident alike. However, Select Chorus was an elite group for only the best singers. You had to audition and be selected. The problem, I would soon find out, was that I couldn't sing.

I don't just mean I didn't have a future as a potential *American Idol* winner. I mean, I had a better chance at TV stardom as one of the humiliating *American Idol* auditions they show solely for laughter and shock value. However, at that time in my life, it never occurred to me that I couldn't sing. So, when the Select Chorus roster was posted on the gray-and-blue cinder block wall in the hallway the next week, I thought there was some mistake that my name wasn't listed.

Not making Select Chorus was just one of the many rejections I experienced in my already awkward tween years. I also tried out for the basketball team, cheerleading squad, and student council. I didn't make a single one. I felt pretty good about being accepted onto the track team until I found out that, like the general seventh grade chorus, they accepted anyone. It was the first time I realized there were things I wasn't good at. Sadly, I had no idea that natural talent and strength played a role in the things I should do.

Since then, I've discovered many other things I am not good at, such as softball, details, and parallel parking, just to name a few. But I have also discovered things that come naturally to me. Because I am creative, outgoing, and extremely energetic, public speaking, coaching, and teaching are effortless for me. However, learning the difference between what I'm good and not good at didn't happen overnight. I will tell you, though, that finally discovering my strengths, along with ways to stay in them, is the primary reason I've been able to reach the goals I've set throughout my life.

Some things will come easy to you. And some things, despite how much you work on them, will always be a struggle. Whether it's singing or sewing, accounting or web programming, you are not good at everything. I'm not either—no one is. The key to your success in your business—and life, for that matter—is knowing the difference. That's why we are going to spend this chapter discovering your strengths.

Your business should be based on something you're naturally good at. That's important because you're going to spend a lot of time doing it. On top of your core business, however, you will be juggling hundreds of day-to-day things to keep it running. Some of those things will be easy for you, but others won't. That's why discovering all of your strengths—and, as a result, your weaknesses—is so important. When you know the difference, you can spend the majority of your time in your strengths and backfill for your weaknesses. This allows you to have the most fun and make the most impact with the least amount of effort. When you focus your efforts primarily on what you're good at, you're more successful too. The overall quality of your work will be much higher when you run your business this way. And when you get help for the things you aren't good at, you allow others to stay in their strengths as well. Identifying your strengths is the first step in Tier 2 of your business plan. So let's talk about how to do more of what you love and less of what you don't.

HOW TO KNOW WHAT YOU'RE GOOD AT

Before you build your business around your strengths, you need to know what they actually are. You might already have some idea of your strengths—maybe you took an evaluation as part of a job interview or training. Great! This is a good place to review and affirm your skills. But if this is your first introduction to discovering your strengths, then this part will be really fun. I love helping women assess their gifts. It's always fun to hear them say, "I thought so!" or "Ever since I was little, this was the thing I could do well." The good news is that, regardless of what you might or might not already know, there are some great tools you can use to identify or affirm your strengths.

Strengths Assessments and Personality Tests

Personality assessments are fast and easy ways to discover your strengths. Several options are available, including the Clifton StrengthsFinder assessment, The Myers-Briggs Type Indicator, and the DiSC model test. I've taken each of these tests, some multiple times. It's always fun to see how eerily accurate they are. Taking an assessment or personality test is a great way to gain understanding into the unique person you were created to be. And because these tests are so comprehensive, they provide insights into how to be the strongest version of yourself at work, in relationships, and life in general.

The Five "E" Questions

If you don't want to take an assessment or personality test, you can still easily discover your strengths. I developed a series of "E" questions I use when coaching clients. These five questions are a quick way to gain valuable insight into your strengths.

Question 1: What Do You Enjoy?

One way to discover your strengths is to think about what you enjoy doing. With the exception of those few misguided *American Idol* contestants, the things we enjoy are almost always our strengths. After all, we don't typically like to do things that highlight what we aren't good at. I'm great at planning parties, so I am always quick to volunteer to host whenever a friend is having a shower. However, the moment a friend needs help with administrative tasks that require details and organization, I'm not the one for the job. I would screw up their efforts and hate my life in the process!

When we think of strengths this way, it becomes easier to figure them out. Maybe it's been a few years (or decades!) since you've even thought about things you love to do. After speaking at Purdue University several years ago on the topic of life balance, I was approached by a woman with tears in her eyes. She said, "I loved what you said about spending time on things you love to do." She paused and stared off into space for a second. "But to be honest, it's been so long since I've done what I love, that I have forgotten what those things even are."

Even if they are buried deep in our past, the things we love—the things that bring us joy—are still a part of us. Life just tends to get in the way and we forget to take the time to enjoy them again. Tom Rath, author of *StrengthsFinder 2.0*, says,

> Although people certainly do change over time . . . scientists have discovered that [passions and interests] are relatively stable throughout adulthood. Our natural talents and passions—the things we truly love to do—last for a lifetime. But all too often they go untapped.[34]

Most of the things we enjoyed in the past are things we still enjoy. That's because the things we love to do aren't just an optional ornament in our lives; they are a part of who we are.

So what do you enjoy? What do you do just because it's fun? I love how bestselling author and creativity expert Austin Kleon puts it, "One thing I've learned in my brief career: It's the side projects that really take off. By side projects I mean the stuff you thought was just messing around. Stuff that's just play. That's actually the good stuff. That's when the magic happens."[35] Think about what you enjoy because that is probably where the magic happens for you too.

Question 2: Where Do You Excel?

Sometimes discovering what you're good at comes from seeing how you perform in relation to others. As a kid, I went to the local roller skating rink every weekend. My friends and I would go for both weekend nights and every day during the summer. It was our hangout, and we never missed an opportunity to go.

We skated for hours and each night when the rink was closing, after everyone had turned in their skates and changed into their tennis shoes, we had foot races. Kids lined up by age group and sprinted from one end of the rink to the other. One night I worked up some nerve and competed in my age group, which was made up of both boys and girls. To my surprise, I beat all of the girls *and* all of the boys! I won a coupon for a free Icee but that paled in comparison to the excitement of discovering something I was good at. I competed every night after that. And every single night, I won.

As silly as it sounds, realizing that I was a natural runner was an incredible moment for me. There was something unique and special that I could do well. It clearly stuck with me as I continued to run for fun, even to this day.

This type of learning by achieving is another way to discover your strengths. What do you excel at? Where do you perform above average? Where do you stand out in relation to others doing the same thing? Don't get all squirmy about answering the question. Being honest with yourself about how you perform in a certain area is different than boasting or bragging. You're simply acknowledging something true *about* yourself *for* yourself. You aren't doing anyone any favors by dismissing or downplaying your strengths—if you're naturally good at something, own it!

Question 3: What Do Others Encourage in You?

For years I thought I was a really bad writer. And honestly, it took a whole lot of people telling me over and over again that I was good before I even considered it a possibility. But, a little at a time, I started to believe it. The positive feedback I got encouraged me to work harder. And as a result, I became a better writer. Now, years later, I'm doing something I would have never dreamed of: writing a book!

Sometimes discovering your strengths happens through the gift of others' compliments. We can be our own worst critic and focus only on our flaws. But oftentimes, other people can see something in us that we can't. They may recognize a particular gift, talent, or skill you have. When someone compliments you on something you do, don't dismiss it. And when you see a theme repeatedly popping up, like I did with writing, lean into that. You're on to something. And if you're not sure or can't remember what others notice about you, ask them! Ask family or friends what types of things they think you are naturally good at. You might just be surprised and encouraged by what they identify as your strengths.

Question 4: What Comes Effortlessly to You?

Another way to discover your strengths is to think about what comes naturally to you. Most often, those things that don't take a lot of effort are your strengths. But because they are effortless, they are easy to dismiss. That's because we assume anything of value must take a lot of effort. But that's not the case when it comes to your natural talent. Those things will generally come easily to you. Of course, you will still need to practice in order to improve, but because it's a strength, you'll likely improve faster.

For example, Alyssa is outstanding with people. She can walk into a room full of strangers and win them over within minutes. She has a public relations business, and she's incredible at leading press tours, working with journalists, and engaging with all types of people. When I pointed out how talented she was, she laughed and said, "Oh, I guess so. I don't feel like I'm doing much. I'm just being me." That's what working in your strengths feels like. It's as effortless as breathing and, like Alyssa said, it's just you being you.

Question 5: What Gives You Energy?

A great way to discover your strengths is to recognize that your strengths don't drain your energy; instead, they actually give you energy. I'm so thankful I get to work every day doing things that energize me. Working in my strengths actually fires me up! Work that fires you up? Imagine that!

You'd think that after speaking at our Business Boutique event where I was on stage, teaching, for two straight days, I would be exhausted. But after our first event in Nashville, when I was finished and had left the venue, I didn't go crash in my bed. Instead, my husband and I went out to dinner where I proceeded to talk a hundred miles per hour, recounting every detail of the event and how amazing it was. Even after my full teaching and speaking schedule, including the months of practice and preparation, I was still on fire and full of energy. That's what working in your strengths looks like. You are more energized after you've done the work than before you started. So what gives you energy? What fills you up instead of drains you? The answer might reveal a strength you've been overlooking.

Keep Growing and Keep Going

Just because you're good at something doesn't mean you can sit back and coast on cruise control. Being successful requires you to *start* with your natural strengths, but it's on you to grow, develop, and improve from there. Jackie, for example, was always crafty but she wasn't a trained seamstress by any stretch of the imagination. However, when she posted a picture of her cute "experimental project," a clutch purse, on Facebook, it went viral and resulted in hundreds of orders. She realized then that, even though that first little experiment took her seven hours to create, she was going to have to learn how to sew. Over time, through classes, reading, online videos, research, and a lot of practice, she has become a talented seamstress. As a result, she can now create a new purse in a fraction of the time that first one took.

Like Jackie, we can take our natural strengths to a higher level of performance and impact, but it's on us to do the work to get there. It takes a lot of effort to make things look effortless. Just because you start with something that comes easy to you doesn't mean you get to stay there. You need to regularly find ways to grow yourself and your business.

WHAT TO DO WITH YOUR WEAKNESSES

It's fun to find out what we're good at, and we know we need to spend the most of our time on those tasks. But what about everything else? What about all of the items on your to-do list that you don't enjoy, that you don't excel at, that are not effortless, and that just plain drain you? Over the years, I've discovered several options for tackling challenging tasks, and the best part is, none of the options involve you having to do them yourself!

Barter

A few years ago, my client Nora was trying to build her fitness business by creating a website. She started working on a simple website template, which quickly became a weekend-long project that involved her trying to figure out coding, widgets, and plug-ins. After two full days and late nights, Nora wanted to throw her computer out the window. She was trying to do something she didn't know how to do and wasn't good at.

After her unsuccessful weekend, I encouraged Nora to have someone build her website for her. She didn't have extra money budgeted for that, so we brainstormed people she could barter services with. As it turns out, Nora had a friend of a friend who was a web programmer. She reached out to him and pitched the idea of a service trade. She would coach him toward his fitness goals and he would build her a website. For every hour she coached him, he programmed her site.

It was a successful arrangement that benefited them both. The best part was that Nora didn't have to try to learn coding and web design to do it. She got to do what she loves and is good at (fitness coaching), and her friend got to do what he loves and is good at (web programming)—and they *both* got what they needed. It was a win-win opportunity for everyone involved!

Outsource

If you don't have a mutual friend to barter with, you can always pay someone to do what you need. Before you start objecting about not having the money, hear me out. I'm not recommending you spend money you don't have. Instead, I want you to go make more money.

For example, I spoke with someone just this week who needed help with taxes. Let's say that you, like her, need a tax professional for your business (you do, by the way), but you don't have the $500 or so it would cost to hire one. I want you to find a way to earn $500 more doing your thing in order to pay for the accountant. When you do this, you get to stay in your strengths and do what you love, *and you* protect your business because you've hired a professional to do what they are good at and love. Again, it's a win-win!

Automate

There are probably things you do for your business that you don't want to do—and don't *have* to do! For example, other than a few spontaneous posts of family pictures, I don't particularly enjoy keeping up with social media. If you use social media occasionally, just for fun to scroll Internet memes and keep up with friends, that's great. But if your business, like mine, is built on social media, then you have to maintain it consistently as a critical part of your operations.

Because social media is so important for my brand, and because my schedule is crazy and I can't trust myself to keep up with the frequency needed, I automate it. Every Monday, I write and schedule all of my posts for the week. Then, as the week goes on and I get busy writing or speaking or traveling, my social media upkeep doesn't suffer. My posts automatically publish several times a day, but I don't have to think about it.

What in your business is taking up your time but doesn't have to? What can you automate? What if you program your social media in advance or preset your email marketing? Even if you can't automate something entirely, you cut down on the amount of effort you spend by taking advantage of the endless apps, software, websites, and tools that support many different areas of your business. They are changing and improving daily, and all it takes is a quick Internet search to find one that can work for you. You can streamline everything from billing and invoicing to scheduling and record keeping. And when you systematize parts of your business that you're currently doing yourself, you give yourself a precious gift: more time.

Delegate

As business owners, we are control freaks. No one loves our business like we do and no one can do it as well as we can! But that's the problem. We can't get out of the weeds of the day-to-day and remove our sticky fingers from every darn detail of what's going on. We won't even give up the things we aren't good at! And as a result, growth slows and the business suffers. If you have team members who can help, that is the quickest way to take things off of your full plate. Assign the work to one of your competent and trustworthy employees. Give them instructions and then, without micromanaging them, let them do it. If your team members are not competent and trustworthy, you've got a bigger problem on your hands!

You can even reframe what you mean by "employee." If you have some cooperative, competent kids at home, don't hesitate to put them to work filling boxes or sticking on labels. You might be surprised to find kids enjoy working routine tasks in exchange for a little money, ice cream, or a special treat. And, as a bonus, it helps instill confidence and work ethic. I know many adults who credit their work ethic to being in the family business as a young kid. I know I certainly do!

Ask for Help

Another option, slightly different than bartering, outsourcing, or delegating, is to just ask someone for help. You might be amazed at how many people are willing to lend a hand when you need it. In fact, they are honored when you approach them for help with something they excel at. So just do it. For example, as a part of my planned giving (which we will talk more about later), I give away a percentage of my time to coach small-business owners for free. I also know a woman who lets people "shadow" her on the job for the day. Most people, if they are able, love to help someone who is a little earlier in their career or dream. Sometimes putting our pride aside can really pay off. All you have to do is ask. As Oprah Winfrey says, "You get in life what you have the courage to ask for." Amen to that!

Ignore

The last option for tasks and to-do items that feel overwhelming or that you're not good at is to simply ignore them. You heard me right. Ignoring things is always an option! Many of the tasks we stress over don't really deserve our nerves. We stress because we wanted to send Christmas cards to all of our customers, but we got behind. We stress because we were going to decorate a fancy booth for the local craft fair, but it turned out plain. We stress because we wanted to put all new updated photos on our Etsy page, but the lighting turned out terrible.

You didn't do something on your list you wanted to do, intended to do, or planned to do. So what? You didn't write Christmas cards because you were too busy fulfilling actual orders. That's a good thing! Your booth at the craft fair looks simple but people are seeing your products! Get over it! Your photos didn't turn out right so you have to use old ones. Let it go!

If something on your list is not turning out right, not working, or is just all-around stressing you out, ask yourself if it has to be done—I mean, *really* has to be done. Other than paying taxes, more often than not, I bet it doesn't. You can ignore it and move on to doing more of what you love.

YOUR VALUES MATTER TOO

When you're just starting a side or small business, you *are* the business. It's sometimes hard to distinguish where you end and the business begins. That's because you're doing everything—all the development, all the tasks, and all the follow-up. But over time, if you're wise, you'll start treating the business as its own separate entity. Some aspects of the business will always reflect you, your strengths, and your personality, as we've covered. But the business will also always reflect your core values, the things you care deeply about. In addition to building your business around your strengths, you also want to build it around your values. This is the second step in Tier 2 of your business plan. Your strengths are what you're good at and your values are what you care about.

Your Values Shape Your Decisions

Core values are more than just a warm-and-fuzzy idea. They are essential to building a business that's true to you. Even if you've never taken the time to think about your business (or personal) core values, you still have them. And whether you realize it or not, they are the context for your decisions. That's why it's so important to take the time to identify and write down your core values.

When you are intentional about your core values, you increase your speed of decision-making, avoid costly mistakes, reduce your stress, and ultimately stay true to yourself. Think about it: What do you want people to know about you and your business? What is important to you that should be important in your business? Let's say you hate calling a business and being instructed to press an endless series of numbers, never actually getting to talk to a real human being. For you, then, personal interaction may become a core value for your business. Remember, though: Your values impact your decisions. It's not just what you *believe*; it's what you're going to *do* about it. In this example, it means every time someone calls your business, they are immediately greeted with a cheerful, real-life human being on the other end of the phone.

Or maybe you love details and personal touches, so you decide that every outgoing order will have a handwritten thank-you note from you or one of your team members. Perhaps you've interacted with companies in the past, never to hear from them again. So maybe your value is follow-up. You commit to responding to every inquiry within twelve hours.

What do you value that the business also needs to value? The answer will help you make decisions for your business. Then you'll continue to grow a business that is built around the very best part: you.

WHAT YOU CAN DO IS AMAZING

In addition to the writing I do for books, media, speaking events, or videos, I've written two blogs per week for the last several years. Each piece I write represents an idea, something I've created and want to share with the world to help, inspire, or encourage others. And every time I sit down to write, I have the same thoughts. *Everyone knows this. Why are you writing about it? This is so obvious! Everyone will read it, roll their eyes, and say, "Duh. Everyone knows that."* In fact, leading up to my first Business Boutique live event, I wrote hours and hours of stage content to teach women about their businesses. And with every session of teaching, slide, or workbook page I created, I had those same thoughts. *Everyone knows this! This is so obvious! They are going to boo you off the stage!*

But I'm not alone. I know that those voices may nag at you too. You discover your strengths, but you downplay them. You know what you're good at, but you underestimate it. You want to create a product or add a new service to your business or share part of your heart with the world, but all you can think is, *Everyone already knows this. Everyone already has this. Everyone already does this.* We assume everyone can do what we do, so what's the big deal? The big deal is that we're wrong.

I want to remind you of something I've tried to remind myself of daily for the last several years. What's obvious to you is *not* obvious to everyone else. What's easy for you is *not* easy for everyone else. What's simple to you is *not* simple to everyone else. Your strengths are unique, valuable, and important. And friends, the world needs you to step into them.

We undervalue our strengths because they may seem easy and obvious to us. But don't let that stop you from sharing them with the world. Because what's obvious to you might be amazing to someone else. There are people out there right now who can benefit from the gifts that come so effortlessly to you. So don't downplay your strengths or dismiss your values. Instead, build your business around them and go for it. There are people out there right now who need what you have to offer!

chapter 7 action items
LET'S APPLY WHAT YOU'VE LEARNED!

Strengths

Let's identify your strengths by answering the Five "E" Questions:

1. What Do You *Enjoy*?

2. Where Do You *Excel*?

3. What Do Others *Encourage* in You?

4. What Comes *Effortlessly*?

5. What Gives You *Energy*?

Now we need to find a solution for the tasks that don't fall into your strengths. Fill in the chart on the next page with things you aren't good at or just plain don't want to do. Put them in the appropriate column to indicate how you'll still get those things done for your business.

	Barter	Outsource	Automate	Delegate	Ask for Help	Ignore
1.						
2.						
3.						
4.						
5.						

Values

What is important to you that should also be important to the business? Customer service, speed, or affordability? It's your business, so you get to choose. Write your core values below.

1.
2.
3.
4.
5.

Way to go! You're one step closer to building your business around the best part of it: you!

chapter 8

THE LOVE-HATE RELATIONSHIP WITH MONEY

Your Guilt-Free Guide for Making
More and Stressing Less

We sat across the table from each other, silent, neither of us sure of what to say. To be honest, we both just felt stuck. I had been coaching Margaret with her nutrition business for a few weeks. Margaret helped clients develop a healthy eating plan. She did regular weigh-ins with them, and she customized shopping lists and recipes for them. She had a good client base and she believed in the value she offered. She had worked through her business plan and executed her marketing efforts successfully. Despite all that, her business had one big problem: week after week, she struggled to make money.

After noticing a pattern, I sensed Margaret's issue wasn't her marketing, clients, or bank account. It wasn't her bookkeeping, and it wasn't how well she served her customers. The root of her problem wasn't the issue of *making* money at all. The real problem was her *belief* about making money. Finally, I asked her point-blank, "Margaret, do you believe that making money is *bad*?"

She stuttered some. She squirmed a little. Then finally she admitted, "Yes, I just feel like I shouldn't be taking money from other people." I felt for her. I could tell it was a genuine struggle.

My response was kind but direct. "Then you will never make money. If you don't believe in the goodness of business and making money, then you will never have a good business or make money."

Margaret's attempts to run a profitable business while not believing that making money was a good thing wasn't going to work. That would be like her trying to coach a client toward proper nutrition when they didn't believe healthy food was good for them. Impossible! Margaret's dilemma isn't uncommon. Sure, any business can struggle to make money at times. But I've seen a recurring theme in my research and coaching: sometimes, like with Margaret, the problem is not someone's *ability* to make money; the problem is their *belief* about making money.

When you consider how many people get into business by gradually charging for something they had previously done as a hobby, it makes sense that money isn't their primary focus. But this creates a common challenge. It's often tempting for people to call something a "business" but continue to treat it like a hobby. In order to treat your business like a business, you need to understand the difference between a hobby and a business. A business *makes* you money; a hobby *costs* you money.

It sounds obvious, but it's surprising how many people I work with who miss this reality. They say things like "Oh, I don't care about the money. I just do it because I love it!" Of course, a hobby is something you *should* love, but love isn't enough to make a business work. You also need to make profits to keep it going. Not only is earning a profit critical to your business success, but it also helps validate the time you invested in it. If your business is not making you money, it's pretty tough to justify spending ten, twenty, or thirty hours a week or more away from your family on something that has no financial return just because you love it. A business can and should be fun, but it has to make money in order to grow and last. The fact is, if you're not making money, you're out of business.

THE MEANING BEHIND MAKING MONEY

It's easy to underestimate the necessity of making money. We think of money as a bonus for doing something we love. But earning money in business isn't optional.

That's why it's important to remember what I told Margaret, if you don't believe in the goodness and importance of business and making money, then you'll never have a good business or make money. Think about it: you are never going to put effort and energy toward a result that you believe is bad.

In his excellent book *Thou Shall Prosper*, Rabbi Daniel Lapin says, "Few people can truly excel at occupations about which they entertain moral reservations."[36] So, if we feel guilty for making money, being successful, or winning, then of course we aren't going to try to make money, be successful, or win.

Making Money Is Good

Making money is not immoral. It isn't about greed or taking advantage of others as some people might believe. Making money actually allows us to do a long list of other things—*good* things.

First, when you have a successful business, you can serve the marketplace well. You are meeting customers' needs, providing products and services they want and are willing to pay for, and you're contributing to the economy. Rabbi Lapin, now a friend with whom I've shared the stage several times, often says to our audiences, "When you serve your customers well, they will give you certificates of appreciation with presidents' faces on them." They will give you money because you did a good job—that's not a bad thing; that's a good thing!

Second, when you have a successful business that employs team members, you are providing jobs for other people. You are giving them a source of income and work they enjoy. That's a good thing! When your successful business creates profits, those profits enable you to take a paycheck home to your own family and provide for them. That's a good thing! When we understand that making money is a good thing, it becomes something we not only want to do, but something we can be proud to do.

Money Is Necessary

Money is also a tool that allows us to do things we need—and want—to do. Almost everything in life requires money. Want to get married? Weddings are expensive. Want to have children? They cost a lot. Want to get in shape? Gym memberships and healthy food aren't free. Want to travel, take time off, or buy gifts for others? All those things require money. Even noble things, *worthy* things, require money.

Want to build wells in Africa, provide clean water to third-world countries, or bring people out of poverty? All of those things require money. The late Zig Ziglar used to say, "Money isn't the most important thing in life, but it's pretty close to oxygen on the 'gotta have it' scale." When we realize how necessary money is in business and life, we can start treating it with the importance it deserves. Money is a tool that helps us create the life we want and allows us to make the difference we want to make.

Money Doesn't Make You a Bad Person

A few years ago, I sat down with a close friend to help her with her business finances. She was barely breaking even and didn't even have any profit left to bring home to her family. When I suggested some changes that would increase her margin and make more money, she interrupted me and said, "Well, I mean, I don't want to get rich."

We're close so I knew I could shoot straight like good friends do. I got wide-eyed and said, "You are barely breaking even, so no worries there. You aren't even close!" We both laughed, but it made me realize that there seems to be a common belief that people who have "too much" money are somehow bad people. But that's not true. Money isn't bad and having it or not having it doesn't make you a good or bad person. Money is amoral. It's not inherently good or bad. Think of it like a brick. You would never look at a brick and think, *Wow, that's a really kind brick.* Or, *That brick is so hateful.* It's just a brick! Money is like that. It's just money. It's neither good nor bad, and it doesn't have any character qualities, values, or morals attached to it.

But when you put it in the hands of a person, money can be used for good or harm, just like the brick. Like the example of the bricklayers in chapter 4, we can build a cathedral with that brick. Or we can take that brick and throw it through someone's car windshield. But the brick doesn't decide. The person using it does. Money is just like that. In the hands of a person, it can also be used for good or bad. Money doesn't define your character. It *reveals* it.

Nonprofit Does Not Mean No Profit

If you're running a nonprofit, you might think this chapter doesn't apply to you because you aren't running a business for the purpose of making a profit. Except, you are! It's the number-one myth about nonprofit businesses. Nonprofit doesn't mean you don't have to worry about money or manage your operation like a business. Nonprofit also does not mean your business is inherently holy, worthy, or noble. Nonprofit is a tax status. It's an IRS designation. That's it. You can do work that matters and make a difference in people's lives regardless of your tax status.

You need income—*profits*—whether you are a for-profit or nonprofit business. In fact, do you know what a nonprofit organization that doesn't have any profits is called? Out of business! If you run a nonprofit, you have the same responsibility to manage your business like a business, to create profits, and to take care of your customers as every other business does. The mission of your business may be different, but the requirements and responsibilities are the same.

LIES WE BELIEVE

I have worked with many women whose businesses have been limited by a few fundamental lies they've come to accept about work and money. But for every lie, there's an important truth for us to discover. Let's look at the lies that sometimes hold us back and the truths we need to hear to be set free and win.

Lie: Earning a profit is greedy and selfish.
Truth: Earning a profit is responsible and smart.

A few years ago when I was deep in research on women in business, I noticed a pattern: many women feel guilty about charging for their work. Since my mom has been in business my entire life, I decided to get her perspective on this issue. We were pushing my son in the stroller through my neighborhood one day, and I asked her, "Mom, why do you think people, women specifically, feel so guilty about charging for things?"

She said, "Well, for me it's because I know the actual cost. When I tell a customer that a cake is going to be forty-five dollars, there's a little voice in the back of my mind telling me that it's really only about four dollars' worth of ingredients.

Sometimes, in my mind, the difference between forty-five dollars and four dollars feels like I am taking advantage of them."

My mom's perspective is surprisingly common. Many women feel guilty or greedy when they see the profit they earn on their products and services. They consciously, or even unconsciously, feel like they shouldn't earn as much profit.

But earning a profit isn't selfish; it's smart. That profit isn't just bonus, fun money. You need that money to run your business. In chapter 12, we will dig into the details of managing your money, but for starters, you need a profit to pay taxes and expenses, to save and invest back into the business, and to pay yourself. Without a profit, you can't do any of those things. While some people think of profit as additional money they are "taking" from the customer, it is actually built into the financial equation as a critical element to operating a business.

Lie: If you want to make a difference, you won't be paid well.
Truth: Your compensation doesn't dictate the meaning of your work.

When I worked at the YMCA right out of college, I loved doing work that mattered. I didn't just collect a paycheck and go home. I was passionate about the difference I was making every day in the lives of others. The mistake I made, though, was believing my work mattered simply because I worked for a nonprofit and barely earned an entry-level salary. In my mind, a nonprofit company meant making a difference while earning a small paycheck and a for-profit business meant work that had no purpose but paid a good salary. Meaningful work has always been more important to me than the money, so I assumed I would work in nonprofit, making a difference but barely getting by, for the rest of my life. I assumed it was the sacrifice I had to make if I wanted to do work that mattered.

It never occurred to me that I could have both. What I now know is that you don't have to work in nonprofit or a ministry to do meaningful work. You don't have to be paid a tiny paycheck and barely get by for your work to count. You can, believe it or not, work in a for-profit business and make good money all while doing meaningful, purposeful work that makes a difference and changes lives. Many employees in for-profit companies impact others with their work and change lives or help people every day, all while earning a good income.

Lie: I need to take out debt to start (or grow) my business.
Truth: Start with what you have and grow slow.

I hear it all the time: "I need a new computer system (or a new building or more employees) to get started." This is the hurdle that intimidates many business owners before getting started. They think they have to buy new equipment, take on a lease, or hire employees—and go into debt to do so. They think it's the only way to start or grow a business. Even if they don't carry personal debt, they believe the myth that somehow business debt is different—that it's justified, as if the debt isn't really theirs. Let's get real: the business's debt *is* your debt! At the end of the day, regardless of how the business is doing, someone is still responsible for paying the bills. And that someone is you. Business debt is no different than any other type of debt. It's all a risk, it's all yours, and it's all a bad idea.

The good news is that you don't need it anyway. You can start small and grow slow. For example, Christa Pitts and Chanda Bell, creators of the popular *Elf on the Shelf* books and products, started by hosting book signings with family and friends for their little self-published book. Sarah Blakely, the founder and CEO of Spanx, started her multimillion-dollar business by cutting the feet out of her panty hose so she could wear them under white pants. Everyone, even the supersuccessful, start somewhere. Start small with what you have.

Let's be honest. Sometimes, we think we *need* to buy something, when really we just *want* to validate what we're doing. Like when I graduated college and I "needed" a new suit and briefcase to interview for jobs—as if I didn't already have a closet full of perfectly acceptable interview clothes. You don't need loans to buy more stuff to build your business. Instead, start small and grow slow.

MAKING IT WORK (WHILE ACTUALLY MAKING MONEY!)

That last lie leads to something else I often talk to business owners about. In many instances, I coach people who focus on having the perfect setup before they make their first sale. They spend time—and money—trying to buy everything they could ever need for the business before they buckle down and get to work. This can sink a start-up before it has a real chance in the marketplace. Big purchases don't validate your business; you do. And more than that, profit does. So instead of trying to justify big purchases to make your business feel legitimate, do the exact opposite. Focus on spending less. The less money you spend, the more money you keep in your business—and in your pocket.

Here are three ways to bypass whatever expenses you think you "need" so that you can build a business that will make money and ultimately last.

Get Creative

Creativity allows you to avoid many start-up expenses. Who in your network might be able to assist you? Nick Pellegrino, a successful restaurateur in Franklin, Tennessee, is a great example. When he was starting out, he saw a creative opportunity in a meat-and-three restaurant that was only open until 2:00 p.m. He approached the manager about subleasing the restaurant on weekend nights when the location was closed anyway. His idea turned into the successful Italian restaurant Mangia, which has reservations booked months in advance thanks to creative word-of-mouth marketing.

Similarly, my friend Jake of Jake's Bakes started his cookie delivery company much like my mom started her cake shop: by subleasing a catering space that already had all the equipment he needed. He baked at night so he wouldn't interrupt the daytime business, and he didn't have to pay for the equipment to get started. The connections you already have can help you get around your biggest expenses—like workspace. With a little creativity, you have more options than you think.

Use What You Have

When you look at your resources with new eyes, you'll be amazed at how much you already have. What do you have right now that can be used for your business? Use your home office instead of renting space. Use your old clunky, embarrassing computer instead of buying a new one. Regardless of what type of business you own, challenge yourself to be as resourceful as possible with what you have. It can help you save a tremendous amount of money. Jeremy Cowart, who has been named by the *Huffington Post* as the "Most Influential Online Photographer," started his photography business with a basic three-megapixel digital camera and by reading *Digital Photography for Dummies*. He continued shooting with that camera even as he got more successful and began photographing musicians and celebrities.[37] What you already have will probably work better than you think.

Barter for Everything Else

We talked about bartering in the last chapter, and it's a great way to cut costs. You have something to offer that people need, and other people have something to offer that you need. What can you trade in exchange for services or supplies you need to get your business off the ground?

Years ago, when the TV show *Dancing with the Stars* was just becoming popular, I decided to take Latin and ballroom dance lessons. After a few lessons, I realized I couldn't afford to keep up my expensive new hobby on my just-out-of-college salary. But since my dance teacher and I had become great friends, we worked out an arrangement where I would do all of the marketing for his side business, and he would give me dance lessons. It sounds crazy, but it worked! I had so much fun learning the waltz, tango, and fox-trot as well as the cha-cha, rumba, and swing, and his new video training launch was a huge success. It was a win-win!

Whether it's dancing or marketing, web programming or teaching, be sure to give yourself credit for the valuable talents you have, and don't be afraid to offer them in exchange for things you need from others. Ultimately, it's not what you buy or how much you spend that will help you win in the marketplace. It's your determination and fierce persistence that will make your business sink or swim. When you get creative, work with what you've got, and barter for the rest, you'll have what you need to get your business going.

IT STARTS WITH YOU

My friend Stacy doesn't think her in-laws like her. That feeling makes her act weird when she's around them. As a result, her in-laws act like they don't like her. It's a bad cycle that's unfortunately all too common in relationships. In our minds, we create self-fulfilling prophecies that then play out in real life. It's not all that different in business.

We think making money is bad so we don't try to make money. Or we think people aren't willing to pay for our products so we never ask for the sale. The truth is, everything about winning in business—and making money—starts with you. Like I told my fitness trainer-friend Margaret, if you don't believe in the goodness of business and making money, you'll never have a good business or make money.

The good news is that the opposite is also true. If you do believe in the goodness of business and making money, you will have a good business and you will make money. You will unapologetically offer what you have to the marketplace because you believe that winning in business is good and noble. You get to decide. You can shrink back, shrug your shoulders, and apologize for your business. Or you can stand and speak up on behalf of this thing that you care so deeply about. I'm in your corner, and I can tell you from years of personal experience and years of coaching others that, friend, we need you. We need your boldness, your bravery, and your business. We need you to go out there and win!

chapter 8 action items
LET'S APPLY WHAT YOU'VE LEARNED!

Lies and the Truth

Lie: Earning a profit is greedy and selfish.

Truth: Earning a profit is responsible and smart.

Write out a list of all of the things you can do with the profit you earn from your business:

Lie: I need to take out debt to start (or grow) my business.

Truth: Start with what you have and grow slow.

Starting or growing your business doesn't have to be an expensive venture like many people believe. You can bypass many costs by thinking creatively about your options, using what you have, and bartering. First, list expenses that you have coming up below:

1.

2.

3.

4.

5.

Now, brainstorm ways around them. Take as many items as you can off of your expenses list and place them below in the appropriate column. This will help you think of other solutions and cut your costs. The more money you save, the more money you make!

Get Creative	Use What You Have	Barter
What's a different option around it?	*What do you have on hand that you can use instead?*	*Who might be available for a trade?*

Congratulations! The simple actions you took in this chapter will help you charge more, spend less, and make a larger profit. That's good for the business and good for you.

chapter 9

MAKE THE MOST OF YOUR RESOURCES

Planning Your Money, Time, Schedule, and Space

Picture this scenario. You finally made the leap. You work for yourself and you couldn't be more thrilled. No more early alarms. No more uncomfortable work clothes. No more traffic during your commute. No more cubicle or noisy and annoying coworkers. No more schedule. And best of all, no more boss telling you what to do. Working for yourself is a dream—right?

But then something happens. As the days and weeks go by, the sparkle and sizzle of working for yourself starts to wear off and the dream doesn't look quite like you thought. You stay in bed late every day, because you can. You don't get out of your pajamas until 2:00 p.m. (if at all) because no one sees you, so what's the point? You don't have any coworkers, so there's no one to bounce ideas off of, get help from, or just talk to. The house gets quiet (assuming the kids are at school) and sometimes downright lonely. Your kitchen is your workspace and last night's dinner plates are sitting on top of your customers' orders. Shipping boxes are covered in laundry. You have trouble keeping track of what you've accomplished because you don't have a schedule and no real deadlines to meet. And, since you don't have a "real" boss to report to, you don't have much accountability to stay on track anyway.

You end up feeling discouraged and disappointed, uninspired and unmotivated. If this sounds familiar, you're not alone. I've not only coached women in this situation, I've been in this situation myself—many times! I used to write from home during the day, but that lasted less than a week because what I just described was me, to a tee. I was less energetic, less excited, and certainly less productive. I've talked to many other women running businesses out of their homes who described themselves the same way. But here's the thing: we're not lazy. We aren't afraid to work and to work hard. Just the opposite. The problem is, we don't set ourselves up to be successful working from home. With a few practical steps, we can stay sane when working from home and live the dream we had in mind when we first started.

BUILDING YOUR BUSINESS AROUND YOUR LIFE

The great thing about going into business for yourself is that you can build your business around your life versus the other way around. You don't have to adjust your life to accommodate your nine-to-five job, missing events with your kids, pushing personal appointments to after-work hours, or even delaying vacation time. You can plan your business around anything you want, from working out, to dentist appointments, to your kids' class parties and field trips, to sports games and vacations. Your life gets to come first and you can schedule your business around the things you don't want to miss. Not to mention, you can keep things going at the house all day when you're there. Laundry can be running and the Crock-Pot can be simmering while you're getting work done.

However, in order to shape your business around your life, you need to set yourself up accordingly. After all, you don't want to end up in your pajamas and feeling bad about yourself every afternoon, focusing on all you *didn't* accomplish. That's why we're going to look at your resources—money, time, schedule, and space—and help plan your business and life in a way that both can be successful.

It's Not Just Yours

When we worked through your *why*, dream, vision, mission, and goals in Tier 1 of your business plan, I intentionally didn't mention family. This business is *your* heart and *your* passion, so I wanted you to dream without anyone else in mind. (Unless you are in business *with* your family, and then it's a given that they are involved at that stage.) However, now in Tier 2, as you build your business around your life and your resources, it's important to think about how your business affects your family. The last thing you want to do as you lean into your dreams is push your loved ones away in the process.

That's why it's so important to get your family on board with the decisions you want to make. After all, your money is not just your *money*; it's your family's money also. Your *time* is not just your *time*; it's your family's time also. Your *schedule* is not just your *schedule*; it's your family's schedule also. And your *home* is not just your *space*; it's your family's space too. So talk to your family. Talk about your *why* with them. Share your dream, vision, mission, and goals. Talk about your shared resources. When you have a conversation about these things, you're not just talking time, money, schedules, and spaces. You're really talking about values and priorities. This brings a new level of unity to your relationships because you're a team and you are all working toward the same goals together.

My friend Joanna did this several years ago. Joanna has always loved politics and in 2012, she had the opportunity to work on the presidential campaign. While it was an incredible opportunity, it also meant many months of travel and time away from her young family. I remember her saying, "We had a big family meeting, and I told them what this meant to me and the impact it would have on the family. We talked about how we could make it work and the benefits we would get to experience as a result of our family's sacrifice and commitment. We all discussed what it would look like, and everyone agreed on the decision." So Joanna hit the road that year and had a successful campaign season, which has opened even more doors for her since. And she was able to do so with her family's buy-in.

At the end of the day, you need the home team on board with the business. And if you're one of the many single women running a business, that's awesome. This chapter is for you too. You have even more freedom and options to build the business exactly like you want.

WHAT'S THE MAGIC NUMBER?

The first resource I want you to think about is money, specifically, the amount you're willing to invest in the business to get it off of the ground. Identifying this number is the next step in Tier 2 of your business plan. Clients always ask me, "What's the right amount to start with?" The answer is: start with *your* amount.

I've coached women who don't want to contribute a penny to their business from their personal funds. They start small so the business can earn money from day one. That's because they start with what they already have, or they build their business in such a way that customers pay up front before orders are fulfilled—so they have cash in their account before buying supplies. Melissa Hinnant, owner of Grace and Lace and a *Shark Tank* success story, told me that when she started, she vowed to never put a penny of her own money into her business. It was just something she wasn't willing to do.[38] I've also worked with women who started their businesses with $10,000 or more of their own money that they had saved up. If you're debt-free and have the savings to invest in your business, it's completely your call. Neither option is right or wrong. It's a value decision. It's your business, so you get to decide.

While there's no magic number to invest, there is also no right amount of time to wait to turn a profit either. Some people want their business to start earning the first week, while others are comfortable waiting six months. Again, it's a value decision and you get to decide what you want to do. While Melissa was not willing to wait even one day for Grace and Lace to make a profit, I know other people who anticipate their business just breaking even many months after starting. If you have the cash, time, and patience, it's up to you to decide how long you wait to turn that first real profit. Just don't wait too long. Your goal should be to have the business fund itself as soon as possible because the sooner it starts making money, the sooner it becomes a legitimate business. Having a deadline will push you to get moving and make it work.

As you're deciding on your start-up investment amount—whether it's zero or thousands of dollars—it's also important to think about what type of business you're building and what's required to get it going. Melissa was sewing boot socks when she started Grace and Lace, so it didn't cost much or take long to turn a profit. But if your business is flipping houses, you're on the other end of the spectrum. You are looking at a significant investment of money and a long time frame before you'll see a return on your investment. When you take into consideration the type of business you have, as well as your value system and comfort level, then making a decision about how much money to invest and how much time to wait becomes much easier.

Decide in Advance

While neither scenario is right or wrong, it's important for you to decide in advance how much you're comfortable contributing to your business. If you don't, the business will quickly drain your personal accounts and "twenty dollar" you to death. It can be like a teenager who treats you like a twenty-four-hour ATM.

> "Mom, I need $20 for a field trip."
> "Mom, I need $20 for the movies."
> "Mom, I need $20 for the game."

If you aren't careful, the business will do the exact same thing. It's like a black hole that can suck you dry of all you've got.

What you spend isn't always obvious, either. You may have already determined how much you're willing to spend on the business, but it can easily get away from you. Say you're shopping for groceries at Walmart when you decide to spontaneously get a few materials for your business. Or you purchase a few household items on Amazon and decide to add in some fabric for your sewing business. Suddenly you've mingled your personal and business finances and you've exceeded your business spending limit—and you didn't even realize it. Overlapping work and personal expenses often means that your personal cash vanishes into the business. We will talk later about how to manage your money, including purchases for your business, so this disappearing act doesn't happen. But I can't stress this enough. Decide your amount, and stick to it.

Building the Business into Your Family Budget

Whether you're starting or growing your business, if you're going to invest your personal money, you need to plan for that amount in your personal budget. If you don't want to contribute any personal funds to the business, that's great too. But if you do, you want to plan for it each month, on purpose. When it comes to budgeting, I suggest you hold what Dave Ramsey calls a Budget Committee Meeting. Sit down with your spouse at the start of every month and talk about your personal budget. Like I said earlier, this is *family* money, not just *your* money. When you do this, investing in the business becomes a line item you plan for, and everyone agrees upon it. The amount may be a one-time cost up-front or a smaller sum budgeted over several months. It doesn't matter how you plan for it, only *that* you plan for it.

Several years ago, I had a client named Lisa who had a great idea for an adoption consulting business. She had been through the adoption process several times and was passionate about helping others through what is often a tedious, exhausting, and overwhelming process. Her idea was awesome, but in all of her excitement about getting it off the ground, she left her family behind in the planning. She made purchases for website templates and hosting, paid for advertising on several other adoption websites, and spent money that her husband didn't know about. Unfortunately, what started out as a really good idea turned sour quickly as it led to fights between her and her spouse over purchases they hadn't agreed on.

So, before you spend another penny on your business, do some planning. Decide on the maximum amount you can spend, talk to you family, get them on board, and then factor the amount into your family budget. If you do this, it will not only keep the business from draining your personal bank account, but it will also save you stress, headaches, and family fights in the process.

PUTTING IN THE TIME

In addition to thinking through how much money you want to invest in your business, you also need to think about how much time you will spend on it. This is the next step in Tier 2 of your business plan. Do you plan to work ten hours per week? Maybe twenty or thirty? Are you going to work forty or more? Don't take your time for granted. It could be your most precious resource, which means it's also one of the greatest investments you'll make to your business.

Break It Down

Planning your time gives you an opportunity to use what you learned about goal setting in chapter 6. Rather than choosing a random number of work hours per week, start with your big goal and work backward to get your weekly microgoal. Then determine how many hours per week you need to work to accomplish your microgoal. You do this by taking your weekly microgoal and dividing it by your work speed. For example, my current goal is to finish writing this book and my microgoal is to write 8,000 words per week to reach it. But in order to determine how much *time* I need to spend writing each week, I need to know how fast I work. I average approximately 800 words per hour. So I just divide my weekly microgoal of 8,000 words by my hourly work speed of 800 words per hour and I get 10. Now I know that I need to write at least ten hours per week to complete my first draft.

This formula is a guideline and isn't always cut-and-dried. Following the sales example in chapter 6, if your microgoal is to get 100 new orders per week, it might be difficult to accurately measure how long it takes you to get a new order. But what you can do is estimate how long your efforts take to create new orders—efforts such as sales calls, networking, placing ads, follow-up emails, and so on.

Let's say that when you send out an email campaign, you gain roughly forty new orders from that effort. And let's say it takes you two hours to create an email campaign. When you take your campaign results (40) and divide by effort hours (2) you get twenty. You gain approximately twenty orders per effort hour. Since your goal is one hundred orders per week, you can calculate that you need to work five hours per week to gain one hundred new orders. Now you can calculate how many hours each week you need to commit to your goal, in addition to your other business responsibilities.

When you set your goal, calculate your weekly microgoal, and determine the number of hours per week you need to work to meet your goal, it's easier to estimate how much time to spend on your business. The next step is to determine where to find that time.

Making the Time

People ask me all the time how they can find time to do everything. The answer is simple: You don't find time. You *make* time. If you want to work on your business and reach your goals, you have to *make* the time to do it. But this brings up a dilemma. I hear women say they want to spend ten, twenty, or thirty hours a week on their business, but they don't want to give up anything to do so. They just imagine that they'll create those extra hours out of thin air and do everything they're currently doing *as well as* their business work. Or they have this idea they can spend just a few hours each week on their side business expecting it to be able to replace their full-time job in a few short months. Either scenario is a setup for failure.

The truth is that your business will grow in direct proportion to the amount of time you commit. You can't expect to work three hours a week and produce the equivalent of a full-time salary. If you want to reach your goal, you've got to make the time. Your time is finite. You can't get more than twenty-four hours in a day. In fact, you can get more of almost anything in this life, except time. Management expert Peter Drucker said, "Time is the scarcest resource and, unless it is managed, nothing else can be managed."[39]

When you know how many hours you want to add to your schedule, you have to choose where those hours will come from. What are you willing to give up so you can use that time for your business? Will you give up sleep hours to wake up early or stay up late? Maybe you'll decide to outsource or automate some tasks to free up time, like hiring a housecleaner or converting your bills to autopay. Maybe you'll hire childcare so you can focus and get work done instead of being distracted trying to be Mom at the same time. Whatever you choose, and it may be a combination of things, you need to decide what you're willing to give up in order to reach your goals. If you wait until you have some time left over to start working on your business, it's never going to happen. It's up to you to make the time.

Resetting Goals

After figuring out how many hours per week you need to work on your business, you might realize any one of the following things:

> *I don't have that many hours available.*
> *I don't want to give up anything to create that many hours for my business.*
> *I just don't want to work on my business that many hours, period.*

Seeing your goal in the form of hours needed per week can be a reality check for many people. You might realize that your goal is too big or too soon, or that you don't want it that bad or aren't willing to work that hard to achieve it. And, while that may seem discouraging at first, it's actually great news that you're realizing it now rather than spending week after week spinning your wheels and falling short. The whole point is to set you up to win, so if you realize the cost of hitting those goals is too high, you may need to revisit and reset those goals.

If that struck a nerve with you, don't worry. It doesn't mean your dream is dying. All it means is that you'll need to reassess what you can accomplish with the time you're realistically able to commit toward it. In the sales example, maybe you push your deadline back six months to give yourself a little more time. Or maybe you decrease your big goal of five hundred new orders and aim for two hundred fifty instead. Whatever you decide to do, don't feel bad about it. Remember, this is *your* business. You can make it anything you want it to be. Reset your goals, refocus your effort, and recalculate the time you're going to be able to commit to making it happen. This is about setting yourself up to win, so give yourself permission to regroup and then do just that!

SCHEDULING YOUR TIME

Once you have determined how many hours per week you're able to work on your business, you now have to schedule those hours. Remember, if you wait to work on your business until you have time left over, it's never going to happen. You're more likely to focus and be productive if you develop a schedule with self-imposed start times and deadlines. You'll reduce distractions and maximize your efforts when you prepare for and anticipate each day. That's why setting your schedule is the next step in Tier 2 of your business plan.

Putting the Hours in Place

The good news is that, like your time and money, your schedule can look any way you want. There's no "right" schedule, and you certainly don't have to abide by a nine-to-five day. You can be creative and make your schedule work for you and your life. In order to do that, I want you to think about three important things:

What Immovable Things Must I Work Around?

Sure, everything technically *can* be moved, but some things you may not be *willing* to move. For instance, you will likely want to sleep at night when your family and the rest of the world are sleeping, so those hours are out. You might also have commitments like another job, church on Sunday morning, committees you are responsible for, or other recurring meetings that cannot be moved. When you start by blocking off the times you know you *can't* work, you start to identify what free space you have left for your business hours.

What Other Activities Do I Want to Work Around?

Once you've identified commitments you *have* to work around, you might also have activities you *want* to work around. Let's say you walk your kids to school every day, you really enjoy it, and it's important to you. That's certainly something the business can flex around. Maybe you want to start your day by working out in the morning. You can adjust your work schedule to accommodate that. Look at your calendar and fill in things you currently do or would like to do. Having these commitments set first will help as you schedule your work hours. You'll be shaping your business around your life instead of shaping your life around your business.

When Am I the Most Effective?

I remember days in college when my roommates would wake up, make coffee, and get ready for their 8:00 a.m. class while I would still be awake in my bedroom working on a project from the night before, having never gone to sleep. This was partially because I can be a terrible procrastinator. But working through the night is when I worked best. Not much has changed. In fact, most of my writing is done at night, after my husband and sons are asleep—including this chapter right now!

However, late nights aren't the right time for everyone. The key to setting your schedule is knowing what works best for you. So many people get caught up in the "right way" to accomplish something. Experts have written countless articles on the benefits to waking up earlier to get things done, work out, or "be your best." As a result, people think that's the only way to be successful or reach their goals. Have you met yourself? Maybe that's right for you—but maybe not.

The secret is to know what *you* need. For me, I need to be rested. I need a clean working area so I don't get distracted. I need clear objectives of what I want to accomplish. I need to be alone. I need to have some caffeine and an open night. What do you need? What time of day are you at your best? When are you the least distracted? When do you have the most creative energy? When do you *want* to work on something? In what environment do you work best? If you can identify what you need in order to be your best, then you can create your schedule and actually start to do that. Then you can quit setting your alarm for four in the morning and hitting snooze every ten minutes until your normal wake-up time at six, never having gotten your work done and annoying your spouse in the process. (Not that I know anything about that.)

Now that you've determined the things you want your schedule to work around and when you're the most successful, you can identify when you'll work on your business. This is when you start to plug those hours into your calendar with a helpful little trick called "time-blocking."

Blocking Your Time

Time-blocking is a widely used and successful technique to manage your time. It is what it sounds like; you actually block out time by creating appointments on your calendar for each of your activities. Not just the big commitments, but everything. Even things like running errands, reading, or cooking become "appointments"—a committed time for doing a specific activity. Blocking your time this way gives you a better handle on your schedule so that you can make the most of it.

In order for time-blocking to be effective, though, you need to be specific with your scheduling. Instead of just blocking time to "work," take it a step further. For each work block, include an agenda or objective of what you intend to accomplish during that time. For example, if you were to look at my calendar right now, you would see several time blocks each week for "writing." However, in the notes section of my appointment, I included what I am going to accomplish as well:

- Finish writing Chapter 9
- Edit Chapter 6
- Reorganize Chapter 10 outline

When I list out objectives for what I need to achieve during my "writing time," it keeps me on track to complete what I need to. Without having an agenda for work time, I can easily become distracted, and I'll bet the same is true for you.

Master Multitasking

Ah, multitasking. You probably think time-blocking isn't for you because who would want to be limited by doing only one thing at a time when you could do lots of things at once? One of the ways many people try to manage their lack of time is to multitask. Instead of cutting things out, they just do more, all at one time.

Women in particular seem to be good at multitasking, which, if done well, can be a great solution to making the most of your time. Someone once told me that men's brains are like a waffle, with each separate compartment requiring individual focus, whereas women's brains are more like a bowl of spaghetti, with many different things running together in a tangled mess. I don't know how scientific this analogy is, but it makes sense. In general, women multiply their time by doing several things simultaneously.

However, there is a right way and a wrong way to multitask. One way is beneficial while the other is harmful. For example, I'll listen to leadership podcasts on my phone while I put on makeup in the morning instead of listening to music. Or, when my son is being clingy, I'll put him in the baby carrier and talk to him while I do laundry. When you combine something that needs your attention with something that is automatic and doesn't require concentration, you can multitask effectively.

But when we try to combine two things that require our attention, one—if not both—will slip. Have you ever tried to have a conversation with someone while they're texting? Yeah. They aren't listening. Think about talking to a customer while balancing your bank account. Or answering emails while trying to help your child with homework. You run the risk of accidentally agreeing to the wrong order, messing up your finances, or misdirecting your child. When you try to divide your attention, something always suffers. But if you want to multitask less demanding tasks, go for it. Just be sure that only one of the tasks actually requires your attention. Then, even if you're busy, you're able to focus on what matters most and multitask the *right* way.

SETTING YOUR SPACE

After you've determined how much money you're going to invest, how many hours you'll spend each week, and how to schedule your time, the last step in Tier 2 is to establish your workspace. When women tell me they feel scattered if they work from home, it's usually because they don't have a specific, consistent spot to work. They just see the entire house as their office and begin to feel like the business is taking over their lives. Because it is! Kids' toys are covering up the computer and order forms get lost in the stack of household bills. Without a dedicated space for work, things quickly get cluttered and confusing.

Having a space or "office" that you set and protect is important for several reasons. First, it keeps you organized. All of your work things go in that space and all of your home things stay out of that space. Second, when you're in your space, it's a trigger for your mind to click into work mode: you are in your office to accomplish things for your business. If your space is in your home, it also provides a visible cue for your family—when you're there, your spouse knows it's your business time, and your children know that "Mommy is working." For little ones who don't understand schedules, this is an important signal. Finally, this physical boundary helps you keep your work and home life separate. Separating the two is important because when you work from home, it can feel like you're never "off." In a traditional office setting you show up for work, clock in, and clock out. But when you work from home, there is no difference. Home and office are one in the same. Setting a separate space allows you to go to work and "clock in" and when you're finished, you can walk out and "clock out." Doing so enables you to honor the schedule you set and gives you permission to enjoy life outside of your business also.

How to Choose the Right Space

If you're just getting your business going, you need to decide where to establish your workspace. And if you've had your business for a while, now's a good time to evaluate your current setup and determine if it's the best arrangement for you. Here are three things to consider when selecting your workspace:

What Space Is Available?

If you work from home, do you have an existing, usable area in your house? Maybe you have a bonus room, garage, home office, or craft room with space for your work. The first step is to figure out what's available for you to use. If you don't have the space, you can get creative. Maybe you have a dining room you don't often use or a guest bedroom that can double as an office. Or maybe it's a borrowed space outside of your home. Regardless of how unconventional it may be, you just need a space that will work for you.

Is It Conducive to Your Business?

What do you need in order to be successful where you work? If you're an artist, you probably need a spot with good lighting or if you write, you need a space that is quiet. Also, consider what distractions might creep up. Your bonus room might not be the best spot if the kids use it frequently. If you teach piano lessons, you need a space away from the noise of your family's traffic pattern. Think through what you need before choosing where you'll work.

Do You Want to Go There?

When I was in college, my roommates and I lived in an old house where the washer and dryer were in a dingy, dark, damp, and possibly haunted basement. I avoided doing laundry at all costs because I hated going down there. You might have a garage, attic, shed, or basement that is available—but it's probably only available because no one else wants to go there either. Pick a location that you get excited to go to. Then you won't avoid your work like I avoided laundry in college.

Thinking through where you work on your business is more important than you might realize. How it's set up, where it's located, and how it makes you feel when you go there all affect whether or not you get work done. That, in turn, directly affects your ability to build your business and reach your goals.

YOU'RE THE BOSS

When you work a traditional job, the company usually has different policies, procedures, schedules, and deadlines to keep you on track and accountable. But when you work for yourself, the accountability—the boss—is you. The only one in charge of you is you. Working for yourself can be a dream if you're intentional about managing your money, time, schedule, and space. To be successful at reaching your goals and stay sane in the process, you've got to treat your business like it is a real job.

So picture this: Instead of waking up late and staying in your pajamas until two in the afternoon, you wake up at a set time and get ready for the day. You shower, put on makeup, and get dressed for work. Sure, you don't have to, especially if you know you'll be home alone all day. But you're not doing it for someone else. You're getting ready for work because you know you're more alert, energized, and productive when you do. In fact, research shows that how you dress affects how you feel. [40] I don't know about you, but I like myself more when I look cute. Maybe you're like me and you even enjoy your work more when you get yourself ready for the day. Then you head to your workspace, which is a place you actually want to go. You work for your set time block and accomplish the objectives on your schedule. When you're finished, you leave your workspace, with the permission to be "off work" because you finished all of your tasks. You spend the rest of the day doing whatever you want. You go to bed that night fulfilled, satisfied, and proud of the work you did and the way you managed your day.

That's a much different scenario from what I described at the beginning of the chapter. Instead of chaos, it's calm. Instead of feeling overwhelmed, you're organized. Instead of regret, you see real results. You're working for yourself and at the same time doing what you love. That's what it looks like when you create a business—and life—you love.

chapter 9 action items

LET'S APPLY WHAT YOU'VE LEARNED!

Money

1. How much money are you going to spend on the business from your personal funds until the business supports itself? $_____

2. How long will you wait until the business breaks even? _____

Don't forget to talk to your family about this amount and put it into the family budget.

Time

3. How many hours per week do you need to work on your business goals? Fill in the graph on the next page to calculate your amount based on the goals you set in chapter 6.

	Weekly Microgoal (from Chapter 6)	Units Per Hour	Hours Needed (Divide microgoal by units per hour) This is the amount of hours you need to work per week.
Ex. New orders	100	20	5
Ex. Christy's book	8,000 (words)	800 (words per hour)	10
Your goal:			
Your goal:			

I need to work on your business goals _____ hours each week.

Schedule

4. What things in your life do you need to consider when scheduling your work hours? List out the following items:

Things I *have* to schedule around:
(Ex. Sleep, another job, etc.)

Things I *want* to schedule around:
(Ex. Walking your child to school, working out, etc.)

Times when I am most *productive*:
(Ex. Morning, weekends, when the kids are in school, etc.)

Space

5. What space will you use to work on your business?

   _____

   Remember, it should be available, conducive to your business, and somewhere you actually *want* to go!

Congratulations! You've taken one more step toward creating a business—and life—you love!

Tier Three

UP AND
RUNNING

Way to go! You're finished with one half of your business plan. Now we are ready to dive into Tier 3, where you'll plan for the operational side of your business. Here, we cover the nuts and bolts of your business plan. In the next few chapters, we'll cover ten elements: products and services, location, logistics, platform, point-of-sale, records, competition, policies, protecting yourself, and pricing. Don't worry, it's easier than you think. By the end of Tier 3, you will not only have more clarity about what your business does, but you'll also know how you want to operate and manage it. Let's get to it!

chapter 10

THE FOLLOW-THROUGH
Figuring Out the Operational Side of Things

Anyone who knows me knows that I have five hundred ideas running through my head at any given moment. I'm creative (sometimes scattered), resourceful (occasionally scrappy), and spontaneous (a little unpredictable). Most of the creative, entrepreneurial people I know are like this too. We thrive on the energy of developing new ideas, products, or concepts—and we love thinking about what comes next. We don't want to have just one business; we have ideas for multiple businesses.

Having new ideas is an excellent advantage in business. But when you act on all of your ideas—including the bad ones—you dilute your efforts. You reduce your efficiency and ability to grow one business well, and you confuse the heck out of your customers. More importantly, when you jump from idea to idea like a game of hopscotch, it can be a struggle to follow through with any of them.

Most of the women I know have one challenge in common: they all have a lot going on in their lives. If you're reading a book about how to start and grow a business, I bet this is true of you too. You probably have a lot going on because you're good at many things. And because you can do many things well, it's tempting to see each of those ideas, skills, talents, or hobbies as a business opportunity.

Maybe you're a talented photographer and you decide to write a blog for your photography website. Then you discover you like writing so you think, *I could start a separate blog and try to market that!* But while you're online, you notice other women successfully selling quilts on Etsy and think, *I could do that.* After all, you know how to sew pretty well and you have a sewing machine up in the attic. Meanwhile, you found out your neighbors rent out their spare room on Airbnb and, since you already love being the hostess with the mostest, you decide you've gotta get in on that!

And any one of these ideas could, hypothetically, become a new business. But just because you *can* do something does not mean you *should.* Not every opportunity is the right opportunity for you. Because when you try to be a Jackie-of-all-trades, you truly do end up being a master of none. I know it's hard to resist doing everything. Trust me, I fight the urge daily! After all, our culture encourages us to wear busyness like a badge of honor. But if your resources are spread too thin, you'll wind up scattered and unsuccessful. And most of all, you'll have a hard time seeing any one idea through. That's one of the many reasons I created the Business Boutique plan—to give you what you need to focus, put your ideas into action, and follow through so you can make your business successful.

We are going to get technical, practical, and operational in this chapter. Sure, it's not supersexy, which causes some entrepreneurs to lose their enthusiasm by this stage. Their wide-eyed business ideas start to lose their sparkle when they have to bring them down to earth and switch into tactical mode. But this stage is the gateway to even more fun stuff like marketing and making money! So grab a cup of coffee and stay with me. In this chapter, we'll plan for your products and services, location and logistics, platform and point-of-sale, and finally, record keeping. As you do this, you'll have more focus, momentum, and success. And, of course, you'll set yourself up to actually see your idea through.

PRODUCTS AND SERVICES

What is your core business? And by core business, I mean singular business. What is the one area that you are focused on? Put all your attention here, and develop products and services that are "like things" that fit within that area. I know this level of focus is easier said than done for many people—including me. But giving specific focus to the one thing you want to build your business around is critical for your long-term success, not to mention your sanity.

Stay Focused

It can be tempting to base your business products and services on all the things you enjoy or can do well. For example, I love riding horses, writing, ballroom dancing, traveling, running marathons, and speaking. I can do all of those things pretty well. I do not, however, have a website or Facebook page that says, "Christy Wright: Sign up for horseback-riding lessons or my class on public speaking. I can teach you to dance, write, or run long distances. Buy now!" You would be so confused. Instead, if you go to my website, you'll immediately discover my focus: I'm the Business Boutique woman. I help women start and run businesses. That's it. That's not to say that I can't do other things. I just know that I am going to be the most successful and help the most people when I pick the one thing I want to be known for and do it well. So all of the products and services on my website relate to Business Boutique. The same should be true for you. You should know your core business, and your products and services should only be "like things" that go together.

Let's say you have an Etsy shop. Etsy can seem like a free-for-all, like an online thrift store or flea market, but it's no different than any other business. I see people who use their Etsy business to sell a wide variety of crafts they've been experimenting with as well as old junk they don't feel like taking to Goodwill. Don't do that! Even a successful Etsy business requires focus. Instead, you might choose to have an Etsy shop for handmade women's accessories that includes purses, wallets, belts, and hats. Those are "like things" that go together. A shop with a simple and clear product line will always stand out from the random garage-sale junk that clutters too many shops. Keep it simple and keep it focused.

So now let's look at your current offerings. Listing out your products and services is the first step in Tier 3 of your business plan. What products do you provide? What services do you offer? I want you to write down your list—every product or service you offer, big or small. Then, when everything is on one page, make sure it only includes "like things" that go together and support your core business. When you narrow down your products and services to only "like things," you brand yourself in the mind of the customer. In other words, they'll know what to come to you for.

The most successful companies know this. Chick-fil-A doesn't sell hamburgers, and Starbucks doesn't publish magazines (although they tried, and failed, in 1999).[41]

Why? Because those products aren't "like things," and they aren't their bread and butter.

That's why, instead of chasing every brilliant idea that pops into your head, I want you to figure out what you want to be known for and focus your business on that. Then narrow down your products and services to only the "like things" that support your core business.

You Can Have Both

Right now, your business might be product-based (it produces tangible products such as jewelry or cookies) or a service business (it provides services such as accounting or music lessons). The truth is that you might start as one, but your core business might evolve over time to include both. There's actually good reason to make this happen. While this might sound contradictory to what I just said about focus, it's actually not. As long as your business offers "like things," then you can offer both—products and services. In fact, offering both allows you not only to diversify your income, but also grow and scale your business.

Let's say you have a wedding planning business. That's a service business. But you want to scale your business—generate more revenue while doing the same amount of work per client—by offering upsells and other items. You decide to add a product line to your wedding planning business. You begin to acquire an inventory of tablecloths, centerpieces, vases, string lights, and banners that you make available for your clients to rent for their special day. Now you can offer services (wedding planning) and products (rentals), which gives you the opportunity to make more revenue per client while doing essentially the same amount of work as before.

Or let's say you have a product business sewing quilts. When you create a product such as a quilt, your ability to earn money is completely dependent on your efforts, or in this case, your time sitting at the sewing machine. That is, unless you want to hire someone, which we will cover later. If you don't want to hire anyone (and many people don't) but you still want to find a way to make more money without spending every minute behind the sewing machine until your fingers bleed, you can add services. Since you've already branded yourself a master seamstress, you can offer group sewing classes. That way you can teach many people at once, still doing something in your core business, and earn more money per hour.

When you start thinking about how to scale your business, there's no limit to what you can do and how much you can earn. Just make sure to keep your ideas in the "like things" category. The goal is to expand what you're already doing, not to use this as an excuse to sneak in other business ideas.

CHOOSING A LOCATION

In addition to planning your products and selecting your services, you also need to think through where you will operate the business. Step two in Tier 3 of your business plan is choosing your location. If you want a Big Mac, you know you have to go to a McDonald's location. That's their place of operation or where you'll find their products. So where will you operate?

Space vs. Location

In the previous chapter, we talked about planning a business space. However, space and location are often two different things. Your space is where you work on the business; your location is where you operate the business. If you run your entire business out of your home, then your location and space might be one in the same. Maybe you have a freelance writing business. You do your business upkeep in your home office. That is, you do all the management, marketing, planning, and record keeping there. And you operate—you do your actual writing—there, as well. You don't need a separate location because your home office space is sufficient for both. Or maybe you have a retail storefront with an office where you work on the business and operate the business.

But it's also possible that your space and location are in different places. If you teach swimming lessons, for example, your workspace could be a home office and your location could be the community pool. If you do custom monogramming, your workspace could be your craft room at home and your location could be a local boutique. You need a space where you work on the business and a location where you actually work the business. They may be the same place or two difference ones, but you need both.

Your Location Can Always Change

Where you operate the business is up to you. Over time, your location may change. For example, Jake, who I mentioned earlier, just took his bakeshop, Jake's Bakes, into his first retail place, and he's doing better than ever. You can always grow and change locations, but at any stage of business, you need a place to operate.

THINKING THROUGH LOGISTICS

After you've determined your products and services and decided where you will operate your business, you need to decide how you're going to provide those products and services. This is where logistics come in, step three in Tier 3 of your business plan. Logistics are the technical details such as making purchases, keeping inventory, fulfilling orders, and managing shipping. The number one goal of planning logistics for your business is efficiency. The more efficient you are, the more time you save and the more money you make.

I've talked with so many clients who run their businesses inefficiently by making purchases whenever they run out, fulfilling orders as they come in, scheduling services around the client's availability, and shipping products as they are completed. That may not sound like a big deal, but when you calculate the incredible inefficiency of running your business that way, you are talking about weeks, possibly months, worth of time and potentially thousands of dollars wasted over the course of the year. Instead, let's look at a few practical steps to help you streamline your operations, become more efficient, and therefore save you time and money.

Purchasing

The cycle of purchasing for your business will vary depending on the type of business you have. The key to efficient purchasing is knowing the rate at which you use the items needed to run your business.

For example, I go through approximately one box of diapers per month for my oldest son, Carter. Since that's pretty predictable, I have put diaper purchases on a monthly subscription through Amazon. I actually save money because I got a good deal on a subscription service, and his diapers are automatically delivered to my door at the frequency I need them. Plus, this saves me from ever running out, which in turn prevents stressful late-night trips to the store!

You probably already think about your personal shopping this way; now you just need to apply that to your business. Maybe you use approximately one hundred business cards, five reams of paper, and eighty shipping boxes per month. You can multiply those numbers by three (three months' worth) and put those items on an ordering schedule every quarter so that you don't have to run to the store every time you run out of supplies. In fact, you don't even have to think about it. And as a bonus, you often get a better deal because you're buying in bulk.

For things that aren't as predictable as business cards or diapers, you can establish a monthly purchasing day. Once a month, time-block an appointment on your calendar to take account of your supplies and note which ones are running low. And by running low, I mean you will run out in the next two to three months. Maybe you're running low on a particular type of bead for your jewelry business or ingredient for your bakery or thank-you notes for your coaching business. Determine all the items you need to replenish and add them to your next order or shopping list. By focusing just once a month on these items, you eliminate having to stop and order multiple times during the month.

Doing these two things—automating regular purchases and lumping all irregular purchases into one scheduled day—will help you operate most efficiently. No more wasted time making unnecessary trips to the store and no more stress of running out of something.

Keeping Inventory

I'm often asked how much is the "right" amount of inventory to keep on hand. A good rule of thumb for most established businesses is three months' worth. In general, when you have three months of inventory available, you aren't making too many small (translation: more expensive) purchases and you prevent the chance of running out of something, even if you have a really big month.

However, if you're just starting out, you might want to start with lower quantities of product to lower your risk. For example, you might order less stationary, boxes, custom-sized materials, and so on until you know how much you will actually need on a regular basis. Then, once you've been in business for more than a year, you can easily calculate how much inventory you use during a year. You simply take the total amount for the year and divide by twelve months. That gives you a rough estimate of your monthly inventory needs. If you're just starting out, it will be more of a guess that you reassess every month during your first year.

Now, we all know that business isn't consistent. Most businesses have some type of seasonality. Product businesses, especially, are heavily weighted during the fourth quarter as people make purchases for Christmas. If you teach swim or paddleboard lessons, you will have more business in the summer, obviously. That's why it's important to track the amount of materials, equipment, and supplies you use each month. When you do this for one full year, it becomes much easier to forecast the next year. You'll want to anticipate growth for the next year, of course, but it gives you a baseline to start from.

Order Fulfillment and Shipping

Many people fulfill product orders as they come in or schedule appointments or sessions around their client's schedule. While it may seem like a fantastic way to serve your customers, it's actually a fast way to stress yourself out and fall behind. If your website says items are shipped within twenty-four hours of receipt of order or you accommodate your client's schedule instead of setting your own, what you're really saying is that you are on call 24/7. Unless you're a doctor saving lives, you probably don't want to be on call 24/7. Sometimes, believe it or not, I want to be off work and unavailable!

This is where your schedule comes in. In chapter 9, we covered the importance of setting your work hours. During those work blocks on your calendar, you work. During the other blocks, you don't work. That means your customers can expect you to fill and ship their orders and reply to their emails during your working hours. It's perfectly reasonable, and smart, to put your work hours on your website, blog, or Etsy page. Remember, it's your business, so you get to make the call!

If your business involves shipping products, you might include something like this under the shipping details or FAQ page: "Our hours of operation are Monday–Wednesday, 8:00 a.m.–2:00 p.m. CT. We ship all orders received by 2:00 p.m. on business days within 24 hours. Orders received outside our hours of operation will be processed the next business day." This sets clear expectations for your customers. It also allows you to streamline your shipping by only making one trip to the post office per business day. If your business "closes" at 2:00 p.m., for example, you could just plan on taking that day's orders to the post office every business day at 2:00 p.m.. That kind of routine is essential for an efficient business.

When it comes to fulfilling orders, it's a good rule of thumb to build in more time than you need. You might get sick or have a crazy week, and you don't want to fall behind because you've set an unrealistic expectation for fulfillment time. Always underpromise and overdeliver for your customers.

If you have a service business, your website might read something like, "We schedule appointments/sessions/lessons Mondays, Wednesdays, and Fridays between the hours of 10:00 a.m. and 5:00 p.m. CT." This teaches your clients that they don't set your schedule, you do. They can choose their appointment time based on their availability and your operating hours. The client doesn't get to dictate your hours any more than they can control their doctor's availability or their grocery store's hours. Teach your customers what to expect from you and stick to it. By doing this, you control your work schedule, and as a result, you can have a life outside of work.

When you plan the logistics for your business intentionally and efficiently, you'll be amazed at how much time you free up and how much money you save. As a bonus, it will make the rest of your work a lot more fun.

PICKING A PLATFORM

After you've narrowed down your products and services, selected your location, and planned your logistics, the next step in Tier 3 is to choose your platform. Your platform is simply where your business will live online. It can seem like the options to choose from are endless. That's why you need to think about what's right for you and your business before setting up shop online. Let's look at some of the most popular options available today. Keep in mind, however, that platforms are always changing. Something new could be released anytime.

Etsy

Etsy is a perfect place if you're just getting started selling products. Etsy is like a "business in a box," but online. Etsy handles the hosting, provides the tools to create a profile page and presence, and handles order intake. They also accept payment for you. Etsy is a great incubator site for your business. It's a low-risk, low-cost way to put your ideas in the marketplace and start making sales.

But because Etsy handles everything for you, there are some limitations. You've got to operate within their rules and guidelines as well as pay them a percentage of your profits. You are limited in how you represent your shop online. And when you use Etsy, you're essentially setting up your shop in a giant online mall with 1.6 million sellers competing for the same 25 million customers.[42] Even if you don't sell on Etsy.com for long, it's a great place to try things out and get your idea off the ground.

Blogging

You might have thought about creating a blog to drive sales for your business. Blogging is appealing because it's easy to get started and, because you write and control the content, it's a great way to advertise your name and brand. A blog platform can be much less intimidating to set up than a full website, and it can drive a lot of traffic toward your business.

But before you run out and set up a blog, I want you to consider if a blog is right for you. I work with many women who set up blogs for no other reason than, "Everyone else is doing it, so I figured I had to." The scenario goes like this: You decide to start a blog. How hard could it be? You set up a WordPress theme, select fonts and color schemes, and spend hours choosing photos. But when you sit down to write, you discover any combination of the following:

- You don't have anything to write about.
- You don't like to write.
- You aren't good at writing.

As you can imagine, this is frustrating. But because you feel like you have to blog, you write long sentences about nothing. Then you have to promote your efforts. So you tweet, email, text, and send smoke signals to link back to your site. But all that effort did nothing to grow your business. It only exhausted you, distracted your marketing efforts, and confused your potential customers.

Blogging isn't for everyone. If you have a natural love and gift for writing—and if the blog drives your business in some way that you can identify and monetize—then by all means, blog! If not, let it go. Not every business needs a blog. I don't know about you, but I couldn't care less if my child's piano teacher blogs. I just want her to be able to read and play music, and to teach my child how to do the same. When you let go of this pressure to write, you can instead choose a platform that's right for you and your business and spend your time doing more of what you love.

Website

Whenever I'm asked, "Do I need a real website?" people emphasize the word *real*. That's because creating, building, or paying for a professionally programmed website is pretty intimidating to most of us. The great part about a website is that you have endless options for how it looks and works. The bad part is that you have endless options for how it looks and works. It's overwhelming!

Plus, you can spend a shocking amount of money to buy, build, and maintain a site. So in light of all that, do I think you need one? Maybe. A website might be for you and it might not. Here are some examples.

You might need a *real* website if:

- Your Etsy store has been booming for a while and you're ready to grow and expand with fewer limitations and more options.
- You have a business that needs to professionally showcase what you do in order to drive sales. Examples may include real estate, accounting, or legal services. These industries in particular have a standard of excellence and professionalism that only a quality website can convey.
- Your business is in the field of technology, design, or marketing. This one is tough, because your business site will also serve as your résumé

and sample to potential clients. If you can't design a good site for yourself, no one else will pay you to design one for them.

If none of these options describe your business, then you may not need a professional website. You can potentially bypass the headache, intimidation, and cost by finding a different solution.

Many people believe a fully customized and programmed website is their rite of passage into legitimacy, but that's simply not true. With so many options for promoting your business online, you don't necessarily need to have the added expense and upkeep of a custom website. This is great news, because it means you can focus your efforts on something that will actually make you money—such as fulfilling orders, serving customers, and making sales. Later on, when the business is stable and your revenues justify it, you can create a professional website—if it makes sense for your business.

You can choose any of those platform options or something else entirely, but your business does need a place to live online. There are over 3.4 billion Internet users worldwide, so if you're not online, on one platform or another, you'll miss the opportunity to get business from billions of people.[43]

Monetizing Your Efforts

Most women I work with get excited about the potential to earn money from their platform. They know from watching other successful online businesses that the site itself can actually make them money. But they have no idea how. Where does the money come from? The Internet fairy? The truth is, making money from your blog or other website comes from more places than you may realize.

When I interviewed *New York Times* best-selling author Crystal Paine, famously known as "the Money Saving Mom," for our first Business Boutique event, she said the income from your blog or website will come from two different sources, and both are crucial to your success.[44]

Residual Income

The first is residual income. This is a way to scale your business. You do a little work on the front end that makes you money over and over again, even when you're not working. Residual income is a good thing in blogging or business. Some examples of residual income can be:

- **Advertisers**

  Advertising is a great way to make money on a blog, but it's definitely not a get-rich-quick scheme. Growing ad revenue takes time. I asked Crystal about this, and she suggests starting by adding Google AdSense ads to your site. Google makes it extremely easy to get started and, with a few tweaks to your site, Google can insert small, unobtrusive ads on your blog pages. You get paid based on how many people see the ad, so your ad revenue will grow with your readership. You'll probably start with something like a dollar for every thousand people who see the ad, which means you'll only make $10 or so for every ten thousand people who see your post. Don't let this freak you out, though. Sure, you need a lot of readers to build this up, but it takes almost no effort on your part to maintain. Then, once your readership gets really big, you can even sell ad spots or sponsored posts to companies that match your readers' interests.[45]

- **Affiliate Links**

  If you're constantly recommending specific books, resources, or supplies to your website readers, you could actually make a little money every time one of your readers buys something you recommend. Companies offer affiliate programs that enable you to link to certain products on their sites, and, if one of your readers follows that link to make a purchase, you get a small percentage of the sale. Amazon has a great affiliate program, and other companies like Zulily and Stitch Fix offer extra incentives for affiliate links. Crystal warns, though, that these simple text links should be a natural part of the content and not an overt, in-your-face ad. So if you're talking about a specific book in a blog post, it would be fitting to put a link to that book on Amazon.[46] When you do that, just use your affiliate link.

- **Online Courses**

  If you love to teach and have a marketable skill, why not create an online video training course as a product? You invest your time and money into creating the course once and getting it online, and then you get paid every time someone buys it.

- **YouTube Videos**

  Have you ever noticed the pre-roll ads that play before most YouTube videos? Companies pay to have their ads placed there. You could add other companies' ads to your videos, or you could invest in creating your own ad to run before other people's videos to drive traffic back to your business. Just search for "YouTube advertising" to find out more than you ever wanted to know about this.

Multiple Streams of Income

In addition to residual income, you can also create multiple streams of income. For example, you may have opportunities to earn money from other sources, such as speaking, self-publishing an e-book, or writing product reviews. Just remember to stay in the "like-things" category.

Small Paychecks, Big Earnings

Many people think that if you make money online, you get one big check every month, but that's not the case. More often, whatever you earn from your blog or website, whether that is $1,000 per year or $1 million per year, is usually made up of hundreds or even thousands of tiny paychecks ranging from three dollars to thirty dollars to three hundred or more. Three dollars doesn't sound like much money in and of itself, but when you are paid three dollars every time someone clicks your affiliate ad, that three dollars scales quickly to hundreds or even thousands of dollars. Overall, earning money from your blog or site usually comes from many different, smaller sources but your ability to increase your income is limitless.

POINT-OF-SALE AND RECORDS

Speaking of income, you need a plan for accepting payment and record keeping. Hopefully, if you're already up and running, you have a system in place. But if not, now's the time to do so. The good news is that like choosing an online platform, there are many inexpensive and easy ways to do both.

Payment Options

Choosing your point-of-sale is the next step in Tier 3 of your business plan. Getting paid for your work is obviously a big deal. If no one pays you, your business will go under. Make the payment process as simple as possible. If your customers and clients have an easy way to pay you, you'll get paid faster and with fewer problems.

For example, services like PayPal, Square, and Venmo can make your life much easier. With a couple of taps on a smartphone, your customers can pay you quickly and easily. This is great for all businesses, but is especially helpful if you're selling products face-to-face. Your customers can pay you with their debit cards or directly from their checking account without ever pulling out their wallets, which works great at craft shows and flea markets.

Depending on which web platform you're on, you may already have some built-in payment features. For example, Etsy will process payments for you for a small fee. If you have a blog, you can actually use plug-ins and widgets (add-on features) that allow you to take payments directly on your blog site.

And, of course, there's always cash—something we at Ramsey Solutions are fans of! Regardless of which option you choose for accepting payment, just make sure it's compatible with your record-keeping systems. Which brings me to . . . paperwork.

Embracing the Paperwork

Ah, paperwork, the least fun part of business—and life—in my opinion. As I've said, I'm not great with details. But because your records affect things like your taxes, they are really important. That's why I surround myself with people who are strong in areas where I am weak. I've learned a lot about small business accounting from my friend Shane Gibson, CPA and Business Boutique guest speaker. Shane goes beyond tax preparation and even offers tax and accounting classes for small-business owners because he loves it so much.

At a recent Business Boutique event, Shane taught that small business record-keeping needs to include two main systems: an accounting system and a document-management system.[47] Your accounting system is how you track money coming in and going out of your business. We'll cover how to do this later when we dive into money management. For now, you just need a method for tracking your business finances. It can be as basic as an Excel sheet, or it can be new, trendy, and beautiful like Freshbooks, Xero, or Wave. The point is, you need a program to help you track the flow of money through your business.

Your document-management system is simply how you keep a record of documents such as invoices, receipts, files, and so on. It's fine if you want to keep physical copies of your paperwork, but you also need digital versions in case those files get lost, get coffee spilled on them, or the dog eats them. For your digital records, a cloud-based online system such as Evernote or Xero is key. That way, if your computer crashes or, heaven forbid, your house burns down and takes your computer and backup drive with it, your financial records and receipts will still be safe and sound. That's called an off-site backup, and you need it. Some programs and services include photo storage, which allow you to take pictures of or scan your receipts and file them digitally with two clicks so you never have to store the paper. Now you can get rid of that shoebox you've been storing crumpled receipts in for years.

As long as you maintain your sales orders, tax receipts, and customers' information, the format doesn't matter. We often get so caught up in having the right software that we can waste countless hours just trying to figure it out.

Whatever is easiest for you will usually take the least amount of time and prove the most effective. It's not important how you stay organized, just that you stay organized. When you do, it will mean less time searching for misplaced information and more time growing your business and making a profit. Plus, the easier your system is to figure out, the more likely you are to actually use it.

SAVING TIME AND MONEY WITH BURNT TOAST

Thinking through the operational details is probably not why you got into business in the first place. And I know it's not what gets you out of bed in the morning. But this practical stuff allows you to be more efficient, which saves you time for more of the fun stuff in life. That way you can do more of what you love and less of what you don't.

Sportscaster Jim Nantz is a good example of this. Apparently, he really loves burnt toast. I don't mean dark toast or crunchy toast. We are talking toast the color of charcoal. Because he is on the road so often, he eats his burnt-toast breakfast at a restaurant nearly every day of the year. The problem Jim had was that for years, whenever he ordered his burnt toast, it never came back burnt the way he liked it. I presume that's because no other human on the planet actually desires charcoal toast, but that's not the point. The point is that every time he didn't receive his toast singed like he likes it, he would send it back requesting that it be more burnt.

After years of this, he calculated that every time he sent his toast back, it cost him ten minutes per day, six days per week, which amounted to four hours a month. When he did the math, he realized that this problem of un-burnt toast was costing him forty-eight hours—two full days—per year! Jim's wife, Stacy, got tired of hearing him complain about his time being wasted waiting on burnt toast, so she decided to do something about it.

She found a picture of black toast. She printed it out as a wallet-size photo, laminated it, and insisted that her husband carry it with him. Now when he orders his breakfast—three eggs scrambled with bacon and black toast—he shows the picture to his server. He gets weird looks, not only because he likes toast that looks like the remains of a house fire, but also because he has a laminated picture in his wallet of said toast. But you better believe that now his toast is served black, just the way he likes it. And the best part is that Jim is no longer wasting time waiting for his toast order to be fixed. Over the course of ten years, he has added twenty days to his life. Twenty precious, entire days![48]

Imagine what you could do with twenty days added to your life. Or just two days, this year. Or just two hours. The possibilities are endless. With a little work on the front end, streamlining these elements of your business will not only set you up to be more efficient but will also help you follow through. No more abandoned ideas, now you'll see them through. No more lost time and inefficient systems, now you'll finish what you started. And your follow-through will pay off in the long run when you have more time and money for the things in life that matter most. And luckily, you won't have to live your life with a laminated picture of black toast in your wallet to be able to do so.

chapter 10 action items
LET'S APPLY WHAT YOU'VE LEARNED!

Products and Services

What products do you provide? What services do you offer? Remember, these need to be "like things." Write them here.

Location

Where do you operate your business? This may be the same as or different from the space in your home where you work on your business, as discussed in chapter 9. Write your location here.

Logistics

Below, write your plans, processes, and procedures for the technical details of how you are going to operate your business.

Plan for Purchasing

Process for Keeping Inventory

Procedure for Fulfilling Orders

Process for Shipping

Platform

Where will your business live online? For example, it may be on Etsy, a blog, a website, or some other platform. Write your main platform here.

Point-of-Sale

Where and how will you accept payment?

Records

At a minimum, you need an accounting system and a document-management system. Write which systems you will use, or are using, here.

Accounting System

Document–Management System

Other Record–Keeping Systems

chapter 11

BEST BUSINESS PRACTICES
Running Your Business Like a Pro

It was my spring semester of eighth grade at McMurray Middle School, and I didn't have any plans for spring break. When I asked my mom if we could go to Florida, she said yes and as a bonus, I got to pick a friend to go with me.

I went out on a limb and asked a girl named Jill. Jill was sweet and normal and fun. Even though we weren't really close at the time, to my surprise, she wanted to go and her parents approved. That spring break my mom took us to Destin, Florida, where Jill and I hung out, laid on the beach, and pretended we were older than we were. We drank virgin daiquiris, rode Jet Skis, and listened to Jewel's *Pieces of You* album on repeat, screaming the words to "You Were Meant for Me" every time it came on. Jill taught me some important lessons about life such as how to apply makeup, that brown shoes do not go with a black belt, and that short overalls are not cool when you're thirteen. Jill was wise about these types of things, and I was not. She learned all of this from her older sister, a wonderful source of guidance that I didn't have as an only child. Jill and I became best friends on that trip, and we were inseparable from then until we graduated high school.

But because we were always together and involved in similar activities, a strange thing happened. Comparison and competition crept into our friendship. When we both played soccer, people commented on who was better. When we both ran track, people compared us. And we were inevitably compared when we were both nominated for homecoming court. This went on all four years of high school. Though we remained best friends, it put a strain on our relationship that we battled our entire high school careers as we were pitted against each other for roles, dates, and awards. Senior year, she was student body vice president and I was student body secretary. She was voted "Miss Overton" and I was "Most School Spirit." To this day, Jill and I are still friends and, thankfully, the competition and comparison struggles are long gone. But back then, as immature and insecure teenagers, we didn't know then what we know now. In high school it seemed like it was always Christy or Jill, when all along it should have been Christy *and* Jill.

Unfortunately, being in business—especially being a woman in business—is not all that different from my high school experience. The insane peer pressure that pits women against other women is everywhere. It's the constant peer evaluation of everything about our lives including our looks, parenting, finances, business, homes, vehicles, bathing suits, baby names, and every other detail you can imagine. You see it in magazines with sections called "Who Wore It Better?" and you see it in business with reviews and comparisons of who makes the cutest product and has the most customers. And don't get me started on social media! As my good friend Rachel Cruze says, "Social media is the vehicle that leads down the road to comparison." We are constantly evaluating ourselves and others by who has the most Facebook comments or page likes. It's no wonder being a woman—especially in business—is tough. Even if you're a confident person, a quick online review about how your product is too expensive or your service isn't as good as someone else's and suddenly you feel like the rug is pulled out from under you.

That's why it's so important to round out Tier 3 by talking about competition, policies, protecting ourselves, and pricing. Because, if we're honest, we sometimes struggle with these things. Figuring out how to set ourselves apart from the competition without elbowing them out of the way is awkward. Setting policies can be challenging, and protecting ourselves without coming off as a jerk can be tough.

Finally, nailing down the right price point can be so overwhelming that we'll dedicate the whole next chapter to that topic. Tackling these elements of your business plan will not only help you battle the constant comparison and competition all around you, but it will also help you be more confident and better prepared when weird situations come up. Because, trust me, in business and in life, weird situations will come up.

COMPETITION

Even if you're doing something incredibly unique, you will be able to find other companies doing something similar, faster, better, or cheaper than you. But believe it or not, not all competition is bad. In fact, we can learn from our competition. Researching your competition is the next step in Tier 3.

Get Educated, Not Intimidated

Researching and getting to know the competition can be tricky, because honestly, sometimes learning about our competitors can scare the heck out of us! We can feel pretty good about our little idea and dream, but when we see what other people are doing, comparison creeps in, intimidation takes over, and we start to get worried. Suddenly our little idea doesn't seem so promising anymore. That's why I want you to follow this rule of thumb. Research your competition enough to learn from them but not so much to be intimidated by them. If you can look at what they do without stressing yourself out, you can:

- determine the industry standard (generally accepted criteria) for your particular type of business,
- discover best practices (a best method for accomplishing something) in your specific industry,
- get a baseline idea for pricing,
- learn from their mistakes without making them yourself, and
- appreciate what they do well and incorporate that into your own business.

In his awesome book *Steal Like an Artist*, Austin Kleon talks about how to learn from the best ideas out there and make them your own. He says, "Your job is to collect good ideas. The more good ideas you collect, the more you can choose from to be influenced by."[49]

For example, you might see that another seller incentivizes advance orders and you decide to adopt that strategy so you can prepare for the summer selling season. Or you might see that another Etsy seller offers twenty-four-hour shipping just days before Christmas, and you know that sounds like a nightmare. You want to spend your Christmas Eve singing carols and drinking hot chocolate with your kids—not running back and forth to the post office. So you learned what not to do. When you take a look at what's happening in the marketplace, you can be more strategic about how you run your own business. And what you find might also help you realize how unique, different, or excellent your product or service is.

Simple Research

Researching your competition doesn't have to be time-consuming or difficult. I'm not talking about hiring a research firm or finding a focus group. You don't need to do a six-month survey of the marketplace. You just want to see what's already out there. By doing a simple Internet search, browsing similar social media sites, or talking to people in your network or community, you can gain significant insight into what your competition is doing.

Start with the following questions:

- What are they doing well that I can learn from?
- What are they doing that I don't agree with and want to avoid?
- What makes them unique or different, and how can I can set myself apart from them?
- What are their prices?
- What are their policies?
- What types of customers do they have?

Do your research and collect answers, but here's the key: don't let it get to you. Remember how I saw an article by a well-known author that was almost identical to something I was working on? It scared me and made me want to quit. That's partially because I was in the early stages of getting started, and it didn't take much to shake me. But seeing others do something similar, or in some cases, better, can be intimidating. That's why your research needs to stay research. Don't let it slide down the slippery slope into stalking and obsessing!

When you find yourself reading the owner's bio page and comparing her child in a monogrammed smock dress to your wild-child currently making mac-n-cheese art on your kitchen walls, you've gone into new territory. Her bio, children's outfits, or the cleanliness of her home has absolutely nothing to do with you learning best business practices! That's when you close out the screen, step away, clean up the mac 'n' cheese if you're so inclined, and then get back to work—your work, the work that you are called to do. Remember, like Jill and me in high school, it's not you or her. It's both of you. Sure, she's there doing her thing, but never forget, there's room for you too.

POLICIES TO LIVE BY

Several years ago, I got a letter in the mail from my dental insurance company. They were notifying me that my policy had been canceled due to nonpayment. I was shocked. I pay my dang bills! I called the company and explained that they must have made a mistake, that I pay my dental insurance annually as soon as the bill comes in the mail. But I hadn't received a bill, so I didn't know anything was due.

The representative, whom we will call Jane, told me that the bill was sent two months earlier. Confused, I asked her what address she'd sent it to. She said, "We don't mail them anymore. We email them. We've become a paperless company." Ironic, I thought, because you sure didn't mind killing trees to notify me of my cancellation! Apparently in the last year, they had decided to become a paperless company without any notice to their customers. Frustrated, I asked her what email address they'd sent the bill to. She read an old email address from many years ago, before I was married.

"Well that explains it," I told Jane, assuming I could just pay, have my insurance reinstated, and be done with the whole thing. "That is an old email address from years ago. I'd like to pay the bill now and have my insurance reinstated."

In a flat tone, Jane responded, "You can't do that. Since you let it expire, you cannot pay it now and reinstate it."

Through gritted teeth, I semigrowled, "Let me understand this. I would like to pay you for insurance and you are telling me that you will not accept my payment? You actually do not want my money?"

With a dismissive tone, she replied, "Ma'am, that's our policy." The phrase "that's our policy" makes my blood boil, especially when the policy makes no logical sense whatsoever. And what she said next blew my mind. "Now, if you'd like to reapply for insurance in three years, we will accept your application and evaluate if you are approved."

Three years! If I wanted to wait three years to reapply, then maybe, possibly, if I am very, very good between now and then, they would consider taking my money. I get worked up just thinking about it.

Good Policies Are Necessary

Here's the reality about policies: more often than not, they suck. I don't know of a single person who loves a particular business because of its policies. You never hear people say things like, "Oh, I always get my accounting done there—I love their policies!" Or, "My favorite salon is right down the road. They have the best policies." No one says that! Policies are not what connect you with your customer. If anything, they are what push your customer away. However, you still need to be prepared for situations that come up. That's why I believe every business—including yours—needs to have some policies in place for those situations, and setting those policies is the next step in Tier 3 of your plan.

Policies set expectations and teach your customers how to do business with you. But policies aren't for your average customer or the general public; most people know how to behave and treat you the way they'd want to be treated. Policies are for people who don't know how to act right. They're for the people who assume their needs are more important than yours. You know who I'm talking about, don't you? You can probably picture one or two difficult customers right now. These are the ones who are always pushing the limit and never seem to be aware that you are actually running a business. They're the reason you need policies.

Policies You Need

What policies do you need for your business? In general, you need to cover a few things: cancellations, refunds, terms of payment, shipping, and hours of operation. You need a cancellation policy so you don't waste your time blocking your schedule for people who never show up. And you need a return policy for situations when your customer might be unsatisfied or when they simply change their mind. You need a policy regarding terms of payment for the customer who thinks they should be able to pay you next year instead of when you complete the job. And, like we covered in the last chapter, you need shipping policies and operating hours.

If you have a policy for these things, you will go a long way toward ensuring that you aren't taken advantage of. Having policies will help you protect yourself from the most difficult situations, but at the end of the day, people always trump policies. If you have a twenty-four-hour cancellation policy and someone calls you twenty-three hours before their appointment and you know you can fill their slot, give them a break. If someone ordered the wrong product by mistake and asks for something different, help them out. Unless someone is trying to take advantage of you, just take good care of people and you won't have to worry about policies that often.

PROTECTING YOURSELF

Even with good policies, you will still have to deal with difficult people. There will be crazy people, high-maintenance people, and people who get on your last nerve. You will encounter people who disregard your policies and drive you nuts. A person may try to steal your pattern, secret sauce, and peace of mind. People will ask for a cheaper price, either at cost or even for free. And then you could get the downright crazy people you don't know what to do with. That's why, even when you have good policies, you still need a strategy to protect yourself when these people show up. Planning for this is the next step in Tier 3 of your business plan.

Get ready, because they will show up, and it's on you to handle it. You teach people how to interact with you. Motivational speaker Tony Gasikins Jr. says, "You teach people how to treat you by what you allow, what you stop, and what you reinforce.”[50] In other words, what you allow is what you will get. So let's look at the three types of difficult people you might encounter, and how to handle them.

The Thieves

"Thieves" are people who, instead of buying one of your precious, handmade dresses, ask you for the pattern. Instead of buying a jar of your grandma's special spaghetti sauce, they ask for the recipe. These people are thieves. That may seem like a strong word, but what else would you call people who are trying to steal your stuff?

I had a client, Pam, who struggled with this. On more than one occasion, Pam gave away her patterns when someone asked for them. She didn't want to, of course, and she regretted it immediately, but she was so caught off guard by their audacious requests that she gave in without even thinking about it.

I don't want this to ever happen to you. That's why I recommend coming up with a reply ahead of time. Think about how you would handle a situation like Pam's and script a response. It'll allow you to determine, in advance, how to handle a difficult situation—without the pressure and awkwardness of being on the spot.

So how do you respond when someone asks you for your methods, patterns, or styles of work? You can say something like, "We built our business on that information, and we actually don't give it out." Or you might say, "That's actually what makes our business so special. I'm happy to chat with you about prices for (insert your product or service here) if you're interested in buying one." You can be kind but firm. Regardless of how you go about it, you need a plan—a script, if you will—for how you'll handle the thieves who want to steal your stuff.

The Cheapos

"Cheapos" are the people who might not ask for your pattern or secret sauce, but they will ask you for something below your price. They might try to ask for it at cost or straight-up ask for it for free. From my years of experience, the biggest offenders are family, friends, and Facebook connections that come out of the woodwork. Your cousin Bill's ex-wife's sister-in-law saw that you were an accountant on Facebook and well, she really needs some help with her taxes, so couldn't you just help her out "real quick?" It's family after all. Or that guy you kissed during a game of spin the bottle in middle school twenty-seven years ago saw on Facebook that you make custom jewelry, and he would really like one for his new girlfriend, so could he get one for half price, since y'all go way back and everything?

Here's the thing. You cannot run your business if you are always giving your stuff away. As a general rule and good business practice, you need a plan for how to handle the Cheapos. Like with the Thieves, you need to script your response ahead of time. That way you're not put on the spot when someone asks for something at a discount or for free. Instead, you can tactfully restate your price to make it clear that you don't give things away. You can say something like, "Oh, I'd love to make you that picture frame! It's twenty-five dollars. Just let me know what color you'd prefer and I'll get started on it."

How about when an old friend asks for something at cost? You could say something along the lines of, "We don't have any discounts or specials for that item right now, but you're welcome to check out our sale page to find something you might like."

Or let's say you have a florist shop, and someone wants to negotiate your product or service for less than your listed price. You might respond with, "That large arrangement is forty-five dollars, but if you're looking for something less expensive, you might be interested in this one that's only thirty." Preparing your response ahead of time will save you the mental angst you experience when you're in the moment and not sure what to say.

That's not to say you can't help people out. I'm not against blessing people and, if you want to help someone, by all means, go for it. You might decide to plan your giving ahead of time, like I mentioned in chapter 7. This is where you give a percentage or amount of your time or products free of charge to help others. But your gift should be just that—a gift that you plan on purpose—not something you give away out of guilt, obligation, or manipulation. Regardless of how you decide to respond to people who are trying to pay less than your asking price, planning your answer in advance will not only save you stress and headaches, it will save you from giving away goods or services and then resenting and regretting it later.

The Crazies

If you've worked with the public for any length of time, then you know 10 percent of your most difficult customers take up 90 percent of your time. And when you're already juggling family responsibilities, a business, and the rest of your life, it's not a good use of time to spend hours trying to make an impossible, unreasonable customer happy. That's why I want you to identify your crazy customers early on and fire them. That's right: fire them. You have more important things to do and less demanding customers to serve. If you can identify the Crazies before they drain your time, money, energy, and peace, you can politely fire them and move on. Here are a few red flags that signal you might be dealing with a Crazy:

- Their questions are accusatory from the get-go and resemble an FBI interrogation.

- When you answer their questions, they still don't seem to be satisfied or pleased. No answer you offer is good enough.

- They look for any and all ways to pay less while simultaneously asking for more.

- They act like they're doing you a favor by ordering, and they expect you to jump at their every request.

- They've already friended and unfriended you on Facebook three times since you met an hour ago.

Your business isn't for everyone, and that's okay. You will be doing yourself and your demanding customer a favor when you part ways before you both end up disappointed and frustrated. You can do this by politely explaining that you don't think your business is a good fit for them.

When my mom has a bridezilla on her hands (or more often, a momzilla!), she politely says, "I get the feeling that you aren't going to be happy with my cakes, and I really want you to be happy. I recommend you go somewhere else because I don't believe I am a good fit for what you're looking for." Another option is to simply tell the Crazy customer that you're not available to take the specific order they're requesting. You might say something like, "The scope of that project is more than I can take on right now, but I am sure there are others who would be able to give you exactly what you want." You get to choose how to fire them.

And I promise, if you're willing to take this brave step in protecting yourself and your business, you'll be more successful, and you'll have fewer gray hairs in the process.

If you can decide in advance how you're going to handle the Thieves, Cheapos, and Crazies, you'll be prepared to protect yourself when weird situations come up. While it might take some effort, the end result is that you'll have less stress and a business you can be proud of.

WOMEN CHAMPIONING OTHER WOMEN

When you learn from your competition without letting them intimidate you, when you set policies to protect yourself, and when you anticipate your response to difficult customers, you will possess an amazing gift in business: confidence. Confidence allows you to hold your head high, talk about your business with pride, and pursue your dreams without fears holding you back. You can love your business like you never have before. And one of the greatest benefits of being secure is being confident enough to champion other women too.

Right around the time Jill and I were singing our hearts out to Jewel in 1995, two other girls were becoming best friends across the country. They were in their early twenties and each was just starting her career. They were both insanely talented and, like Jill and me, often went after similar opportunities. But instead of letting competition creep in, these women figured something out, something that has enabled them to stay friends throughout their lives and propel their success even more. They discovered the power of women championing other women. Early on, regardless of the competition in the marketplace, media, or culture, these two women were determined to cheer each other on. They knew that the success of one didn't mean the failure of the other. They saw the power and potential in loving and learning from each other regardless of the competition and limited opportunities for women in their particular industry. Back then, when no one was watching and no one cared, they championed each other.

Today, we all know them as Tina and Amy, Amy and Tina. Both Tina Fey and Amy Pohler are beautiful and brilliant, hardworking and hilarious, sassy and successful. And it's obvious that championing each other hasn't taken away from their opportunities and careers; it's only added to them. Plus, their friendship and support has set an example for women everywhere. They've redefined how powerful, successful women can interact with other powerful, successful women.[51]

I love what Tina and Amy are doing, because, you see, the world is not a place of scarcity, my friend. It is a place of abundance. There are not a limited number of spots at the top. There's a spot for you wherever you make it. Just because another woman is winning doesn't mean you're losing. And celebrating and supporting someone else doesn't take away from you; it only helps you. These are lessons I've learned over the last decade coaching professional women who are trying to make it in this world. And these are the very things we intentionally model at the Business Boutique events. Every speaker that steps on stage is incredibly talented. And every one of us supports each other, compliments each other, and lifts each other up. Like Tina and Amy, the women of Business Boutique have seen the power of women championing other women, and we want to help others do the same.

Dave Ramsey's daughter, Rachel Cruze, and I are a good example of this. We are in the same business doing the same kind of work. Like me, she coaches people, writes, and speaks. We are both talented at similar things, and we both have similar opportunities. We are together a lot—for events, tours, and radio programs—and Rachel has become one of my closest friends.

I am so proud of her and all she has done to teach people in our generation the life lessons she learned growing up as Dave Ramsey's daughter. Beyond that, she has taken her dad's message of financial peace to a new level with her voice, passion, experience, and most of all, her heart. She's a gifted speaker, amazing on video, graceful during interviews, and so fun to be around. And I tell her that, often. In the exact same way, she's quick to encourage me, champion me, and support me as well. Just like Tina and Amy, Rachel and I have discovered the importance of women supporting one another.

And that's what I want for you: the power that comes from women championing other women. Whether it's the boutique down the street that is similar to yours or someone across the globe competing for the same online customers, whether you've met her or not, there's room for both of you. While you may feel pressure to elbow your way to the top, I want to share some good news: you don't have to. Because ultimately, it doesn't have to be her or you. It is both of you—out there busting it, doing the work you are called to do.

chapter 11 action items
LET'S APPLY WHAT YOU'VE LEARNED!

Competition

1. Who is your competition? List them here.

2. For each business you listed, answer the following questions (use a separate sheet of paper if you want):

   1. What are they doing well that I can learn from?

   2. What are they doing that I don't agree with and I want to avoid?

   3. What makes them unique or different, and how can I set myself apart?

4. What are their prices?

5. What are their policies?

6. What type of customers do they have?

Policies

Write out your policies in the following areas:

1. Hours of Operation

2. Terms of Payment

3. Shipping

4. Cancellations

5. Refunds

Protecting Yourself

Write out your responses to the following requests and situations:

1. Someone asks you for your method, pattern, or secret sauce.

2. A family member asks for something for free.

3. A friend asks for something at cost.

4. Someone asks for a lower rate than your listed price.

5. You have a demanding customer you need to fire.

chapter 12

HOW TO MAKE MONEY AT THIS

Understanding Profits, Pricing, and Paying Yourself

Several years ago, I spoke at a business conference for dentists. I was invited to speak on the topic of money because, while many dentists (and other medical professionals) are brilliant at what they do, they sometimes struggle with the business side of things. Generally, in all of their years of education, medical professionals never learn the basics about money management or running a business. Unfortunately, regardless of how talented or skilled they are at treating patients, money can become one of the main problems they deal with on a regular basis. So, in my keynote presentation, I talked about the benefits of avoiding debt, managing money, and growing a business with more wisdom and less risk.

After all my speaking engagements, I like to stay for a while to meet people and answer questions. That's what I was doing at this particular conference when a large man approached me with a confused look on his face. He said in an exasperated voice, "I have a question for you. I heard everything you said about managing my money in my business and personal life, but I just don't get it. You talk about avoiding debt, but it doesn't make any sense to me. Why would I want to save up and pay for a car with cash and have to wait years to get it, when I have a BMW right now and only pay $1,500 per month in a car payment? I don't understand!"

Just then, his assistant piped up and said, "Oh that's just the start of it. He has so many credit cards and they are all maxed out, and he has multiple loans against the practice. Sometimes he can't even make payroll and pay us!"

I was speechless. It wasn't that he thought $1,500 per month was a reasonable car payment. It wasn't that he had taken out loans. And it wasn't that he clearly didn't listen to anything I had said. It was that I knew he wasn't going to make it. No matter what I said, he didn't get it. I was so sad for him because I knew, based on how he handled his finances, his practice would likely never survive.

Unfortunately, whether you're running a medical practice or a little Etsy shop out of your home, more often than not, mismanaging your money will be the thing that brings your business down. *Inc.* magazine reports, "[Most businesses fail] because they can't pay their bills. Most entrepreneurs either are (or start out as) financially illiterate. They go out of business because they don't manage their cash and can't pay their bills."[52] That's why, in this chapter, we are going to go over the practical steps you must take in order to manage your business finances—so you can protect not only your business, but yourself, as well.

If you think this chapter is going to be about investors, capital, and small business loans, think again. Thankfully, what you need to build, manage, and protect your business is simple. You need three things: separate bank accounts and budgets for home and work, a good profit margin, and solid pricing for your products and services. That's it. Did you just relax a little? I did. These elements will help you win with money in your business. As simple as they are, these are the three things most small-business owners miss! Let's unpack each of these and make sure you're set up to win.

DON'T MIX THE MONEY

This may sound crazy, but go with me here. I want you to take a little oath for me. You ready? Repeat after me: "Business money is for business stuff. Personal money is for personal stuff. I will never use personal money to buy business things, and I will never use business money to buy personal things. So help me God." Good. Now that you've made that commitment, let's talk about why keeping your personal and business money separate is such a big deal.

You Need Separate Accounts

I need to be super clear here: you need separate bank accounts for your personal finances and your business finances, and you should never mix them. Like I mentioned in chapter 9, don't buy groceries out of the work account, and don't buy product supplies with your personal account. This just opens you up to more trouble than you can imagine.

This is so easy, but despite how simple it is, no one does it. Even my clients running large businesses with multiple team members still conduct business transactions through their personal accounts. This is a recipe for disaster for so many reasons. First, your business and personal finances are combined, and the funds are so comingled you cannot possibly know what's been spent for personal use and what for business use. Second, the balances aren't separate, so you can't identify your business profit and don't even know if you're actually making money. Third, you have a nightmare on your hands when tax season rolls around and you try to sift through receipts and sort which Walmart or Office Depot trip was for business and which was for personal stuff. And heaven forbid if you have business and personal purchases on the same receipt! Good luck untangling that mess at tax time. Finally, your records are a royal mess, which opens you up to IRS fines for inaccurate business receipts if you get audited.

I can't stress enough the importance of this simple step in managing your finances. It's so important, in fact, that I want you to commit to taking care of it this week. All you have to do is go to your bank and set up two separate accounts: a checking account for all of your business transactions, and a savings account for saving and reinvesting in the business. It will only take a few minutes, and it shouldn't cost much (if any) money. Doing this one simple task will protect you from endless headaches. Once your accounts are set up, run every single transaction for your business through your business checking account. We'll talk about what to do with the business savings account later, but for now, every dollar of revenue you receive for a product sold or a service rendered goes into your business checking account. And every purchase you make for the business, big or small, in person or online, comes out of that account—no matter what. I don't care if you are in a rush and accidentally grab your personal debit card instead of your business card. And I don't care if you're snuggled up on your couch shopping online for your business and you don't want to go get your business debit card. No matter how inconvenient it might be, always use your business account to make transactions for the business. If you do that one thing, you will not only reduce your stress and protect yourself, but you'll also make every other aspect of money management easier on yourself.

Separate Budgets

Remember, when you decide to treat and run your business like a real business, it becomes its own little entity. It's no longer a part of you or your personal finances. That means your business has its own bank accounts, and it means your business has its own budget, as well. As we covered in chapter 9, you might have a line item in your personal family budget for a short time until the business funds itself, but after that, the business doesn't have any place in your personal budget.

The business budget, like your family budget, is something you'll create every single month. And while it's similar to a personal budget and easy to establish, your business budget will be different in two main ways.[53]

First, while you budget your personal income based on a consistent salary, you'll forecast your business revenues based on the previous year. If you're just starting out and have been in business less than a year, you're not totally off the hook, but you do have a lot more grace since you don't have a baseline to work from. Your budget will be more of an educated guess that will be adjusted month to month. Regardless, your business budget will be formatted like your family budget. It will list income (projected revenue) and (projected) expenses.

Second, for your personal budget, you need a "zero-based budget." That simply means budgeting every dollar on paper so that your income minus your expenses equals zero. That ensures that you're accounting for every dollar you bring home, which helps avoid "accidental" spending. The business budget, however, is slightly different. Here your projected revenues minus your projected expenses equals projected profit. We don't want that to be zero! I will share later about what you do with profit, but for now, just make sure you're projecting a profit. Your profit each month, by the way, will directly affect your personal budget because that's where the money you bring home comes from.

Once you've established your budget, you need to reassess monthly, quarterly, and annually. At the end of every month, quarter, and year, you will want to review your actual revenue, expenses, and profit against what you budgeted and expected. Look for overages or shortfalls and readjust your budget more accurately as you go. As I mentioned in chapter 10, because most businesses have some level of seasonality, a budget can help you anticipate the expenses of inventory so you can survive the crazy, hectic months as well as the dismal, slow months.

Creating a budget for your business puts you in control of your money. John Maxwell says, "A budget is telling your money where to go instead of wondering where it went." And when you're intentional with your money this way, you'll be able to reach the milestones you set in Tier 1 and build your business into what you want it to be.

BUILDING UP PROFITS

A lot of people I've coached through the years think they have businesses when what they really have is a hobby. Like I said before, the difference between a hobby and a business is that a hobby costs you money while a business makes you money. But because some "hobby businesses" have money coming in, the owners mistakenly believe they are making money. Let me clarify the difference between bringing in money and actually making money. When you bring in money, it simply means you have money coming in through transactions. When you make money, it means your business is making more money than it's spending. That means you are earning a profit. It doesn't matter how much money is coming in if you aren't making a profit. If you spend $1,000 a month operating your business and you bring in $1,000 a month in total revenue, you've got a hobby, not a business.

Profit isn't only necessary to survive in business, it's also the report card of how well your business is doing. Your profit is your measure of success. When you have good profits, your business is doing well, your costs are low, and your income is high. On the other hand, small profits mean your costs are high and your income is low. I want you to have a profit so that you have more money and more options to grow, expand, and reach your goals.

Understanding Revenue and Profit

If your business is working as a CPA or bookkeeper, then you're probably already familiar with terms like gross revenue, gross profit, net profit, operating expenses, cost of goods, retained earnings, and on and on and on. If you get excited about stuff like that, more power to you. Personally, all of that makes my eyes cross. If you're like me and don't get fired up about spreadsheets, then don't worry. You don't have to have an MBA to manage your business money well. I can give you some basic guidelines that are easy to understand (and follow) that will work for almost any business.

The first thing to know is that the money you have coming into your business, either through people buying your products or paying for your services, is your revenue. The second thing to know is that your revenue is not the same thing as your profit. So don't get carried away and run to the mall when you get a big check from someone. Unfortunately, not all of that money is yours.

Let's look at the whole month at once. Add up all the money you were paid throughout the month. That's your gross revenue. The first thing you do with that money is pay for your cost of goods. For example, if you make custom clothes, your cost of goods refers to what you spent on fabric, thread, patterns, and all the hard costs you put into making your product. Your revenue minus your cost of goods gives you your gross profit. But you're not done there because your gross profit still has to pay for things.

From there, you take your gross profit and subtract your operating expenses. That's everything besides cost of goods that goes into running your business. That could include rent (if you lease a storefront, for instance), gas money for making deliveries, cell phone bills, Internet service, and so on. The money that's left is your net profit.

So far, then, the flow of your business's money looks like this:

Gross Revenue
– Cost of Goods Sold
———————————
Gross Profit
– Operating Expenses
———————————
Net Profit

Next, you're going to divide your net profit four ways, and you'll do it in exactly this order:

1. Taxes. How much you need to hold back varies a little based on your income, but it's a good rule of thumb to hold back 25 percent of your net profit for taxes. This is critical. You might even want to open a separate bank account just for stashing your tax money. This keeps it out of your normal business account so you won't be tempted to spend it before tax time. So many business owners are stunned at tax time when they get a huge bill from the IRS. You're going to owe taxes, so prepare for it! Don't save it all for once a year, either. If you're self-employed, you'll need to pay quarterly estimates to the IRS. There are a million rules around this stuff, so I recommend business owners work with a great tax professional to make sure you won't be surprised at tax time.

2. Emergency Fund/Savings. After you've held 25 percent of your net profit for taxes, you need to save a portion of your net profit into a business savings account. This account will help cover you for any expensive emergencies like a broken sewing machine or a fried computer. The specific amount to save each month varies for every business and business owner. If you're just starting out, it's wise to be more aggressive with your savings until you build up a good-sized buffer between you and any emergencies that may pop up. Three to six months of business expenses is a good rule of thumb. Like your personal emergency fund, this is money that you don't use unless a true emergency comes up.

3. Upcoming Expenses/Reinvestment. This is another chunk of savings, but this money has a more specific purpose. This is money you're saving for any big expenses in the near future. For example, if you know you want someone to design a website for you in three months, you need to save one-third of that amount each month from now until then. Or, if your computer is getting old and acting up, you can assume you'll need to replace it soon. Unless it suddenly crashes, this should be a expense that you planned for ahead of time.

4. Paycheck. Finally, once you've taken care of everything else, it's time to pay yourself. Hooray! If you've accounted for all the expenses we've covered so far, then you can take home whatever is left and know that your business is in good shape. That's the paycheck your business pays you for all of your blood, sweat, and tears.

So, the complete flow of the money coming into and going out of your business should look like this:

Gross Revenue
– Cost of Goods Sold
———————————————
Gross Profit
– Operating Expenses
———————————————
Net Profit
– Taxes (25%)
– Emergency Fund/Savings
– Upcoming Expenses/Reinvestment
———————————————
Your Paycheck!

Again, this is a simplified version of your business's cash flow. You could probably manage this system yourself for a long time if you want to, but my best advice is to find a tax pro to help walk you through it.

Paycheck Wake-Up Call

Once you calculate your paycheck (called your net income), you need to take an honest look at your revenue and expenses. When you do the math, you might feel discouraged by your paycheck. You might discover you're averaging $2 an hour and would be better off serving at a restaurant making tips. But unlike working in a restaurant, you are in complete control of the income you create in your business. You have the freedom and ability to adjust your business as necessary to get your personal income where you want it to be. Let's look at how to do that.

In order to increase your personal paycheck, you need to increase your net profit. You can do this by increasing your revenue (how much money comes in) or decreasing your expenses (how much money goes out), or possibly both. You can increase your revenue by selling more units, serving more clients, or raising your prices—or all of the above. You can decrease your expenses by finding cheaper materials, buying in bulk, or maybe putting off large purchases until later. Just think of each one of these areas as little dials you can turn as you try to "fine tune" your business. And if that level of financial tinkering sounds intimidating, don't sweat it! We came up with a tool that makes all of this drop-dead simple. Our Profit Potential app will ask you a few easy questions about your business, and then it'll show you your projected revenue, profit, taxes, and more. Then, while you're looking at those numbers, you can use easy sliders to see how big a difference raising your prices, making more units to sell, or bringing down your costs can make to your monthly and annual profits. Best of all, the tool is completely free for you to use! Just visit www.businessboutique.com.

Whether you use our Profit Potential app or not, I can't stress enough how important it is to think through all of these factors. When you look at your expenses and realize every dollar spent is a dollar not in your pocket, you start to rethink that expensive camera or new computer. When you see that spending money on your business doesn't always make you money in return, you reconsider that bedazzled clipboard and monogrammed computer case you had your eye on. You start to understand you're not only cutting into your profit margin but you're also taking away from your personal income. That's why it's so important to pay attention to your net profits and adjust if needed. When you do this, you set yourself up to win at business and support yourself at the same time.

MASTERING PRICING

If you want to earn a profit, setting the right price for your product or service is key. However, pricing can be a struggle for most of us. And I say "us" because I've been there too. First of all, it can be hard to know what to charge. And even if we land on a price, we might not feel good about it. That's because, when it comes to pricing, there is a lot more going on than just the numbers. I know because I hear it again and again when I'm coaching women. They say things like:

"I feel weird about putting a price on myself."

"Talking about my price makes me uncomfortable."

"I don't want to come across as pushy or arrogant when I tell people my price."

If you've ever felt like this, you are not alone. Sixty-six percent of women I've surveyed said they worried about pricing.[54] But if we try to base our price on our feelings, we make mistakes. In fact, I probably see more errors in pricing than any other business finance issue. I don't want you to make those mistakes, so let's take a look at what not to do when setting your price.

Mistake #1: Pricing Yourself as the Cheapest Option

Trying to be the cheapest is a bad pricing plan. If the only advantage you have over your competition is being the "bargain-bin brand," you might want to rethink your entire business. I'd be willing to bet you have something more to offer the marketplace—something people are willing to pay for. Besides, when you under-price what your products or services are worth, you not only cut into your profit and personal income, but you also make it difficult to increase your prices later.

In his book, *Start with Why*, Simon Sinek says, "Selling based on price is like heroin. The short-term gain is fantastic, but the more you do it, the harder it becomes to kick the habit."[55] You'll have a hard time increasing your profit margin if you're always trying to undercut the competition. Further, you'll miss the section of the market that wants to pay more because they want your higher-quality product. When you're thinking through your pricing strategy and model, being the cheapest should not even enter your mind. In fact, being the cheapest is a race to the bottom where whoever wins, loses.

Mistake #2: Pricing to Compete with the Wrong Businesses

Pricing to compete with the wrong businesses is a bad model too. I see this happening two ways. First, some side-business owners try to compete with multimillion-dollar big-box stores. When you do that, you're competing with businesses that may have things you don't have. For example, Walmart and Amazon have billions of dollars and resources to run their well-oiled corporate machine with maximum efficiency, high sales quantities, and unbelievably low expenses because of their bulk purchasing. They are not your competition. I don't care if Walmart or Amazon sells something similar to you. You're not in competition with them, and your pricing has nothing to do with what they charge, so don't bother trying to match them.

Second, you're not in competition with other people selling their hobbies online. Take Etsy, for example. Some of the stores are just hobby-businesses. And because they aren't pricing their products to make money, they aren't in the same business as you. Don't try to compete with them.

In order for your price to work for you, you need to know who your competition is and who it's not. It's not big-box stores, and it's not other business owners running hobbies. Don't base your pricing on what the wrong people are charging. Instead price for your business and your customer.

Mistake #3: Pricing for the Wrong Customer

Not every person is your customer. You have a certain type of customer—your target market—that we'll talk about later. Your target customer is who you should price your product or service for. For example, one of my friends and colleagues is entrepreneur coach Ali Brown. Ali's client base is women who make over seven figures in their business. She prices her services accordingly. She doesn't try to price her coaching for everybody; her services would be way too expensive for many people. But she knows who her customer is, and she prices for them.[56] In contrast, if I charged for my services like Ali does, I would miss the entire market I am actually trying to serve—women dreaming of starting or currently running side or small businesses. I like to help people get started and grow their business from the ground up. Maybe one day my clients will grow their businesses to the point that they'll become Ali's clients. That would be awesome! But for now, I fill a different space in the market than she does, and we both price our products and services accordingly to reach and serve the right customer.

Knowing the mistakes to avoid is a start to determining the right pricing for your business. When you know what not to do, you can focus on what to do.

The Formula for Pricing

If you aren't going to price to be the cheapest, compete with the wrong businesses, or serve the wrong customers, how do you price? Pricing can be easier if you're charging for a physical product. Because it's a tangible item, you start with your expenses, your hard costs, as a baseline amount and set the price from there. However, that's not the case with a service-based business. If your business is vacation planning or web design, for example, you do have some hard costs and expenses, but for the most part, your price is based on your time. That can feel a little awkward. Instead of putting a price on a product, you're putting a price on yourself. You're having to force yourself to ask, What are my time and skills really worth?

Additionally, service-based businesses have a much wider price range. For instance, if you're going to buy a pie, it will probably cost you somewhere between ten and forty dollars. The hard costs for the ingredients, baking, and packaging help set the price. But, if you are going to hire a fitness coach, lawyer, professional speaker, or photographer, the prices can range from one extreme to another. Some professional speakers charge one hundred dollars for a one-hour keynote address and, at the other end of the spectrum, someone like Hillary Clinton charges over $250,000 for a one-hour keynote address.[57] For a half-day session, some photographers charge one hundred dollars and some charge $10,000!

That kind of range can make it hard to determine your price.

Most women just want me to give them a formula. Unfortunately, there isn't one. Pricing can feel like a game of educated guesses. But several variables exist to help you determine the ideal pricing range for your business. Let's take a look at each to help you set your price.

Cost of Goods

As we've said before, cost of goods refers to what you pay for the materials used to create your product. For example, if your product is art, then your cost of goods would be the expense of the paint, canvases, and frames. If you're in a service business and you don't provide any tangible products with your services, then you do not have a cost of goods to factor in your pricing.

Expenses

Your expenses are what it costs you to run your business. This might include paper for orders, boxes for shipping, overhead such as lighting and phones, gas for deliveries, and so on.

Time Invested

You also need to include time invested in your price. Calculating your time, as you probably know from experience, is much more complicated than just adding up the minutes or hours spent creating an actual product; it's the time invested on anything having to do with your product. That means the time spent on the phone taking and writing the order, preparing, creating, cleaning up, and boxing the order, as well as shipping, sending receipts, billing the order, and so on. If you're teaching a lesson or coaching a client, it's the time invested in preparing for a session and following up with homework, accountability, and paperwork. Those are work hours, and you need to include them in your price.

And if the customer makes changes to the order, the price should change as well.

Let's say you bake cakes like my mom, and a customer emails you for a price quote on a small white cake with decorative balloons. You tell them it will be $14.99 plus tax. They agree and pay for the cake. Two days later, you get another email asking if you can make one small change. They want the cake to be half-chocolate and half-white cake with fresh strawberries in the center. "No problem," you say. A day later, they email again. This time, they want the cake to be sugar-free and gluten-free. And instead of balloons, they want a portrait of their dog made out of icing. This is no longer a $14.99 cake!

As soon as your customers start making changes requiring more of your time, the cost should change as well. Factoring in your time invested will help you set a price that reflects the value of all your time.

Quality

Another factor to consider is the quality you're providing. If you're using high-quality materials for your product, you will want to charge more to cover those costs and price your product at what it's worth. Or, in the case of a service, your quality will depend on your years of experience, level of education, portfolio of past clients, and any awards and accolades you've received. If you're just starting out, your goal might be to just get clients. You might want to charge below average while you are still gaining experience and establishing your client base, referrals, and portfolio. But as your experience, education, clients, or awards increase, your price should increase as well.

The photographer my husband and I used for our wedding was insanely talented but also affordable and within our budget. Then, a few months after our wedding, he was named "Best Photographer in Nashville" by a local magazine. Receiving this award meant he could—and should—raise his prices. So, when my friend used him for her wedding pictures a year later, she ended up paying a lot more than I did! That was completely appropriate. Like our photographer, the quality and experience you offer will help determine the value of your service. That, in turn, will help you set your price accurately.

What the Market Will Bear

It's important to think about what the market is willing to pay for the product or service you provide. In general, the higher your price, the smaller the market that can afford it. The goal is for you to find the sweet spot that maximizes your profit while maintaining a strong customer base.

I worked with a woman named June who sells handmade purses from her Etsy shop. We were talking about pricing and working through the variables she needed to consider. When we talked about her time invested, she locked in and ignored the rest of the variables. She said, "Well, each purse takes me about thirty hours to complete. I'd like to make about twenty dollars an hour, so do you think someone would pay $600 for my purse?" No, June, I do not. I do not think that Etsy customers will pay $600 for the fabric purse you made in your attic-turned-sewing room! I didn't say that, of course. I said something similar, but a little nicer.

There's an average selling price for almost everything on the market. That includes Etsy items, handmade items, fabric items, and items from a home-based business. That's just reality. Unless your name is Kate Spade or Tory Burch, you shouldn't be charging $600 for a purse just because you sew as slow as Christmas. You want to be in line with the "average selling price." And that includes services like wedding planning, graphic design, and swim lessons, as well. If you discover your pricing is way above the market average, it's up to you to figure out how to make the thing faster, get more efficient, and get your costs down so you can charge a price that is more in line with what the market is willing to pay.

Competition

A good way to find out what the market will bear is to research prices. If you're on Etsy, see what other sellers are charging for similar products. If you're a free-lance designer, research what other designers are quoting. And if you have a bakery, find out what other bakeries in town are charging. Researching your competition's rates will give you insight into what's working in the marketplace and help you set your price.

Location

If your business is strictly online, then location might not apply to you. But, if you have a storefront of any kind or if you provide services in person, where you operate will impact what you charge. Because the cost of living varies so much across the country, your prices should appropriately reflect your location. For example, I love the show *Fixer Upper*. I am a huge fan and I watch it religiously. I am amazed at the big homes they buy for crazy-low prices.

On the other end of the spectrum, one of my best friends, Susan, lives in Manhattan. What my husband and I paid for our home is about what it costs her to buy a gallon of milk. Where you live will affect your price, and it should. Considering your location will help you price your business for the customers you serve locally.

It's a Range, Not a Point

Remember when I said there's no exact formula for pricing? That's because even when you consider all of these factors, you still won't come up with the perfect price point. Instead, you will find your ideal price range. But it's just that: a range. At no point in business will you land on the "perfect" price that you set and never revisit again. Your business will change, the market will change, and as a result, your price will change. Your range should be something you experiment with, test, and adjust over time.

Charging What You're Worth

Whether you're behind a computer, a sewing machine, or a mixing bowl; whether you're teaching, speaking, or designing; regardless of your "type" of business, the bottom line is you need to charge what you're worth. Like my friend with the $600 purse, don't rely on just one variable to give you the answer you're looking for. Work through all the variables to help you narrow down your price range. I bet you'll discover your work is worth more than you think.

I love the anecdote of the carpenter in the book *Selling the Invisible* by Harry Beckwith:

> A man was suffering a persistent problem with his house. The floor squeaked. No matter what he tried, nothing worked. Finally, he called a carpenter who friends said was a true craftsman. The craftsman walked into the room and heard the squeak. He set down his toolbox, pulled out a hammer and nail, and pounded the nail into the floor with three blows. The squeak was gone forever. The carpenter pulled out an invoice slip, on which he wrote the total of $45. Above that total were two line items:
>
> Hammering, $2.
> Knowing where to hammer, $43.[58]

When you're setting your price, you're not only charging for cost of goods, expenses, and time invested, you're also charging what you're worth. You're charging for the unique gifts, talents, skills, education, knowledge, perspective, ideas, quality, and style you bring to the work you do. So don't just charge for hammering. Charge for knowing where to hammer.

When you do these simple things—when you keep your business finances separate, when you create a good profit margin, and when you get your price range in the sweet spot—it sets you up to win. You won't be one more statistic about small business failure, because you'll have managed your money well. And then you really can make money doing what you love.

chapter 12 action items
LET'S APPLY WHAT YOU'VE LEARNED!

Separate Finances

If you don't have them already, set up separate business checking and savings accounts. You'll also need to build out your separate monthly business budget!

Profit

To practice calculating the profit in your business, use last month's numbers and fill in the formula below.

Gross Revenue
– Cost of Goods Sold
_____

Gross Profit
– Operating Expenses
_____

Net Profit
– Taxes (25%)
– Emergency Fund/Savings
– Upcoming Expenses/Reinvestment
_____

Your Paycheck!

Variables to Calculate Pricing

1. What is the cost of goods for that product/service?

2. What are your expenses in producing or delivering it?

3. How much time goes into it?

4. What level of quality is it? Very high, high, medium, low, or very low.

5. What is the average range of pricing for a similar product/service?

6. What is your direct competition charging for that product/service?

7. How might your location affect your pricing?

Based on the above variables, what is your ideal price range?

Try Out Our Profit Potential App.

Plug your business information into our free Profit Potential App at www.businessboutique.com and answer the following questions.

1. If you have a product-based business, what would your profit potential be if you were to produce 20% more units over the course of a year?

2. If you have a service-based business, what would your profit potential be if you were to take on 20% more work over the course of a year?

3. How would reducing your operating expenses by 10% impact your profit potential? What are some easy ways you could shave 10% off of those expenses?

4. How is your profit potential affected each month/year if you were to work an additional five hours per week?

chapter 13

THE BUSINESS SIDE OF THINGS
Breaking Through the Boring Stuff

I wasn't a great student in high school or college. It wasn't that I struggled to understand my classes, I was just preoccupied with social activities like soccer, theater, student council, and prom. Like most high school and college students, if something didn't interest me, I didn't invest much time in it. And now, like most adults, I wish I had paid closer attention. For instance, I wish I could remember my Spanish vocabulary. And I wish I could recall historical events or the locations of certain countries without needing Google. I only spent time and energy on things I cared about and, unfortunately, Spanish, history, and geography were not on that list.

We sometimes act this way in business too. We naturally focus all of our time and energy on the things we care about, the fun stuff: setting up the Facebook page, printing business cards, picking colors and fonts for our website, writing cute thank-you notes, choosing ribbon for packages, and decorating our space to be "just right." We don't think about the business side of things until we have questions like, *Do I need a business license? What taxes do I owe? Do I need patents for my products? Should I form an LLC? Do I need a lawyer?* And then we hit a wall.

In my research, I've discovered that this wall is where women take one of two paths. Some women take Path One, where they decide they aren't "business-minded" enough. They resolve to keep their hobby a hobby and let their business dream die. But other women take Path Two, where they decide to push through. They get answers to their questions and help with things they don't understand. Instead of turning back, these women get over the wall and go on to reach their goals and grow their business.

I want that to be you! I want you to get over the wall, and I don't want you to give up on your business. That's why we must look at the "boring" business things in this chapter: taxes, accounting, licenses, insurance, copyrights, and patents. However dull they may seem to some people (including me!), knowing about these subjects is crucial to running your business well. I'll warn you up front, this is a meat-and-potatoes chapter. We're going to power through a lot of things that many business owners never think about, but they're incredibly important. Stay with me.

You don't have to be an expert on these subjects, but you do need a basic understanding of them. My hope is that, after reading this chapter, you'll not only feel more confident about the topics that intimidate you, but you'll also have more time to get back to the fun stuff!

DREADED TAXES

There are some things in your business you could just avoid altogether if you don't want to deal with them, but taxes aren't one of them. That's why I'm starting here. Failure to properly plan and save for taxes can sink your business. As crucial (and inevitable) as taxes are, though, they're also potentially the most confusing part of business management. I'll try to keep it as simple as possible, but unfortunately, there's no such thing as "simple" when it comes to small-business taxes. How much tax you owe is dependent on endless variables. Let's make sense of taxes by answering some of the most common questions I get asked by business owners.

Do I Need a Certified Public Accountant or Other Tax Professional?

Yes, for the love of all things good in this world, yes! If you're like me and hate taxes, then you probably dread this aspect of your business more than any other.

Since I hate accounting so much, and since taxes are kind of a big deal (like legally binding and a huge liability), you need help. If you're not a tax professional, you need to hire an experienced, trusted, and qualified tax person to assist you. They will make sense of all the confusing paperwork and accounting associated with running a business.

A tax pro who specializes in small businesses can walk you through important decisions and processes like choosing a business structure and obtaining a business license or permit and obtaining federal and state tax IDs. Sound overwhelming yet? I know, I need a nap just thinking about it! But when you seek professional assistance for your taxes—and other legal aspects of your business—you not only take the burden off yourself, but you also protect your family and your assets. I promise you, money invested in protecting your family and your future is always money well spent.

Do I Owe Income Tax on the Money I Make from the Business?

Yes. As I mentioned in the last chapter, you'll want to set aside 25 percent of your net profits for taxes, and I recommend keeping the money in a separate business savings account until your taxes are due. Keep in mind that 25 percent is just an estimate; your actual tax rate will vary, but this is a good rule of thumb. You will pay your taxes quarterly, which is every three months. This sounds annoying, but it's actually a great system of accountability to make sure you don't forget about them for an entire year and then owe thousands of dollars (that you might not have) the following April. In fact, if you don't pay quarterly, you may be charged a penalty.[59] Your tax professional will be able to help you estimate how much you owe and can help process the paperwork and payments to the IRS.

Should I Be Charging Sales Tax?

Yes . . . usually. This one gets tricky, and you'll want your trusty tax pro to help you sort it out. In general, you need to charge sales tax if you sell to someone in your state. If you have a brick-and-mortar store, you will always charge sales tax on transactions in that store. If you sell to customers in different states through an online business or over the phone, you don't need to charge sales tax on those items. However, if you sell something online to a customer in your state, you do charge sales tax. See what I mean? It gets a little fuzzy. The three main things to know about sales tax are:

1. You charge sales tax on any transactions for retail goods in your state (in person or online).
2. You do not have to charge sales tax on any transactions out of state.
3. You need a tax pro to help you with all of this.

One last thought here. If you physically travel out of state and sell your goods there, you may need to get a temporary sales permit for that state. If so, you'll need to file a sales tax return for that state (and pay sales tax). That's one more thing to talk to your tax pro about.

What Records Do I Need to Keep for Tax Purposes?

Again, a tax professional can help you with a comprehensive list, or you can find one online at the IRS website, www.irs.gov.[60] You should also check with your state department of revenue, since your state requirements may differ from the federal requirements. At a minimum, you will need to maintain records for the following:

- Any business income received, including receipts for all sales transactions.
- Receipts from purchasing supplies used to create a product; we talked about these as cost of goods sold in the previous chapter.
- Receipts for your operating costs of running the business, such as marketing costs, phone and Internet service, gas for deliveries, rent (if you have a storefront), and so on.
- Any expenses you plan to write off for your business.

If you are one of the 10 percent of women-owned businesses that employs team members, you will need to keep employment payroll records as well, which you'll need in order to properly process and pay employment taxes.[61]

Thankfully, you can keep your records in a number of ways. Use your bank statements, deposit receipts, canceled checks, invoices, or some combination of all four as proof of your transactions. Just make sure you have a document processing system, like I talked about in chapter 10, to help you store them and stay organized.

What Can Be Written Off for My Business?

Have I mentioned yet that you need a tax pro? This is one more area where a professional can help you. Sure, you will have to pay them, but a tax professional will likely find several ways to save you money—often more than they are charging you for their service. There are hundreds of variables and technicalities regarding what small business expenses can be used as tax deductions. But, as a general rule, you can write off (deduct from your taxable income) anything that is both ordinary and necessary for your business. Let's look at what that means.

If an expense is ordinary, it simply means it is common in your particular type of business or industry. An expense that is necessary means you must have it in order to run your business. If you own a boutique that sells handmade clothing, a sewing machine would be an ordinary expense for your industry, and it would be necessary for you to operate. If you have a graphic design service, design software would be an ordinary expense for your business and it would be necessary for you to operate. If you have a home organization business, getting fresh highlights for your hair would not be an ordinary expense, nor would it be necessary for you to operate—but it would be cool if it was!

A word of caution about tax write-offs. Many business owners who work from home try to use the home-office deduction on their taxes. I do not recommend this. Here's why. Even though having a space and location are both ordinary and necessary to run your business and even though that space and location might be your home, this can cause you more trouble than it's worth. That's because writing off part of your home for your business can make you a more likely target for an IRS audit. If you really want to explore the home-office tax deduction, I strongly encourage you to work with your tax pro to make sure you understand exactly what you can and can't write off.

So those are the basics to know about taxes, but this is just the beginning. Albert Einstein is reported to have said, "The hardest thing in the world to understand is the income tax." If Einstein didn't understand taxes, I don't feel so bad that I don't, either. But hard as they are to understand, you must get them right so please don't stop here. Protect yourself, your family, and your business by getting help from a tax professional. And, speaking of write-offs, the expense of having a tax professional help you with all of this is, in itself, tax deductible. To find a high-performing tax professional in your area that Dave Ramsey and I recommend, visit www.daveramsey.com/elp.

TYPES OF BUSINESSES

Aside from planning for the nightmare that is the tax system, you need to know what type of business you are. Now, if you're like me, you might be thinking of adjectives that describe your business. Type? Oh I am a fun, entertainment business! I am a cute, boutique business. I am a friendly, coaching business! But no, I'm not talking about your style. Your "type" simply means the business structure or entity category your business operates under. Wah, wahhh. I know—way less fun. But the good news is, deciding your business entity type is actually easy when you take a close look at the options.[62]

Sole Proprietorship

This is a small business run by one person. It's easy to set up and inexpensive to maintain. You report your business financial records on your personal tax return.[63] One downside that scares most people is that you are personally liable if the business is sued. However, the vast majority of side and small businesses are safe to start out as a sole proprietor.

Partnership

Similar to a sole proprietorship, a partnership simply means you own your business with one or more people. As a general rule, I don't recommend partnerships. There are almost no benefits to this structure, and it can be a huge hassle if the partnership goes south. And you'd be shocked at how often the partnership does fall apart. Legally entangling your dream with someone else often leads to damaged relationships and expensive legal business breakups. Protect yourself and your relationships by finding a creative way to do business with others without going into business with others.

Limited Liability Company (LLC)

Getting an LLC means that your business is an entity that is legally separate from you. The primary benefit of this arrangement is that your personal and family assets are not at risk if someone sues the business. The bad news is that an LLC can be expensive to set up and maintain and can often be unnecessary for most small businesses. There are two instances, however, where it makes sense to incorporate.

First, you might want to become an LLC if you have a high-liability company. For example, when I had a farm, I had a dream of opening a horseback riding camp for young girls. But putting kids on unpredictable horses would be considered a high liability. In that case, I would have needed to form an LLC to protect what I own in the event of an accident or injury resulting in an angry parent suing me.

The second reason to become an LLC is if you have significant wealth or the appearance of wealth. As strange as it sounds, having wealth makes you more vulnerable to lawsuits because someone might try to sue you simply because they think they can get rich quick. In this case, forming an LLC and protecting your personal assets (such as your bank accounts, house, etc.) might be a wise decision.

Corporation and S-Corporation

In addition to the above options are two additional options: corporation and s-corporation. These are complex business structures, generally for larger, established companies with a lot of employees. These likely do not apply to you, but if you're interested in finding out more information about them, you can talk with a tax professional or review the IRS Business Structures page online.[64]

So what's best for you? Most small-business owners start and continue to operate as a sole proprietorship until the business gets so big it creates liability and risk that the owners need to protect themselves from. When in doubt, of course, talk with your tax professional.

TYPES OF INSURANCE

After you get a handle on taxes and choose your business type, you might want to protect yourself with small-business insurance. Your business might be small, but your risk could be huge if you don't have the proper insurance in place. Most people are familiar with basic homeowners, renters, car, life, and health insurance, but small-business insurances can be beneficial as well. Let's look at three of the most common types.

Product Liability Insurance

This covers the seamstress who leaves an injury-causing pin in a pair of pants or the barista who unknowingly serves a scalding hot beverage. If you have a product-based business, this insurance might be a good idea.

Professional Liability Insurance

This protects service providers such as massage therapists, hair stylists, and pet groomers against claims of injury or error. This insurance covers your mistakes—and your behind!

Home-Based Business Insurance

This covers you when the poor UPS guy slips on the frozen front steps of your home, which happens to be where you operate your business. Beware: homeowners insurance doesn't generally cover home-based business losses or accidents, which is why this additional insurance may be a good idea for you.

Of course, there are many other types of insurance for small businesses. Your best bet is to talk to a trusted insurance provider before deciding what kind of coverage you need—especially if you have employees.[65] Taking this extra step will help you protect what you've worked so hard to build.

PROTECT YOUR STUFF

In addition to protecting yourself and your business, you might also want to think about legally protecting your products from theft with a patent, trademark, or copyright. Again, legal counsel can walk you through this maze. While these measures aren't necessary for everyone, it's good to know which options are available should you want them down the road.

Patent

A patent is a way to legally protect a unique product. The process can be lengthy and expensive, but, if you truly have a unique idea you want to protect, it might be worth it to you.

If you determine you need a patent, you first need to make sure no patents already exist on the product you want to protect. You can search the United States Patent and Trademark Office at www.uspto.gov for more information. And if your product is not a one-of-a-kind original, that's okay! You still fill a need in the marketplace with what your business offers. It just means you don't have to jump through the patent hoops or pay big bucks to protect it. You can put more energy into building your business rather than wading through reams of red tape.

Trademark

A trademark is any word, name, symbol, or design (or combination of these) that distinguishes your business from another. For example, if you have a specific logo you're building a brand around, you might want to look into registering it as a trademark. What's interesting with trademarks is that you don't technically have to register them. Trademark status is based on use, so if you use your logo regularly for your business, it can be treated as an active trademark. But according to the United States Patent and Trademark Office website, officially registering a trademark has several advantages, such as a notice to the public of your ownership as well as legal presumption of ownership nationwide.[66] It's actually pretty simple to register one. You can visit the same site as you do for patents, www.uspto.gov, to register your trademark online.

Copyright

A copyright just means that you created some text (article, book, lyrics, etc.) and you claim all rights to it. If you create and publish something online or in print, you automatically have the copyright, so you aren't required to file anything. If you do file a copyright, however, it proves that you have the legal rights to your text in the event someone tries to use and claim words you wrote.

Legal Counsel

For help with all of the above, as well as other technical aspects of your business, it's not a bad idea to have professional legal counsel in your corner. Is it required? Absolutely not. Is it expensive? It can be. If you have an existing relationship with a small-business attorney or the means to hire a lawyer, go for it. But don't let a lack of the right connections or funds be a roadblock for you. This one is completely optional.

Aside from paying your taxes and my strong recommendation to hire a qualified tax pro, here's the bottom line: the rest is your decision. It's possible for you to operate your business successfully without ever worrying about trademarks, copyrights, patents, or legal counsel. But should you decide to take these additional measures to protect your stuff, it's important to know your options.

GETTING OVER THE WALL

As I am writing this chapter, my husband is sitting next to me watching an obstacle course challenge on TV. He turned it on right as two teams were racing to get over a giant eighteen-foot wall, the final challenge in this course. I'm amused at the irony, because building a business can sometimes feel the same way.

Of course, getting over the wall of the technical, important, and boring business stuff is not the only or final challenge you'll experience in your business. But this is the point where many small-business owners lose hope. This is where they get overwhelmed with questions, feel unqualified in business, and want to give up.

My client Hannah got to this point in her floral business; it all felt too big and overwhelming. She didn't charge up the wall like those race contestants on TV; she ran smack into it. She decided she wasn't cut out for business and almost gave up on her dream. But, as we talked about it one day, I reminded her of something I want to remind you of now. Even though this business stuff feels really big and important, it's actually a small part of what you need to do in order to be successful.

I know it can feel like the business stuff is 95 percent of running a business, but it actually only represents about 5 percent of what you need to spend your time on. The technical, business side of things are smaller and simpler than they seem.

It would have been easy to give up at the wall like so many people do, but Hannah didn't. She took Path Two and has grown her floral business into multiple locations and is doing more weddings and special events than ever before. She got the help she needed and, she admits, it was easier than she thought. Now she's making money living her dream and helping people in the process.

If you feel like you're ready to give up, don't let a few technicalities hold you back from doing what you love. There are professionals (like tax pros!) and resources (like this book!) that can help you get over the wall and back to chasing your dream. Millions of women across the country are absolutely crushing it in their businesses, and I bet a whole bunch of them hate the boring business stuff just like me. Maybe just like you. But, I promise, if they can do it, so can we.

chapter 13 action items
LET'S APPLY WHAT YOU'VE LEARNED!

Getting Over the Wall Checklist

Check off these items as you complete them. For those you have not yet completed, write a date out to the side and commit to getting it done. But remember, not every item will apply to you and your business. Use this checklist as a guide, not a mandate.

___ Do you have a trusted tax professional?

___ Are you setting aside 25% of your gross profit into a business savings account for taxes?

___ Do you have a record-keeping system for your taxes?

What records are you keeping? Make a list below:

What are you planning to write off for your business? Make a list below:

Circle the type of business you chose.

- Sole Proprietorship
- Partnership
- LLC
- Corporation
- S-Corporation

Circle the type of insurance you currently have or might need.

- Product Liability Insurance
- Professional Liability Insurance
- Home-Based Business Insurance

Circle the following methods you want to utilize to protect your stuff.

- Patents
- Trademarks
- Copyrights
- Legal Counsel

Tier Four

PUT YOURSELF
OUT THERE

Congratulations! You made it past the tough stuff, and you're ready for the fourth and final tier of the business plan. This is the topper on your wedding cake, and it is, in my opinion, the most fun of the tiers. It's also the easiest because of the work you did in Tiers 1, 2, and 3. In Tier 4, you will learn to put yourself out there and tell the world about your business. The following chapters cover your unique position, branding, your target market, social media, and your elevator pitch. It's all downhill from here, so let's get started!

chapter 14

MARKETING YOUR BUSINESS

Four Things You Need to Know to Make an Impact

My last semester of college was dedicated to my Advertising Campaigns class, the final class I had to pass in order to graduate with a degree in Advertising. At the beginning of the semester, the professor divided the class into groups, each representing an advertising agency. The groups (agencies) had to spend the entire semester researching and building a campaign for the sole purpose of competing for a client. At the end of the semester, each group had to pitch their campaign to the board (client), and one group would win the account.

The product we had to pitch was the Smart Fortwo. The car was not available in the United States at the time, so we knew building a campaign would be particularly tricky. Additionally, we started with a slight disadvantage because the rest of the groups had six members, but we had only five. We appropriately named ourselves "Party of Five," because we had a good time, despite not performing well on most of the early projects and assignments. It was discouraging, and we could tell the other groups didn't take us seriously. But we tried to keep a good attitude because the class was important, and we wanted to do a good job.

During the research phase, we had to identify the target market for the

SmartCar Fortwo, but we got stuck. We started by applying all of the research techniques we'd learned. We did surveys. We conducted interviews. We held focus groups. But the results were always the same: everyone hated the car. No wonder. We were in the mountains of East Tennessee, where everyone drove big trucks! We couldn't find anyone who liked the tiny car. And we couldn't move forward to build ads for a target market when we couldn't figure out who they were, why they liked the car, or what they wanted. Then, as I was doing some late-night online research at the library, I came across a petition to bring the SmartCar to the United States—complete with five hundred signatures. Gold! This was the target market! This was information that (I hoped) no one else had, that would help our group build a strong campaign.

The petition listed the names, cities, and states of all the individuals who liked the SmartCar Fortwo. So our team divided the list of names and, acting a bit like stalkers, we tracked down the phone numbers for as many of those people as we could. Then, we hit the phones. Even though some people were confused as to how we got their number, most everyone was kind and cooperative. They answered our twenty-plus questions and gave us exactly what we needed: insight into our target market.

The results were beautifully consistent. They loved the SmartCar Fortwo. They loved the fuel efficiency. They loved how easy it was to park. They loved how practical it was. Knowing their mind-set and using their words, we spent the rest of the semester building a campaign titled, "The SmartCar Fortwo. It just makes sense."

At the end of the semester, we watched on presentation day as the other groups pitched their campaign to the leadership of the advertising college. They had nice, pretty ads and good ideas, but none of them had the research we had. Every other group polled people in Knoxville only and based their campaign on the one or two people who kind of liked the car.

When it was our turn, we revealed the petition and our research strategy, and I could see everyone's eyes widen. We nailed our pitch, sat down, and waited nervously for the results. When the advertising college president came to the podium, he gave a little speech about how everyone had done a great job. Then he cleared his throat, paused, and then said, "And the 2005 campaign winner is Party of Five."

We all stood and screamed and danced like crazy people. All of our hard work had paid off!

When I talked to my professor after it was all over, I told her how nervous I had been throughout the semester. I told her how we really struggled with some assignments because we didn't have the best visuals or the prettiest ads. Then she said something that I'll never forget: "The prettiest ads don't win the campaign, Christy. The best research wins the campaign." And she smiled and walked away.

That one lesson stuck. I've carried it with me ever since, and I still use it in my career today. It's why I spent years researching women-owned businesses, conducting interviews, focus groups, and surveys before we ever marketed Business Boutique to the world. I learned that effective marketing doesn't come from the prettiest ads with the best pictures and colors and catchiest headlines. It's deeper than that. Effective marketing happens when you reach the right people in the right way.

Most people in business know that marketing is a great way to reach customers, and they usually love marketing and advertising—when it works. But too often, they can't figure out what works and what doesn't. It feels unpredictable, confusing, and frustrating. And when they don't see any impact, marketing feels like a waste of time, money, and energy. But it's not! Marketing is not the problem. The problem is that business owners don't understand what makes effective marketing—the kind of marketing that gets results. Impactful marketing doesn't have to be unpredictable or confusing. Effective marketing is surprisingly simple. It is just great communication. In other words, it's being able to talk about your business to the right people in the right way.

In order to do that, you need to know four key things:

1. Who you are
2. Who your customers are
3. Where they are
4. How to talk to them

When you know these four things, marketing your business will not only be easier, but also more effective. You'll be able talk about your business and get results.

WHO YOU ARE

If you want to stand out among the competition, you've got to know who you are and what makes you unique. That's why I had you identify your *why*, your mission, your core values, and your strengths early on. Those pieces work together to enable you to define an essential part of effective marketing: your unique position. Defining your unique position is step one of Tier 4 in your business plan. Before you start to get sweaty palms and feel pressured to do something earth-shattering that no one else is doing, relax. Identifying your unique position just means deciding what aspect of your business to leverage in your marketing.

Finding Your Unique Position

Figuring out your unique position is easier than you might think. Your unique position is simply the angle you want to lead with in your marketing. For example, one coffee shop's unique position might be fast service. They market it by saying, "Get your coffee in less time than it takes for the stoplight to turn green." Their message leverages their unique position (fast service) to make you think, *Great! I'll buy from them because I can get coffee and still get to work on time.*

At the same time, another coffee shop down the street might have the unique position of high-quality coffee. They market it by saying, "You don't have to start your day with lukewarm, translucent coffee from the break room. Start your day with delicious, hand-poured coffee made from organic Columbian beans roasted in small batches for maximum flavor." They leverage their unique position (quality coffee) to make you think, *Great! I'll buy from them so I don't have to drink the terrible break-room coffee at work.*

Your unique position doesn't have to be the only thing you do well, and it doesn't have to be something no one else is doing. In this example, both coffee shops might have fast service and high-quality coffee, but each one chose a unique position they've leveraged to help them stand out among the competition.

Once you identify your unique position, you've taken the first step in knowing who you are and what you want your marketing to be about. Next, you need to decide how you want to represent yourself and your business as a whole. This is the next step in Tier 4—branding.

Building a Brand

A brand isn't just something for advertising agencies or marketing firms. And it's more than colors, logos, and graphics. A brand is twofold. It's the look, tone, and feel of your business that's reflected in all of your marketing. And it's your reputation. Your brand is made up of the design that you put out there and, at the same time, your brand is determined by how customers perceive you and what you're known for. Think about it this way. Walmart and Target have two different types of brands. Both sell similar products, but they are perceived differently. Walmart values low prices. It's what they're known for, and they use that kind of language in the different taglines they've advertised over the years. Target, on the other hand, values a more beautiful shopping experience. That's what they leverage in their branding, and it's what they're known for. Your brand is your reputation, and it reflects who you are.

Look, Tone, and Feel

So what's your brand? As you think about who you are and what you want to be known for, you will be able to build your brand. A great way to start is by making a list of adjectives to describe your business. Start by asking yourself, do I want my business to be more . . .

- Luxurious or necessary?
- Formal or casual?
- Elite or everyday?
- Sophisticated or fun?
- Expensive or affordable?
- Masculine, feminine, or neutral?
- Energetic or calm?

Don't stop here. Brainstorm as many adjectives to describe your business as you can. As you do, your brand will start to emerge. Once you've identified your brand, you'll be able to make decisions about the look, tone, and feel. These things are slightly different, so let's take a closer look at each one.

Look

The look is how you represent your brand visually. It includes the colors, fonts, images, graphics, and design you use. It's the overall style of your website and any marketing pieces like brochures or business cards. It's how you display your products at a craft fair booth or in a retail store. Whether it's on a website or in a store or somewhere else entirely, the look of your brand should be consistent in all locations.

For example, Draper James, Reese Witherspoon's Nashville clothing boutique, is what you might picture a "sweet south'n store" to be. They offer sweet tea when you walk in the door, the colors are rich and bright, and the clothes look like they were pulled straight out of 1930s Charleston. They have pillows embroidered with cute sayings like "Well, bless your heart," and everything is gorgeous, right down to the lemonade pitchers, picnic baskets, and stationary. All of this—the store layout, products, colors, and patterns—is consistent, and it makes up the look of the Draper James branding.

Tone

The tone of your branding is about word choice. Your adjective list will help you choose the right words to fit your tone. For example, if you want your business tone to be sophisticated and formal, then you wouldn't use casual words I use like, "Hey, y'all" and "I mean, come on!" As I've pointed out before, I am specific about the tone I use with Business Boutique. When I talk to people about what we're doing, I say we're "equipping women to make money doing what they love." I do not say that we're "building entrepreneurs and future-enterprise CEOs by acquiring capital investments." See the difference? Your marketing sends the right message and reaches the right people when you use the right words.

Feel

The feel of your brand represents an experience. It reflects how a customer feels when they interact with your business—good or bad. For example, you may get angry when you see the corporate logo for a company that consistently gives you terrible service. That's an example of the feel associated with a brand. Or when you see an ad for your favorite local barbeque restaurant and you're instantly reminded of the delicious scent of fresh brisket in the air and immediately feel nostalgic and happy from all of your fond memories there. That's the feel associated with their brand.

A wide variety of factors contribute to the feel of your brand, including how easy it is to navigate your website, how fast customers get their products, and how friendly and helpful your customer service is. It's the temperature of the store when customers walk in, the smells and sounds present, and even the layout of the merchandise.

You can create a great feel for your customers without spending a lot of time or money. It just takes intentionality. For example, I travel a lot, so I'm familiar with all the airport-related services around Nashville. My favorite parking-lot service near the airport has ice-cold water available for me to grab on my way to the car. I love that! It's a nice touch on a hectic travel day. My favorite grocery store gives free cookies and stickers to my kids when we're out shopping. These are nice touches that make for a great—and memorable—experience. These intentional decisions contribute to the feel of those brands.

Branding Is a Two-Way Street

A brand is not only the look, tone, and feel of your business; it's also what people perceive when they interact with you. You can control the look of your website. You can control the tone you use in all the copy you write. You can even control the feel of your brand by strategically making decisions that create excellent experiences for your customers. But at the end of the day, it's not what you want the customers to experience that determines your brand as a whole. It's what they actually experience. Your good intentions about your brand won't matter if that's not actually what you're delivering.

Whether or not your customers experience what you want them to experience comes down to consistency and integrity. You need to actually be who you say you are. You need to actually do what you say you're going to do. Your policies, processes, practices, choices, and everyday decisions need to line up with your brand. You can put out great logos and you can have catchy tag lines, but if you don't do what you say you're going to do, your reputation will precede you. Actions (the actual experience your customer has) speak louder than words (the catchy tag lines or logos you create).

Several years ago I had service with a cable company that was so terrible and had such an awful reputation that they decided the only way to stay in business was to completely rebrand themselves. They came up with a new name and logo. At first glance it seemed like a new company. But one interaction with their customer-service department, and I was quickly reminded that it was the same old company. A new name didn't change the maddening experience I had with them. You can't expect to restore a failing business by just changing the branding without changing the experience.

The actual experience a customer has forms the brand's reputation. Scott Cook, cofounder of Intuit, said it best, "A brand is no longer what we tell the customer it is—it is what customers tell each other it is." With social media available as a megaphone for your customers all day every day, good or bad, they will talk about you! That's why it's important to make decisions that display consistency and integrity.

This happened when we were planning the first Business Boutique event. I wanted to give cupcakes to all the attendees to create a fun and memorable experience. I thought it would tie in well with the story of my *why* and how growing up in my mom's cake shop was the inspiration behind my passion for the Business Boutique. And, as a bonus, since the first event was in Nashville, the cupcakes could actually be from my mom's shop.

However, in an effort to save money, someone suggested getting the cupcakes from a big-box store instead of my mom's shop, because they were cheaper. While I appreciated that person's thriftiness, I had to explain why it was a bad idea. And believe me, it had nothing to do with my mom getting the order. She could care less at this point in her life! But we have a brand that teaches, supports, and grows small businesses. Buying cupcakes from a wholesale store would not only be hypocritical and inconsistent with our brand, but it would also defeat the entire purpose of having the cupcakes to begin with!

Thankfully, we ended up getting the cupcakes from my mom's shop. And after I shared my story from the stage, all twelve hundred women walked into the lobby and received a cupcake from my mom's shop. And the icing on the cake? Mom was there in her little apron helping to hand them out. You better believe that created a moment and a memory that no one could stop talking or tweeting about. That is great branding!

We were being who we said we were. We had consistency and integrity, and that's why it worked. And the same is true for you. You can choose your look and tone. You can even make intentional and strategic decisions to create great experiences for your customers. But for your branding to be effective, it will always come down to consistency and integrity. Be who you say you are. When you do that, it'll be so much easier to make an impact with the right customer.

WHO YOUR CUSTOMERS ARE

Once you've figured out the unique position and branding you want to put out there, it's time to figure out who your actual customer is. The right customer for your business is called your target market and identifying them is step three in Tier 4 of your plan. Let's talk about who this is—and who it's not.

Who Your Target Market Is Not

The best message in the world won't work if no one hears it, or just as bad, if the wrong person hears it. So, before we identify your target market, let's clarify who it's not. First, your target market is not everyone. Most new business owners are so desperate for sales they try to market to everyone, everywhere. The problem with this shotgun approach is that they end up reaching no one. Your target audience is not everyone. It is a specific type of person, and all of your marketing efforts should talk to them and only them.

Second, your target market is not necessarily someone like you or your friends. Even if your business started by selling to your inner circle, it doesn't mean that's where you should stay. In fact, selling to your friend group can often lead to problems down the road. For example, my client Michelle sells baby clothes. They are adorable handmade outfits that can only be purchased online. But Michelle has a problem. The majority of Michelle's business comes from friends, and while her friends want her clothes, they don't want to pay for them. This is the same problem many side-business owners face: Michelle markets to people just like her.

You see, Michelle started making her own childrens' clothes because she was cost-conscious, crafty, and willing to do it herself. But then she promoted her products to friends and family who were like her: cost-conscious, crafty, and willing to do it themselves. Naturally, they look at her dresses and think exactly what she thought, I could make that myself. Your business exists to help a certain type of person—and often that person is not someone like you.

Defining Your Ideal Customer

So if it's not everyone and it's not necessarily the people in your network, who is your target market? For starters, regardless of the type of business you're in, your target market has two key qualities:

1. They want what you have to offer.
2. They are willing to pay the price you charge.

This might sound simple, but the implications are huge. When you market to a customer who wants what you have, you don't have to beg, push, and pull to convince them to buy from you. They already want it! Additionally, when you market to a customer who is willing and able to pay the price you charge, they don't try to negotiate and lowball you. That makes life (and business) easier and more fun for you and the customer.

The best way to identify and define your target market is to imagine your ideal customer. That's right. I want you to dream up this person. And don't think of a group of people; I want you to think of one person who is your ideal customer. Who is she? Why does she like what your business offers? After you think about why your business is for her, get to know her. Think about what makes her tick. Think about what she wants, what problems she has, what things she values, and so on. And since you're really getting to know this ideal customer, just for fun, go ahead and give her a name.

I coached a woman in Phoenix who needed help figuring out how to market her business. She made miniature flag banners for cakes. She brought one to our session and showed it to me. It was precious, tiny, and cost fifteen dollars. I encouraged my client to dream up her ideal customer and we named her "Angelica." Here's what we discovered: Angelica is someone who does not have the time, ability, or desire to make a mini-cake banner. She cares what her friends think. Angelica is not going to get her cake from the grocery store. She wants to throw a party for her two-year-old that has her friends admiring all of the Pinterest-perfect details while thinking, *How does she do it?* She also doesn't mind paying fifteen dollars for a tiny cake decoration that will help make that possible. Now that I think about it, Angelica isn't all that different from me. I would love a cute cake banner for a party I'm hosting. Imagining your ideal customer will help you understand your target market, and then you can start talking to them.

Your target customer won't be the only person who does business with you. You'll have a wide range of customers, most of whom are probably close to your target audience and then a few stragglers that leave you scratching your head. But, for the most part, your target audience is a bunch of Angelicas! When you start talking directly to your Angelica, your marketing becomes much more effective because you can reach the right person with less effort and more impact.

Ask Your Current Customers

If you've been in business for a while, another easy way to identify your target customer is by talking to the customers you already have. I suggest sending an email survey to past clients or posting questions on your social media. This is a particularly valuable approach because what you learn will come straight from the horse's mouth. If you poll your current customers, try to gather information on these three categories:

- Demographic Information: gender, age, marital status, children, income level, or work
- Geographic Information: location by city, state, region, or country
- Psychographic Information: attitudes, beliefs, values, behavior, or lifestyle

Your research can include any combination of the above.

While geographic and demographic information provide basic data about your customers, psychographic information will provide insight into who your customers are by showing how they feel, think, and behave. In my opinion, this is the most interesting information because you can learn about your customers and adapt your business to meet their needs. Let's say you have a travel agency. Your survey might include the following questions:

- How do you normally plan your trips?
- Do you travel more frequently for work, pleasure, or both?
- What websites or companies help you with your travel planning?
- What problems or frustrations do you run into when planning a trip?
- What would help make your travel planning easier?

When you ask questions and gather this kind of information, you can get to know your customers even better. Plus, you can fix things in your business you didn't know were turnoffs and leverage things you might not have considered before.

Paying Attention

Even if you don't do formal research, you can learn about your customers by paying attention to their reviews, comments, and feedback. What you learn might even point to new marketing opportunities. For example, in developing the Business Boutique event and materials, it never occurred to me to market to men. After all, we are equipping women to make money doing what they love, right?

However, around the time of our first event, I noticed a theme. Many of the women who attended came because their boyfriend or husband bought them a ticket. One online comment read, "My husband surprised me with a ticket, and it was the best gift I've ever received!" By paying attention to what people were saying, I discovered a marketing opportunity I didn't expect. While the target market for Business Boutique is certainly women, we identified a secondary target market: the boyfriends or husbands of those women. Paying attention to recurring comments in your feedback may show you additional marketing opportunities you hadn't thought about.

When you imagine your ideal customer, do research, and pay attention to your current customers, you will be able to understand and define your target market. This is who you're going to talk to in all of your marketing efforts.

WHERE YOUR CUSTOMERS ARE

Once you figure out who your customers are, you need to know where they are. These people are out there somewhere, and you want to find them so you can go to where they are. This might sound difficult, but once you get to know your Angelica—I mean really know her—figuring out where she hangs out isn't that hard. There are several ways to do this—in person and online.

Finding Them in Person

Think of places where your ideal customer hangs out. For instance, if your business is making custom baby gifts, you might sponsor a lunch for a local Moms of Preschoolers (MOPS) group so you can meet and build relationships with women who have little ones—and probably have friends with more little ones on the way! Or, if you offer small-business accounting services, you could bring coffee and donuts to local small businesses and introduce yourself to get your foot in the door. Whatever kind of business you have, your customers hang out somewhere. Go find them!

Finding Them Online

You can also find your customers online through social media. Listing where you will put your social media marketing efforts is the next step in Tier 4 of your business plan, and we will cover more on how to do that in the next chapter. Though the format is different, the principle is the same as finding them in person. Figure out where your ideal customer spends time online and go there.

When I had my horse-boarding business, I decided to market on Craigslist. I know it sounds unconventional, but it's common for Craigslist to have posts on agriculture and livestock transactions. In fact, that's where I bought my horse, mini-donkey, and both fainting goats. Since I knew it was a popular site for my type of customer, I marketed my business there. As luck would have it, I got all of my clients from that one effort.

Your customers might not spend hours a week on Craigslist, but they probably are online somewhere. And they probably have one social media platform that they use more than others. Dig in and see if they're on Facebook, Twitter, or Instagram.

Maybe they use Pinterest or, if your target market is business professionals, LinkedIn might be a better option. Social media can be a cheap and effective way to reach your customers. There's so much to be said about social media that we're going to spend the next chapter talking about it.

HOW TO TALK TO THEM

Now that you know who you are, who your customer is, and where they are, you can start talking to them. This sounds so basic, I know, but there's a right way and a wrong way to talk to your customer. You can say the wrong thing, or the right thing the wrong way, and miss the opportunity to connect with them. Your target customer has one question in mind all of the time: Why should I care? Therefore, your job in all of your marketing communication is to answer that question for them. Let's talk about how to do that.

Mastering the Elevator Pitch

This is where your elevator pitch comes in. Writing your elevator pitch is the final step in Tier 4 of your business plan. "Elevator pitch" is just a marketing term that means how you'd explain your business in just a couple of sentences, in about the time it takes to ride an elevator. This can be surprisingly hard for some people. While most people might not have any trouble talking at length about their business, explaining it in less than twenty or thirty seconds can be challenging. But, as we know all too well, the attention span of the average person is not that long. Most people probably aren't willing to stick around for the ten- or even five-minute version. That's why you've got to be able to capture their interest and communicate the main point of your business concisely—before you lose them. Start with the elevator pitch version and then, after you've captured their interest, you can get into the fine print or five-minute version.

Your elevator pitch describes what your business does. In two sentences or less, your elevator pitch needs to focus on the benefits to the customer, not the features of your business. It's natural when you have a product or service that sets you on fire to want everyone else to see how awesome it is too. But when most people talk about their business, they talk about the wrong thing. They spend all their time pushing the standout features of their product, but unfortunately, no one cares about how great your product is. (Except maybe your mom. Your mom probably cares.) What people care about is what they care about. That's why every word out of your mouth should answer the simple question your customer is thinking: Why should I care?

Let's say you start a ferryboat business that takes people from the coast of Florida to a tropical island. You're pretty excited about your ferryboat because you've worked hard to make it the best ferry possible. So, when people ask you about your business, you start talking about how awesome your ferryboat is. "It has Italian leather seats and surround sound. It has a top deck where you can enjoy the view. It has a snack bar and a full staff to serve you. And it has a 5,000-horsepower engine with all-new safety equipment." (I don't know if a 5,000-horsepower engine is even a thing, but just go with me here.) You go on and on talking about the boat.

All of those things are nice and fine, but they aren't going to compel someone to buy a ticket. Why? Because no one cares about your ferryboat. Instead, talk about what they care about, which, in this case, is the island. Instead you say, "We'll take you to an island that has tropical cabanas right on the beach. You can relax your worries away in hammocks by the sunset. The five-star restaurants are all on the water. And you can watch the dolphins swim close to shore while you enjoy fresh seafood. There are good-looking, tan men ready to bring you fruity drinks with little umbrellas in them." That's when the person you are talking to says, "That place sounds amazing! How can I get there?" And you answer, "Well, I just so happen to have a ferryboat."

You see, when you start talking about what your customer cares about, you pique their interest and making the sale is natural. That's why your elevator pitch, and all marketing language, should focus on the benefits to the customer, not the features of the business. For example, when someone asks me what Business Boutique does, I don't say, "We have events and coaching and video training and a podcast and a book." Instead, I say, "We help women start and grow businesses from their passions and skills. We equip them to make money doing what they love." It's two sentences and completely focused on the benefit to the customer.

In the action items for this chapter is a spot for you to write out your elevator pitch. Give it a shot and practice saying it out loud several times to get comfortable with it. Then, the next time a potential customer asks what you do, you won't hesitate to tell them exactly how your business can serve them. You'll be talking to the right person in the right way. That is great communication and effective marketing.

TELLING THE WORLD

In 2015, a country music singer named Chris Stapleton performed at the Country Music Awards show with Justin Timberlake. Their duet medley of "Tennessee Whiskey" and "Drink You Away" was the hit of the night and it was all anyone could talk about the next day. The headline for *USA Today* read, "Justin Timberlake and Chris Stapleton Stole the *CMAs*."[67] *Rolling Stone* said they "positively slammed" it.[68] And *Billboard* reported, "Wednesday, November 4, 2015, should go down as the day when a guy named Chris Stapleton had his name become the No. 1 trending search term on Google."[69] He was the breakout star of the night, and all anyone could ask the next day was, "Where did this guy come from?"

But the truth is Chris Stapleton had been around for years. He had consistently turned out great music and entertained audiences. It was marketing—in this case, the 49th Annual Country Music Awards—that showed the world how great he is. The CMAs did for Chris Stapleton what great marketing can do for you and your business: show the world how great you are. It doesn't matter how talented you are or helpful your business is or unique your product is if no one knows about it, you can't help them and they can't buy from you. That's why effective marketing is so important. It shows the world how great you are.

So figure out who you are and who your customer is. Get out there and start talking to the right people in the right way. Show the world what you have to offer and, more importantly, just how amazing you are. Then you can put on some great tunes, whether that's Chris Stapleton, Justin Timberlake, or in my case, Taylor Swift, and celebrate this wild journey of putting yourself out there and living your dream.

Unique Position

Write your unique position here:

Branding

List adjectives that describe your business here:

_____   _____   _____

_____   _____   _____

_____   _____   _____

Look

Use those adjectives to make decisions about the look of your branding. Write out some branding choices below:

Colors:

Fonts:

Photos or Graphics:

Design Elements:

Tone

Use those adjectives to make decisions about the language and word choice you want to use. This will become a guide and reference to help you write in a way that accurately reflects your brand and attracts the right customer.

Words to Use
Ex. "Make money"

Words to Avoid
"Capital Investment"

_____

_____

_____

_____

Feel

Finally, use your list of adjectives to make decisions about how you want your brand to feel to your customer. This is where you add nice touches that create a positive, consistent, and memorable experience for them.

Ex. Handing out cupcakes at the event to tie in with my cake story.

_____

_____

_____

_____

_____

Identifying Your Target Market
Ideal Customer

Dream up your ideal customer below. Write out everything you can think of about them and give them a name.

Name:

Description:

Research Current Customers

Write what information you want to gather from your current customers below.

Demographic Information:

Geographic Information:

Psychographic Information:

Create a list of questions to ask that will provide you with the information you're looking for. These questions will be included in your poll or survey.

1.

2.

3.

4.

5.

Where Your Customer Is

Write where you think your customer is hanging out online or in person.

Online:

In person:

Your Elevator Pitch

Below, write out how you will respond to this question: "What does your business do?" Remember: focus on the benefit to the customer, not the features of the business. Two sentences, tops!

chapter 15

THE STORY YOU'RE TELLING
Reaching the Right People the Right Way

Ree Drummond, famously known as the Pioneer Woman, is an award-winning blogger, #1 *New York Times* best-selling author, food writer, photographer, and television personality. As if you didn't already know that. Who am I kidding? She is everyone's virtual best friend and go-to source for home-run recipes. In addition to being a household name, she has appeared on *Good Morning America*, the *Today Show*, and *The View*, and she has been featured in *Ladies' Home Journal*, *Woman's Day*, *People*, and *Southern Living*.

But Ree didn't wake up one day as a *New York Times* best seller or a sought-after guest. It all started in 2006 with a little blog called "Confessions of a Pioneer Woman," now just "The Pioneer Woman" at www.thepioneerwoman.com. She wrote about her journey "from high heels to tractor wheels" with wit, humor, sarcasm, and authenticity that instantly connected with readers. She wrote about her love story with Marlboro Man that made every woman in America want her very own Marlboro Man. She also posted recipes with step-by-step instructions and beautiful photos before anyone else got in the recipe blog craze. In many ways, she was a literal pioneer—in the blogging and cooking world—even if she didn't set out to be.

But do you know what led to Ree Drummond's incredible growth and success? Hint: it's the very same thing that can lead to yours. She consistently posted really, really, really great content. From her stories to her humor to her photos and recipes, Ree paved the way for building a brand—and a full-fledged business—out of nothing more than amazing content. Today, more than a decade later, content is still the main driver for her business and countless businesses around the world.

MAKING GREAT CONTENT

Just twenty years ago, the word "content" was just another word. But now, with social media as the megaphone for individuals and businesses, it's all anyone can talk about.

"You need quality content on your website."
"You need content to drive your email list."
"You need to post interesting content on social media."

The need for "content" is everywhere it seems. But what does it even mean?

What Is Content, Anyway?

Content is really just another word for information. That's it. It can be text, photos, audio, or video, and it can come in many different formats including print, CDs, DVDs, or digital. If you think about it, you probably consume multiple types of content every day. A 140-character tweet by your favorite celebrity is content. A long, rambling post from your distant aunt on Facebook is content. A podcast you listen to, video you watch, and articles you read are all forms of content.

Content is everywhere, but what does it have to do with your small business? As was the case with Ree Drummond, when you have really great content, people can't help but notice. That's why we're going talk about how to use content to drive your marketing so your customers will notice you. After all, being noticed is a key element to making your business successful.

What Your Content Should Be About

Some people don't think their business has anything to do with content. People will complain, "But I don't have anything to say!" Or they'll tell me their business doesn't lend itself to content. "But I have an accounting (or jewelry or gardening or organizing or clothing) business. What type of content would I put out about that?" Well, since content drives growth and leads to sales, all businesses are in the content business. According to Dan Antonelli, CEO and Creative Director of Graphic D-Signs, "When small businesses communicate with their customers by providing information instead of offering a sales pitch, the consumer will listen. The message and the brand are no longer an interruption, but a valued information provider."[70]

Thankfully, deciding what your content should be about is easy. Your content should be about what your business is about. That's it. Your content needs to be something interesting or informative and related to your business. You want to create content that sets you up as the go-to person for anything associated with your particular product or service. This helps build a connection with potential customers because you earn credibility while also meeting needs they're facing.

For example, an accountant might create articles about how to save money on taxes. A handmade jewelry business owner might make videos demonstrating how to clean cheap jewelry and keep it from turning brown. A gardening business might release a podcast with tips on how to keep weeds and bugs out of the garden. A professional organizer might post a photo blog of before and after pictures with simple solutions to use your space more efficiently. Every business has an opportunity to generate content around their thing. Yours does too. And as you do, you not only establish yourself as an expert in your field but you also build a relationship with your customer in the process.

What Makes Good Content

Your content can take many forms. It can be text, photo, audio, or video. It's not enough, however, to simply produce content; you need to produce good content. As you and I know from experience, if something doesn't hold our attention, we move on. That's because not all content is created equal. In order to create good content—the type that people notice and that creates sales—your content needs to have certain qualities.

It's Relevant

First, your content needs to be relevant to your business. Remember, think about what you want to be known for and create content around that thing.

It's Current

Second, it also needs to be current. Now, more than ever, our world is changing at lightning speed, and posting outdated methods, videos, or articles will damage your credibility.

It's Interesting

Next, your content needs to be interesting. You need to hook your reader and draw them in. In most cases, you have less than one second to catch their attention. Think about it this way. If you post an update on Facebook or Twitter, your content has to be so irresistible that it makes your reader stop their rapid thumb-scrolling through the newsfeed on their phone.

It Does Something for the Reader

Additionally, your content needs to do something for your reader. If your content is all about you, unless you are one of the Kardashians, no one is going to be interested. Your content should help, inspire, teach, challenge, encourage, or entertain your reader. Remember, as we discussed in the last chapter, every one of your customers thinks, *Why do I care?* Your content—and everything you write for your business, for that matter—should answer that question.

Let's say you have a fitness business. Maybe you post a blog titled "Five Ways to Boost Your Metabolism Before You Get Out of Bed in the Morning." (If you know how to do this, by the way, please tell me!) See? You want your customers to respond this way. Your content should always have your customer's needs and desires in mind. Mandy Hale, blogger, speaker, and author known online as "The Single Woman," does this. Whether it's a tweet, blog, or book, she always posts things that do something for her reader. If you scroll through her Twitter feed, all her tweets are "You" statements. She doesn't talk about herself. She talks about "You" with posts like, "You are enough," "You are worth fighting for," and "You are beautiful." All of her followers think, *Yes! I am enough! I am worth fighting for!*

I am beautiful! They retweet Mandy's post, which drives more readers back to Mandy's page so they can also like and follow her. And it's working. Since joining Twitter in 2010 as @TheSingleWoman, she has over 600,000 Twitter followers as of this writing—and that number is growing every day. That brings me to the next quality of good content . . .

It's Shareable

Finally, your content needs to be shareable. People often ask me how to grow their audience without paying for advertising. One of the best ways to do this is on social media—with great content that people share. It increases how many people get to see your content by getting your current followers to bring new readers to you. When you post a blog, tweet, or video that your network enjoys and appreciates, they will naturally want to share it. When they share it, their followers are introduced to you. This is how you can grow your audience exponentially with a compounding effect.

When I was in middle school, I put stickers all over my class binder. Stickers from Journeys shoe store, The North Face, Young Life, and Ron Jon Surf Shop. As a tween, having stickers on my binder represented my identity. It was my way of saying "this represents me." Social media is our modern-day version of that. When someone retweets or reposts something on their newsfeed, they're putting a sticker on their virtual binder and saying, "This represents me, what I think, how I feel, what I believe." When you provide content your readers identify with, they will naturally want to share it, which not only grows your following, but your business and sales as well.

That's why good content is so important. It's how you create relationships with your customers and earn the right to be heard. It's how you get people to know, like, and trust you. And, as we'll look at in the next chapter, when people know, like, and trust you, selling to them happens naturally.

STORYTELLING AS A CONTENT STRATEGY

One of the best ways to build a relationship with your followers is by telling stories. According to Mike Wood of *Entrepreneur* magazine, "Storytelling marketing is one of the best techniques you can use to keep people's attention. It also helps with the overall quality of your articles, and it leads to more shares and engagement."[71] Storytelling isn't just for entertainment purposes anymore. It's an effective strategy for building your business online. That's why I always notice great stories and great storytellers.

For example, in the last five years of attending my church, I don't remember most of the sermons. I don't remember what Scriptures were preached or what series we went through. But here's what I do remember: the stories.

In one of those stories, my pastor talked about trying to unwind at the pool one day. He was reading a good book when his youngest son came to him and said he needed to go to the bathroom. Since my pastor was relaxed (for once) and didn't want to get up, he—admittedly, not in his finest moment—told his son, "Ah, just pee in the pool."

A few seconds later, my pastor heard an audible gasp spread across the pool deck so he looked up. That's when he saw his son standing at the side of the pool with his pants down, peeing into the pool. Horrified, he yelled to his son, "What are you doing?"

His son responded, "Dad, you told me to!"

It has been five years since I heard that story, and I still laugh when I think of it. And, being a mom of boys, I am preparing myself for similar hilarious and unpredictable moments ahead.

When I started speaking for our company, I spoke to audiences about getting out of debt. Let me tell you, when you're teaching people about debt, here's what doesn't work:

"Get out of debt."
"Stop spending so much money. Stop it!"
"Cut up those credit cards!"

That never works. Why? Because people don't need more information, they need inspiration. They need to believe and have buy-in, and the best way to accomplish that is through story.

Stories Stick with Us

Whether it's about debt or life lessons or your business, stories are one of the most effective ways to communicate, influence, and inspire people. If you look at the great leaders and communicators of the world, they are all incredible storytellers. They don't talk at people. They don't just communicate information or dictate instructions. They tell stories. For example, Bryan Stevenson, the speaker who earned the longest standing ovation in TED history,[72] spent 65 percent of his presentation telling stories.[73] People listen, internalize, and remember stories more so than any other method of communication.

The reason we remember stories is because they stick with us. They get into our heads and our hearts in a way nothing else can. Believe it or not, our brains are actually wired for story. Years ago, researchers wanted to understand why storytelling is so effective. They did a study where they set up a scenario with a public speaker and a volunteer audience. The speaker and audience members were connected to an MRI machine to show their brain activity. As the speaker told a story, certain areas of the speaker's brain were activated and, at the exact same moment, the exact same areas of the listeners' brains were activated. The researchers called this "brain coupling." Do you understand the implications of this? Through story, you can hack into people's brains! Only for good, of course. So becoming a great storyteller is basically like developing a superpower that helps you lead, inspire, and influence others.

Stories Build Connections

Did you know that our brains are also more active when we hear stories? Carmine Gallo, in his book *Talk Like Ted*, says that PowerPoint slides or flat information only activates the language part of the brain. But stories "do much more, using the whole brain and activating language, sensory, visual, and motor areas."[74] You probably do this every day, even if you don't realize it. When we hear a story, we start to picture ourselves in it. Stories make us feel something. When we identify with a story, it creates a feeling of empathy and connectedness to the other person. That's exactly what you want when you're building a relationship.

If you want to engage readers and find customers, start with a good story. Look at Ree Drummond. Even after a decade and unbelievable success, she still tells stories.

No amount of success (or lack of success) takes away from the need to tell captivating stories. Even Apple's senior VP of retail and online stores, Angela Ahrendts, says, "Great brands and great businesses have to be great storytellers."[75] And this is coming from an electronics company!

Your stories don't have to be long or detailed. They can be a 140-character tweet, short Facebook post, 300-word blog post, 30-second video, or 45-minute podcast. The stories don't even have to be yours. You can tell someone else's story. In fact, many of the examples in this book are stories about other people. When your content is driven by story, you're much more likely to engage, entertain, and impact your audience.

MOVING CUSTOMERS DOWN THE FUNNEL

The reason I feel so strongly about stories and good content is because, in your business and marketing, they serve one purpose: to build a closer relationship with your customers. To help illustrate this, I'll use the common marketing lingo. That means it's time to talk about a funnel!

Understanding the Marketing Funnel

Imagine a funnel. Your goal is to move people down the funnel, and content is what does that. Outside of the funnel, at the top, is white space. That includes anyone who has no idea who you are or what your business does. Your goal is to get those people into the funnel and then move them gradually from the top of the funnel, where they barely know you, to the bottom, where they become loyal, frequent, paying customers.

Most businesspeople think you use social media to sell, but that's actually not what it's for. It's for building relationships. A customer who doesn't know you (white space) is like a stranger passing you on the street. If your first word to someone in your white space is basically, "Buy my product!" it's equivalent to running up to a guy on the street and yelling, "Hey, let's get married!" Unless you're completely out of your mind, you probably know that won't work. The best relationships happen gradually.

The same is true with potential customers. You want to get their attention and invest in the relationship before you try to make a sale. Social media allows you to do that. With social media, you can draw people in from white space to becoming a viewer, fan, or follower. After that, you can get them to visit your blog or business online. From there, you build a deeper relationship and invite them to sign up for your email list. Your email list is where you actually offer your product or service. That level of engagement is where most sales actually occur. Each layer of the funnel is a deeper layer of relationship with your customers, and it looks something like this:

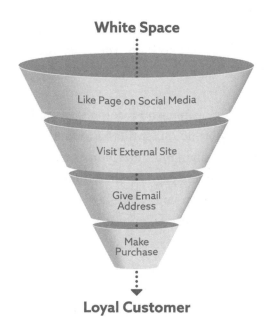

White Space

- Like Page on Social Media
- Visit External Site
- Give Email Address
- Make Purchase

Loyal Customer

Where to Post Your Content

Now that you know you need good content, let's talk about where to put it. We are going to start at the top of the funnel with social media. Because of the sharing feature of social media, this is how most people move from the white space of not knowing you into your funnel where they like your page or follow you. It's important to note that the social media platform(s) you choose needs to be where your target audience is hanging out. That's where you'll want to spend your time, money, and energy because it's how you'll engage people and move them out of white space and into the funnel.

However, with so many social media platforms to choose from, it can be hard to sort out which one(s) are best for you. We'll take a look at some of the most popular platforms on the market right now (as I write this), but new platforms are introduced every day. By the time you read this, this section may already be out of date.

Each platform works in different ways, so we need to stick to a high-level over-view for this to make sense. That way, even when new platforms are introduced, you'll still be able to apply this information to whatever hot social media platform is taking over the world at that time. Learning these nuances will help you decide which ones are right for you, your business, your customer, and your "funnel."

Facebook

With the exception of a few people who live in caves, most everyone makes their way to Facebook. It is the 800-pound gorilla in the social media space and, while you have to play by their ever-changing rules, you can usually reach who you want. You'll want to keep your business page separate from your personal page. Having a separate business page will help you reach more people in the long run because you'll have more flexibility and access to more tools than what's allowed on personal pages.

Twitter

Twitter is typically used for breaking news, article links, and business transactions. Twitter does limit the length of your posts, known as tweets, so content should be concise to fit on this platform.

Instagram

Instagram is a great platform for photos and videos. You can build relationships with your customers and highlight your business at the same time. As of this writing, though, Instagram doesn't allow external links in posts, except for their ads. This can present a challenge for driving traffic to your website.

YouTube

YouTube is an enormous video library and probably the most widely used platform for posting video content. It's a popular spot for DIY and informational videos, and it's generally the first site people search when they want to watch some episode, broadcast, or video everyone is talking about.

Pinterest

Pinterest is an online network where users can search and "pin" online photos, articles with tips, DIY tutorials, and recipes on a virtual pinboard. You can maintain multiple boards, where you collect and pin posts you like, plan to use, or are inspired by. Because users frequently "repin" and "like" content, Pinterest is a high-engagement platform. However, posting doesn't necessarily generate followers. Most often, when someone scrolls through Pinterest, they are focused on the content of the pin, not who created it.

Snapchat

Snapchat is a microvideo platform with a unique distinctive: the posts are deleted every twenty-four hours. That means your content won't live long, and the short shelf life helps create a sense of urgency and FOMO (fear of missing out) around your posts. That gives Snapchat posts a less-polished, more real-life feel than you find on other platforms, and that leads to a greater sense of authenticity with your audience.

You might decide to use one or all of these, or you might start out with one and then switch to another. Most social media platforms are easy to learn and easy to use, so you can get up to speed quickly.

Give More than You Take

Regardless of the platform you use or the type of content you share, you want to follow social media expert Gary Vanerchuck's jab-jab-jab-right-hook principle. In his incredibly popular book, *Jab, Jab, Jab, Right Hook*, "Gary Vee" advises giving more often than asking on social media.[76] Providing helpful, informative, and encouraging content for your audience is a give. Prompting your audience to do something like buy, click, or sign up is an ask. Using a boxing analogy, Gary Vee says that gives are like jabs, and asks are like right hooks. He suggests offering three gives for every one ask. Put another way, don't ask your customer to do anything until you've given them something of value at least three times.

For example, your social media schedule might look something like this for one day:

(Jab) Post #1: Inspiring quote

(Jab) Post #2: Live behind-the-scenes video of your business

(Jab) Post #3: Helpful article with a list of tips

(Right Hook) Post #4: Invitation to sign up for a contest

My friend Steve, a social media professional, says, "A good brand is a generous brand." Be generous in your marketing and social media strategy, and you will build a relationship with your followers. They will become loyal, appreciative, and ready to take the next step with you.

Taking the Next Step

The next step in the funnel is encouraging your followers to visit an external link from your social media page. Up to this point, your fans and followers have only been reading your content on your social media, which automatically shows up in their newsfeeds. They don't have to do much work to view it. Now you are asking them to take an additional step in your relationship by clicking an external link that sends them somewhere else—most likely, your primary business platform. If you remember from chapter 10, your platform is where your business lives online. This might be an Etsy store, a blog, or a full website. Getting your fans and followers to take this step with you is a big deal. They are most likely pre-occupied with whatever else is happening online, so if you get them to not only stop and read what you've posted but also trust you enough to leave what they are currently doing and go to your site, you've accomplished a lot! Once they are on your site, it's time to ask for the next level of commitment in the funnel: their email address.

The Bottom of the Funnel

Once someone has visited your store, blog, or website, you want to capture their email address and build an email list for your business. This list is incredibly valuable because it's further down the funnel and includes people who have raised their hand and said, "Yes, I want to hear from you." This is known as "permission marketing," an idea first introduced by the brilliant marketer and *New York Times* best-selling author Seth Godin. In his book, *Permission Marketing*, Godin explains that people don't want to be harassed and interrupted, so you need to use a different technique and ask for permission to talk to them.[77]

Give Free Carrots

Here's how to get your customer's permission to talk to them. Every time a unique (new) visitor lands on your blog or website, offer them something for free, a carrot. It might be a free download, e-book, video training, or something else that they want. And, by offering them a carrot in exchange for their email address, you get permission to talk to them—and build your list of email subscribers at the same time.[78] You do this by offering something that your customers actually want and by using the right words to offer it. After all, if your customers don't understand or want what you're offering, they aren't going to give you their email address for it.

What Do They Want?

When you offer a carrot in exchange for your customer's email address, it needs to be something the customers actually care about and want. What problems do they have that you can solve? What needs do they have that you can fill? What questions do they have that you can answer? You can solve their problems, meet their needs, and answer their questions through many different ways: a free download, a video lesson, a short e-book, a discount off of your products, or something else creative. You can choose whichever format is easiest for you to create, but it needs to be something different and with a higher perceived value than what you regularly offer. For instance, if you frequently offer coupons and sales, then using a coupon as your carrot won't stand out or be compelling enough for someone to give you their email address, because they know they can get the carrot without giving anything in exchange for it.

Speak Their Language

In addition to offering something your customers want, use the right words to offer it. I once visited the website for a large home improvement store and, as soon as the site loaded, a box popped up on my screen that read, "Sign up for our weekly newsletter to receive exclusive content!"

Now, do you know what I am never sitting around with my friends saying? "Man, y'all, I really wish that home improvement store down the street would give me some exclusive content!"

That never happens! Why? Because "exclusive content" isn't language I use. And your customer probably doesn't, either. Even if you're actually offering content, don't use the word content to entice them. That's not a casual, conversational term; it's a business term and should be used in that context. Instead, use words that are more appealing and conversational. For example, that home improvement store could have offered something their target customer wants (that meets a need, solves a problem, or answers a question), and they could have used clear and conversational language. They could have offered a free download titled, "5 Ways to Improve the Curb Appeal of Your Home," or "Tips to Save on Your Water Bill," or "How to Get Stains Out of Your Carpet." Those are all things their customers want and understand. When you use the right language to offer your carrot, your customer will be more likely to sign up.

Build Your List

By offering something your customers want, you will have eased into the relationship gradually rather than just flat-out asking for their email address first. Because we all get enough junk email in our inboxes, people tend to be cautious about giving out their email. That's why you first want to build a relationship through social media and then offer something of value. When you invest in those relationships first, people will be more willing to trust you with their email address.

It takes time to build a quality email list, but keep at it because your email list is gold. This is basically a list of people who are likely to do business with you at some point. In fact, over time, many of your sales will probably come right from this list. A recent study revealed that email is forty times more effective at gaining customers than Facebook and Twitter combined. The study calculated that "for every $1 invested, email marketing generates an average return of $38."[79] That's a 3,700% return on your investment! I love how social media expert Amy Porterfield explained it during a Business Boutique event: "The energy of your business is directly tied to the strength of your email list."[80] That's because your email list represents trust and permission. Once you have that, all you have to do is make it easy for them to buy from you. Those sales should be effortless because of all the work you've already put into moving your customers further down the funnel.

THE BIGGER PICTURE

Everything we've talked about in this chapter will help you create strong relationships with your customers. However, it's easy to get so caught up in the individual steps that we actually forget the bigger picture in marketing our business.

For example, I'm currently coaching a woman who has been in business for almost three years with little to no success. Sandra's business sells T-shirts and totes designed with statements about adopting animals, preserving wildlife, or enjoying nature. They are beautiful and inspiring, but she can't seem to increase her sales.

During one of our calls, Sandra told me that she grasped the techniques of social media, but she didn't see how it would work for her business. She explained that she wasn't a wildlife expert and wasn't personally rescuing animals off the street so she didn't believe she was solving a problem for her customers. That left her feeling like she had nothing valuable to share. Even though she knew the ins and outs of Facebook and Instagram, she didn't know what to say in her marketing.

I'll tell you what I told her: you have a story to tell. And I'm not talking about the entertaining microstories we tell for content on social media. I'm talking about the bigger-picture story of your business. That's a story worth telling.

I tell a lot of stories on stage and in my writing, but each one is only a piece of the bigger story, my story of equipping women to make money doing what they love. That's the bigger picture of Business Boutique. So, hopefully, everything I write or say points toward that one great, big story.

Sandra didn't think she had a story, but she does! Sandra's bigger story is that she is outfitting world changers—giving people a voice through their clothes and accessories to not only represent their personal beliefs about saving the environment and adopting animals, but also to inspire others to do the same.

And you have a story too. All of your marketing efforts should tell one big story about who you are and what you can do for your customer. Seth Godin says, "Marketing is no longer about the stuff that you make, but about the stories you tell." So tell the story of what you offer. Tell the story of the problems you solve. Tell the story of why this matters. Write your story, and then use your marketing efforts to tell it. Over and over again, tell your story. After all, Ree Drummond started as a woman with a blog—telling her story of moving to the country. And everything we've seen from her since—the recipes, the tips, the photos—has been a continuation of that bigger story. So, if all of the options overwhelm you, don't get discouraged. At the end of the day, just like Sandra and Ree, all you need to do is tell your story.

chapter 15 action items
LET'S APPLY WHAT YOU'VE LEARNED!

Content

What will your content be about? (Hint: this is what you want to be known for.)

What formats will you use to post your content?

Using Stories

Start your story log here. Brainstorm interesting stories you might want to use in your content.

Where to Post Content

Place a check beside the social media platforms you want to use to post content and build your business.

   __ Facebook
   __ Twitter
   __ Instagram
   __ YouTube
   __ Pinterest
   __ SnapChat

   __

   __

   __

Give More than You Ask

Brainstorm things you will give your readers on your social media.

Give

Give

Give

The Carrot

Brainstorm things you can offer for free in exchange for your customers' email addresses. Make a list below.

Ex.: Free e-book download

1.

2.

3.

4.

5.

The Bigger Picture

What is the bigger story that all of your marketing is telling? Keep this front of mind for all marketing efforts to support.

chapter 16

MAKING THE SALE

How to Promote Your Business Without Being Pushy

One rainy Sunday afternoon when I was in college, some girlfriends and I were wandering through the mall headed to our favorite cheap jewelry store. While we were walking and chatting, a man with a clipboard came up and asked if we had a minute to answer a couple of questions. Of course, today I know what these clipboard guys are up to in the mall, but at nineteen, I was a little naïve. As soon as we slowed down and looked at him, he launched into his sales pitch.

He asked if we would be interested in a free, all-expenses-paid weekend getaway to Gatlinburg, Tennessee, which is a beautiful mountain destination spot about an hour from where we went to school. He kept saying the word free, which is a key term when you're casting a sales spell on a group of broke college students. There was only one catch: we had to spend thirty minutes of the weekend attending a short seminar. He said it was just a little video followed by someone talking for a few minutes. And, for that tiny investment of our time, we'd get a free girls' retreat to the mountains. We were in!

One week later, our group of excited girls checked into our cabin. Only two of us had to attend the seminar, so the others hung out at the cabin while a friend and I attended the afternoon presentation. What happened next is kind of a blur. There were videos of families having the time of their lives at different resorts. There were floor-to-ceiling photos of beaches and mountains and hot tubs and spas. There was a tour led by a large, enthusiastic, and fast-talking man who walked me through a maze of photos with his burly arm around my shoulders. He showed me how I could vacation basically for free for the rest of my life—except for the low, low payment of one hundred dollars per month (for ten years). He showed me how happy I would be staying in one of the resorts. He said my future husband and I could relax in the spa and my future children could play on world-renowned waterslides. There were more videos and more photos. And then came the paperwork. Lots and lots of paperwork.

I think someone must have slipped something in my water bottle because, before I knew it, my broke, unemployed, nineteen-year-old self walked out of that office with a time-share payment for the next ten years of my life. Later, when I came to my senses and realized what I'd done, I hated myself . . . and the salesman who sold it to me. That terrible experience took months and hundreds of dollars to get out of. Unfortunately, a terrible experience is what many of us think of when we think of sales. And that fear of the pushy, aggressive salesperson may be holding you and your business back.

THE PROBLEM WITH SALES

Because many of us have had uncomfortable experiences with sales, we are a little hesitant about it and we don't know how to do it well. When we're the ones buying something, we don't think twice about certain types of sales transactions—like buying coffee, groceries, or clothing—because those are impersonal interactions with name-brand companies. But something you sell is always more personal. It can feel weird and uncomfortable to talk about and sell a product you've made. We shift and stumble, and it's certainly not our favorite part of being in business. But if we don't get over our fear of sales, we'll never make any. You know what they call a business that can't make sales? Closed! That's why we're going to spend this chapter looking at how to sell—with confidence. This is a key part of business, and, when you get it right, it's not only easier but it can actually be fun. Selling doesn't have to be uncomfortable. The secret to selling is about shifting your focus. It all starts with the words we choose.

Get vs. Give

In the process of selling something, we often focus on what we are getting. We feel guilty and we doubt ourselves—as if we are being given money for absolutely no reason. Instead of focusing on what you're getting, focus on what you're giving. You are giving value. You are giving a solution to a problem. You are giving something your customer needs or wants. When you stop focusing on what you're getting from them and instead focus on what you're giving to them, you can start to sell with more confidence and less awkwardness.

Make vs. Take

Similarly, it's easy to focus on the word *take* instead of *make* when we're selling something. Most women I talk to don't even realize they're using the word *take*. I hear them say they feel guilty for taking money from someone else. They might say something like, "I couldn't possibly take that much money," or, "It feels wrong to take money from another mom."

Often, because we women are so relationally driven, we focus on the other person. This can be an incredible asset in business, especially in customer service. But, when we think of our business as taking, it can actually hold us back from what we're trying to do. When we say we are taking money, we are implying that we are reaching into our customer's purse and stealing from them. I hope you aren't taking anything!

Instead of taking money, think of it as making money. When you decide that you are going to make money instead of take it, you shift your focus and honor the hard work and effort that went into your sales transaction. You validate the worth of what you made—that is, what you rightfully earned. In that case, I hope you're making a ton of money!

Offer vs. Push

Often salespeople are described as pushy. Are there pushy salespeople out there like my time-share salesman? Sure. I can't walk through the mall without being interrupted, intersected, and interrogated by the dang mall kiosk guys wanting to "just ask (me) a question" while trying to lather up my hands with some special lotion they are selling. I get it. We don't want to be pushy like them. Here's the thing: good selling doesn't have to be like that.

Great sales aren't about pushing; they are about offering. I don't push anyone to buy tickets for an event or buy my book. But I am comfortable offering those to someone who is interested because I believe it will help them. When you focus on what you offer, not what you have to push on people, you can relax when talking about your products or services. People will actually want to hear what you have to say because you aren't pushing them.

REDEFINING SALES

Good sales are not supposed to be pushy, aggressive, uncomfortable, or annoying. Good sales happen naturally and can actually be a lot of fun. That's not to say that you don't have to work hard to sell, because you definitely do. But the work you do is not the pushing and convincing you might imagine. The work of selling is more about building relationships with the right people in the right way. Doing that starts with our attitude. The late W. Clement Stone, philanthropist and author, said, "Sales are contingent upon the attitude of the salesman—not the attitude of the prospect." We're often nervous about selling because we're worried about the customer, but sales don't depend on the attitude of the customer as much as we think. Sales depends on our own mind-set. So let's redefine how we think about sales by looking at other ways to approach it.

Sales Is Sharing

One of the best ways to get past the uncomfortable feeling of selling is to not sell at all. That's right, don't sell anything. Just share your heart. When you share your heart, you can sell your product without even realizing it. Take Angela, my client with the handmade jewelry business. She tells her story whenever she talks with customers. Like she did with me, she talks about the impact her mother had on her. She shares memories of the bond that was built between them. And in recounting the special and meaningful words her mother shared along with each piece of jewelry, Angela's customers see her heart, understand her *why*, and want to buy from her over any one of the other jewelry companies on Etsy. You see, a sale doesn't have to be pushy. In fact, some of the best sales happen when you don't "sell" your business at all. Just tell your story and share your heart and let the sale happen.

Sales Is Serving

There is an easy way for you to help people, meet their needs, solve their problems, and improve their lives by selling. You just serve them. And when you serve your customers well, they will thank you. This happened to me a while back when I had been trying to find shoes for my son. He was learning to walk and had just started pulling up and cruising around, and I was on the hunt for any shoes that would stay on his feet. I tried Velcro closure, elastic strings, and slip-ons, but any shoe that actually fit his foot wouldn't stay on. He'd step right out of them.

My friend Beth has two boys, and she told me to go to a well-known kids' specialty shoe store. I rejected this idea immediately because she said the shoes were almost $50 a pair. But one fateful day at the park changed my mind. My friends and I decided to meet up with our babies so they could play at the playground. I brought Carter wearing the only pair of shoes I could get on his feet.

Within forty-five seconds, he was out of his shoes, walking in the mulch on the playground. Of course, the sticks got stuck in his socks and made him cry. While all of the other babies walked around happily, their little feet protected from mulch, Carter and I wrestled in and out of shoes that clearly were not working.

That was the last straw. I took my crying, mulch-toed, shoeless child from the park straight to the kids' shoe store in the mall. I came in exasperated, and the nice employee asked if I needed help. Yes. Yes, I did need help. She measured Carter's foot and it all made sense. "He's a size five and a half, so we will need a six. Oh, and he's an extra wide. We only make one shoe in an extra wide, so I will go get you that in both colors." Extra wide. Of course! All this time I had been trying to cram his extra-wide feet into normal-sized shoes.

She came back with the shoe, and it slipped on Carter's fat foot like Cinderella's missing slipper. It was so effortless and perfect that I almost cried. I said, "I'll take them in every color you have." So two pairs of shoes and eighty-four dollars later, my problem was solved—and I'd never been so happy to spend money in all my life. That sales representative didn't have to sell to me. She simply served me. She listened to me. She measured my son's foot. She got the shoes he needed and put them on his feet. She got the additional pair I wanted. She took care of my son. She sold by simply serving.

That experience is a good example of how easy, effortless, and even fun sales can be. When you serve people, you don't have to push, pull, beg, or convince them to purchase. The sale is natural, and your customers are not only willing, but happy—thrilled even—to pay forty-two dollars for a pair of tiny tennis shoes.

When you switch your mind-set from selling to serving, it's easy to use words like offering and giving instead of pushing and getting. You're not in the business of sales. You're in the business of serving others.

Sales Is Influence

Whether we're aware of it or not, we are all in the business of sales. That's because sales is simply influence. For example, all day, every day, through blogs, videos, events, coaching, and books, I influence people. I influence people to improve their lives and businesses, to make changes and reach their goals, or to take care of themselves and have better relationships. And do you know what? No one ever responds to my blogs or videos and says, "You're so pushy and aggressive." Why? Because I am just influencing.

But it's not just me; you are too. Do you have a close friend? Great! You influenced someone to let you into their inner circle. Are you married? Great! You convinced someone that you're worth spending the rest of their life with. That's a big sale! Did you get your kids to eat dinner last night? Great! You sold them on the idea to eat their veggies . . . or at least try them. See, sales is just influencing. So the next time you're talking about your business with someone, don't get hung up on your ideas about sales. Instead, just focus on influencing. When you believe in what you are talking about, then influencing—and as a result, sales—will come naturally.

Sales Is an Exchange of Value

My friend and sales expert Tiffany Peterson describes sales as "an exchange of value." What I love about this particular definition is that it takes all the squirmy awkward emotions out of it. It's not about how we feeeel about the sale. It's just a fact: a sale is an exchange of value. When you go into your favorite coffee shop, you pay four dollars and receive a latte. That is an exchange of value. The coffee shop wants your four dollars more than they want the coffee, and you want the coffee more than you want that four dollars. That is a sales transaction. Now apply that concept to your business. You sell your organizing services for one hundred dollars per hour. When you meet with a client, they give you one hundred dollars and you give them one hour of your time, skills, solutions, and organizing. They pay you because they'd rather have access to you for one hour than that one-hundred-dollar bill in their wallet. You give up one hour of your time because you'd rather have one hundred dollars than that time. When you start to see sales transactions for what they are—just an exchange of value—you can start making more sales and stop feeling so weird about it.

When we reframe our idea of sales, we can sell with confidence. Having the right mind-set is the first step. The next step is to follow the right process. By doing this, you can take the pressure off yourself and enjoy selling your product.

KNOW, LIKE, AND TRUST

We talked about our online marketing funnel in the previous chapter, but there's also a progression for making a sale in person. I already mentioned people buy from those they know, like, and trust. Online or in person, if you want to sell to them, you've got to build a relationship with them so they know you, like you, and trust you.

They Need to Know You

This usually occurs through some type of marketing. They may have been first introduced to you online or maybe they were referred by a friend who already does business with you. When you use the strategies we talked about in chapter 14 for effective marketing, you can introduce new people to your business and build relationships with them through the funnel process. All of those efforts help them get to know you. No matter how they are first introduced to you, they need to know you exist before they can buy from you.

They Need to Like You

This is where you build a relationship with your potential customer. It might be through informative emails or some online incentive, or it may be in person, when you drop off some coffee one afternoon as a treat. A great way to make your relationship with your customers more personal is to respond to comments and posts on social media. Many businesses miss this simple opportunity to have a one-on-one connection with a customer online. But when you do, not only does that particular customer feel special that you responded to them, but everyone else sees and appreciates that personal interaction too. As you invest in relationships, customers begin to like you more and more. One warning, though: you're never going to be able to please everyone. Some people will just be hateful because they are hateful. You can demonstrate great customer service by addressing legitimate concerns, but don't try to win over an Internet troll. It's a losing battle, and they'll never buy from you, anyway.

They Need to Trust You

This is where you ask questions. It's also where most salespeople make mistakes. You build trust not by talking but by listening. Remember the time-share salesman? About 90 percent of that "conversation" was him talking at me. It was such a blur that I don't even know what he said. It was a terrible experience for me, and it eventually resulted in a cancellation for him. Instead of talking, build trust by asking more questions. What does the customer need? How can you help? What problems can you solve? As you ask questions, you show humility and genuine interest in them and their needs versus your own agenda to make a sale.

The best part is that you not only get a one-time sale, but when a customer trusts you, they'll usually come back to you as well. They become loyal and make repeat purchases because they had a great experience. That's exactly what happened when my husband went shopping for my engagement ring back when we were dating. In an industry where many customers are under-informed, the salesman was patient, asked questions, and took his time with my husband. Matt was able to look at rings of all sizes and prices and didn't feel pressured. As a result, he felt comfortable enough to make an important purchase at this store. When you take time to ask questions and listen, you build trust.

Sales can be fun, easy, and yes, even effortless. But that only happens when the groundwork is laid first by building relationships with customers who know you, like you, and trust you.

MISTAKES TO AVOID

Selling is a skillset developed over time. The more you do it, the more natural it will become. In my coaching and personal experience, however, I've seen a few mistakes that tend to hold people back from great selling. Let's take a look at four common mistakes and how to fix them.

Mistake #1: Being Sorry

When you don't believe in yourself or your business, your language, facial expressions, and posture will give you away. People will know. I've seen women who have shown such doubt in their own businesses that they basically talk people out of doing business with them. They look down and grimace when they state their price. They say things like, "I know it sounds like a lot of money, but . . ." Or, "I hate to say it, but this costs $100." Or, "I'm sorry it's so pricey, but the materials cost more than I expected." This doesn't just happen in person, either. I've seen websites with long explanations and disclaimers around the price of the goods and services. Come on, people—you're sabotaging your sales!

Remember, in chapter 11 I mentioned that you teach people how to treat you? If you act like you have something to be sorry about, your customer is going to think you have something to be sorry about. If you act like your price is too high, they're going to think your price is too high. Half the time, they wouldn't think to question your price in the first place if you hadn't planted a seed of doubt in their minds. If you don't even think your product or service is worth what you're asking, why should they?

Here's some tough love that you may need to hear: it's not your customer's job to give you confidence. They're not here to pat you on the back and convince you that you can do this thing. You've got to dig deep and find that confidence somewhere else. If you want to serve and influence the customer, then stop being so sorry for everything you think they might, possibly, one day, kind of get annoyed about. You have nothing to apologize for. It's your business, and they can buy from you or not.

Fix the mistake: Say your price and shut up.

I've heard so many women fumble around when giving their price. They'll start by paving the way with a few excuses, then eke out the price almost in a whisper, and then keep rambling to fill any potential uncomfortable silence. This is not the way to close the deal. If you want to project confidence, for the love of all that is holy, just say your price and shut up. (Trust me, the last part is something I struggle with daily too!) Hold your head high, pull your shoulders back, and even if it takes all the strength you have, smile, say your price, and stop talking.

For example, when someone asks how much you charge to make custom invitations, you might say, "That will be eighty dollars, and I'd love to work on that for you." Even if you don't feel confident, just fake it. Smile and pretend. Look them in the eye. Act like you're extremely comfortable, even if you aren't. Let there be silence. Give the customer a moment to think about your offer without you nervously chattering away. Don't try to help them make the decision. You're talking to an adult, so give them the same space you'd want when considering a purchase. When you do this, you create breathing room for the sale to actually occur.

Mistake #2: Not Being Able to Receive

Several years ago, all of my girlfriends took me on a trip to Florida for my bachelorette party. Since they were hosting it, they kindly paid for everything. One morning we were at the pool and I went to the snack bar to get a bagel. One of my best friends since third grade, Sarah, came with me. As I placed my order and got my wallet out, she said, "No, I've got this."

I responded, "No, it's okay. I've got it."

And she said, "No, I am paying for your bagel. It's your bachelorette trip."

You'd think I would just let it go, and I should have, but I didn't. I continued awkwardly, "No, I've got it . . ."

Then she looked me in the eye, got really intense like only a good friend can do, and said, "You have a problem. You cannot receive. I am paying for this bagel and this conversation is over." We both laughed, and she did just that.

That was over five years ago, and that moment has stuck with me because I realized she was right. I was weird about receiving a gift because receiving makes a person feel vulnerable. Giving is often more comfortable than receiving. When you're giving, you're in control, and you have the power. When you're receiving, the roles are reversed. I would rather stand on a stage and give a presentation to three thousand people than stand in a room and have thirty people sing "Happy Birthday" to me. I'd rather host a baby shower for someone than have one thrown for me. Sometimes it's hard to receive, and that's often the same reason many of us struggle to sell. Whether you realize it or not, sales is about being willing to be vulnerable and receive.

Fix the mistake: Receive anyway.

My friend Amy hired a piano teacher, Sophia, for her two daughters. Each week when the lesson is over, Sophia shifts around uncomfortably while my friend writes her a check for payment. It's obvious that Sophia is uncomfortable receiving her payment, but Amy doesn't mind paying her one bit. Sophia serves Amy and her family well. She's taking care of a need they have, and Amy is thankful for the opportunity to pay her for her great work.

If we're honest, being weird about getting a sale is often more about us than it is the other person. So instead of getting in our own way, let's just get over ourselves and be willing to receive. It may feel a little awkward at first but, with practice, we can learn to receive with grace. After all, we won't stay in business very long if we don't let people pay us.

Mistake #3: Giving Up

Sales is vulnerable. It's like giving someone a present or asking someone out on a date. We put ourselves on the line, and rejection is always a possibility. And when it comes, it hurts. It's natural to want to tuck our tails and give up. We might be too embarrassed or scared to try again. But rejection in sales and business—and life, for that matter—is inevitable. Your business isn't for everyone and that's okay. It doesn't matter if you get rejected; it matters how you handle it.

Fix the mistake: Follow up.

Did you know that over sixty percent of sales transactions happen after the fourth interaction?[81] Sixty percent! Instead of giving up when you get rejected, I want you to follow up. As you follow up and build relationships, it's more likely that your work will lead to a future sale. It might not, but, as Nora Roberts says, "If you don't ask, the answer is always no." And, if you follow up and keep asking, the answer might become yes!

Several years ago, there was a guy in my running group who was interested in me. I wasn't interested in him at all, and I was actually dating someone else at the time. But this guy wasn't fazed one bit. He continued to pursue me and, after several months of me turning him down repeatedly, he asked if I would just go have coffee with him. I instantly knew why. He was going to make his case for why I should date him. In order for me to make things clear once and for all, I met him for coffee. As expected, he laid it on the line. He said he wanted to take me out and date me. I told him that I was flattered, but nothing was ever going to happen. To paraphrase Taylor Swift: We are never, ever, ever getting together! To make it crystal clear to him and so I left no room for confusion, I said: "In fact, I am positive I am going to marry someone else."

If you were to ask that guy how he felt after coffee that day, he'd say, "I felt good about it. I knew it was going to happen." If you want to ask him about it, you can. That man is now my husband! See? Following up really can pay off. As my friend Tiffany Peterson says, "The fortune is in the follow-through!" Don't quit when you face rejection. Send a handwritten note or shoot another email. Make another phone call or stop by their business. Keep the conversation going and, instead of giving up, follow up!

Mistake #4: Not Asking for the Sale

Perhaps the biggest mistake people make when selling is not asking for the sale. That seems pretty basic, right? But I've seen it happen time and time again. We can talk about our products, share our story, and put ourselves out there—but when it comes down to actually closing the deal, we toe the line but never work up the nerve to actually cross it.

Once you've shared your story, built a relationship with your customer, and named your price with confidence, the hard part is over. You need to actually "make the ask." Don't let that opportunity slip through your fingers. We are missing sales simply because we aren't asking.

Fix the mistake: Ask for the sale.

It's as simple as being prepared to close the deal. Don't beat around the bush. If you want to be effective, you've got to be direct. You can say something like, "Would you like to place your order now?" Or maybe, "Can I go ahead and book a session for you?" Or, "Can we get you on the calendar?" These are all simple and direct ways to close the sale and create action. Practice saying your closing line out loud so when you're in that moment, it comes naturally. I remind the women I work with, "Don't ask, don't get." That's true in life and especially in sales. If you don't ask for it, you'll never get it.

So go for it. Wrap up that pitch with a beautiful bow and ask for their business. If it's something you've overlooked until now, taking this one step could make all the difference.

FAKE IT TILL YOU FEEL IT

The reality is that you may not become a skilled saleswoman overnight. That's okay. Keep practicing and it will get easier and you will get better. But, until you get to the point that you're comfortable and confident selling your products or services, I want you to do what I did to get my first job. I want you to fake it till you feel it.

After quitting my disastrous first job out of college, where I only stayed for two months, I took the position as the aquatic director at a new YMCA where I built the aquatics department from the ground up. I was responsible for setting and managing a budget of hundreds of thousands of dollars and hiring and leading a team of fifty people. I purchased all the materials for the aquatic area from chlorine to staff uniforms. I created all the aquatic programs, set prices, and did all the marketing for the department. And on and on and on.

Here's the reality: I was twenty-two years old. I was months out of college with little to no real-world work experience. I had zero leadership or management experience, and my degree was in advertising. It was a huge job for anyone, let alone someone who still had dirt on her shoes from the University of Tennessee.

I kept up with the endless demands and performed well as a young manager, but a few months after we opened, we became the fastest-growing YMCA in the country and I realized just how unqualified I was for the job I was doing. I looked around and noticed all of the other directors from other departments such as Wellness, Membership, and Childcare were at least a decade older than I was. Why me? How did I get that job?

I had to know, so one day I asked my boss, Lauren, "What made you choose me for this job?"

She laughed and said, "You know you interviewed against a woman who had twelve years of experience in aquatic management, don't you?" No. No, I did not know that!

"It was easy. Your confidence. In your interview, you were confident you could do the job, so you sold me. You made it easy for me to be confident in you too."

That one quality—confidence—allowed me to jump-start my career at a higher level than most people. I was given responsibilities I wasn't ready for and opportunities I wasn't worthy of. Everything I've been able to do in my career since then has been possible because of that first job. That's how powerful confidence is. Because if you don't believe in yourself, no one else will either.

I don't mean you need to have a blind arrogance or a huge ego. But if you can be confident in yourself and your business, you will convince others to be confident in you too.

I want you to value yourself and what you bring to the marketplace. Stop being sorry for what you have to offer. Share your heart and your story. Because on the other side of every sales transaction is a person who you're helping and serving through your business. When you remember that, selling is no longer about the transactions you create but the difference you make. And that is when sales really becomes fun!

LET'S APPLY WHAT YOU'VE LEARNED!

Changing Focus

To help you stay focused on the right things, make the following lists:

Get vs. Give

List all of the things you give your customer when a sale is made.

Make vs. Take

List all of the work you do in order to make the money you earn.

Offer vs. Push

List examples of things you offer in your business.

Value vs. Price

Before you talk to customers, remind yourself, *The value I offer is* (insert your product or service). Write the value you offer here.

Redefining Sales

Sales Is Sharing.

Share your story here as a reminder of what to talk about with customers.

Sales Is Serving.

Write out the ways that you serve your customers to remind yourself of how you help them.

Sales Is Influence.

Write out other areas of your life where you successfully influence others toward some action or result. This can remind you that you are a successful influencer and therefore a salesperson!

Know, Like, and Trust

People buy from those they know, like, and trust. So it's important to make sure people know you, like you, and trust you.

Know (marketing). Write out ways that you are letting people get to know you and your business.

Like (build a relationship). Write out ways that you are investing in and deepening relationships you have with your customers.

Trust (ask questions). Write out questions you can ask your customers to understand them better. These questions can give you insight into how you can better meet their needs and solve their problems. This will also build trust in your relationship as your customers feel listened to and understood.

Congratulations! You're on your way to selling with confidence.

What's Next?

CHASING YOUR VERSION OF SUCCESS

Congratulations on finishing your plan! But we're not done just yet. In addition to creating your plan, there are a few other things you might want to think about. For one, you might be interested in how to grow your business. In the next section, we'll talk about how to grow and expand to the level you want, when you want. You may also be thinking what many women in business think every day: *How am I supposed to do it all?* We'll cover how to create your own version of life balance so that you walk away with your plan feeling empowered instead of overwhelmed. Let's finish strong!

chapter 17

TAKE IT TO THE NEXT LEVEL

Growing, Scaling, and Expanding Your Business

Stephanie Parker and her husband, Brett, never planned to run a multimillion-dollar business. In fact, she never really planned to run a business at all. In the beginning, she just wanted her baby to sleep through the night.

When her new baby wouldn't sleep through the night due to the child's startle reflex, Stephanie put her basic seamstress skills to work and came up with a tiny toasty sleep sack for her little one. And it worked! The baby (and therefore Stephanie) started sleeping better, and she thought that was that. But then a friend asked her to make one for her. And then another friend. And then another friend. At that point, she knew she was on to something, but she had no idea that her idea would become a nationally best-selling product line.

Stephanie was like many women who accidentally got into business. But after her little sleep sack, now famously known as the Zipadee-Zip, worked for her daughter, word of mouth among her friends and family kept the requests rolling in. After scrounging up enough money to build a basic website to sell them, actual orders from strangers—customers—started coming in. She'd never spent any money on advertising but the rested, grateful moms she served spread the word quickly by telling all of their friends.

Within four months, her company, Sleeping Baby, had $70,000 in revenue, and they were doing all they could to keep up with the demand. They knew they were onto something huge, and they decided to pitch their product on the national television show, *Shark Tank*. To their surprise, they were actually chosen.

But this is where Stephanie and her husband demonstrated wise judgment and made a decision that few people would have made with that incredible opportunity in front of them. They turned them down. They realized after being selected for the show that they didn't have the infrastructure to support the level of growth or exposure that would come with being in the national spotlight—whether they received an investment or not. "We made it on the show after being in business for four months," Stephanie explained. "But we realized we didn't have the manpower to support manufacturing."[82] And at the time, that "manufacturing" referred to the women at the local fabric store that Brett had begged into working for his wife on the side!

They continued growing their business and putting systems and processes in place in order to pitch their idea to *Shark Tank* again in the future. After eighteen months in business, the company had over one million dollars in sales and they felt like they were ready to try again. They were chosen for the show a second time and went into it thinking they had enough product for six to nine months. They sold out within a week! Looking back on that experience, Stephanie remembers, "Zipadee-Zips were selling on eBay for $150!"[83]

That was after they ramped up hiring, production, and processes in order to support the immense growth and exposure that the show would bring. It shows that the Parkers' decision to turn the show down the first time was an intelligent move. Getting that much attention and that many orders before they were ready would have completely destroyed their business. Their decision to better prepare themselves paid off in ways they never could have imagined. And their business continues to grow and reap the rewards of those early wise choices.

Business growth can be an exciting, wild ride—but only if you are prepared and ready to grow in the right way. In fact, trying to grow too big, too fast is one of the top—and perhaps the saddest—reasons that small businesses fail. [84] The business implodes because it can't support the growth. That's why this chapter is devoted to how to grow your business the right way.

You can grow, scale, and expand in several ways. As your business becomes more successful, you might want to make the leap from working on it on the side to making it your full-time job. You may need to hire team members. You might want to move from online to a retail store or from one storefront to multiple locations. Regardless of how you define growth, to be successful you must keep several things in mind. And if you're a dreamer trying to find your idea or if you are just getting started, it may be hard to imagine needing to hire someone or opening a retail location. But as the business grows, your confidence will grow. And as your confidence grows, your goals will probably grow as well. Let's look at a few options to consider when building your business and reaching new goals.

MAKING THE LEAP TO FULL TIME

I'm often asked, "How do I know when I am ready to make the leap and take my business full time?" The person asking is usually working a full-time or part-time job to pay the bills, but they are building a business on the side. They want to know when they can quit the day job and start working for themselves. Or it may be a mom staying home with her children full time, but she needs the business to start bringing in the equivalent of a full-time income.

In either scenario, "making the leap" implies that you are stopping something you're currently doing—whether that's working another full-time job, taking care of the children around the clock, or something else altogether—in order to focus on the business "full time."

This is one of my favorite questions because it means the business is growing enough and the business owner is ambitious enough to consider devoting themselves to their business full time. Regardless of which scenario you are in, I want you to keep three things in mind when transitioning your side business into full time.

Take a Step

First, let's make it a step, not a leap. Steps are a lot less scary and risky than leaps. And when you take just a step, you don't fall as often or as far. You do that by building up your revenues. You want to build your revenues up high enough so that it doesn't feel like a terrifying leap when you leave your "safe" full-time job for your side business. You want to pull the boat up close enough to the dock so that when you take that step, you don't fall into the water. Your revenues should be high enough to provide you enough of a personal income to live on. Which leads me to . . .

Don't Do Assumptive Math

I coached a man a few years ago who worked on his side business ten hours per week, which earned him $10,000 of personal income for the year. He assumed that if he quadrupled his time working on his business, that his income would quadruple as well, earning him $40,000 per year, which would have been enough to support himself. He quit his full-time job and worked on his side business full time, forty hours each week. But the demand wasn't there for forty hours per week yet and, that year, he earned just slightly over what he had earned the year before—only $12,000.

Assumptive math is dangerous. Don't quit your day job and assume the demand will be there. Instead, you have to build your revenues up high enough while working your other job so that when you're ready to make the transition, the money is actually there.

It's important to point out that you don't necessarily have to replace the full income amount you're earning from a day job. You just have to earn enough for you to live on. Maybe you bring home $60,000 from your full-time job and you've built your side gig up to $30,000. Can you reassess your budget and get by on $30,000? If you're prepared to make some cuts and live within a smaller budget, you can transition earlier.

Remember That It's a Season

When you're building your side business up to your full-time income, you may feel like you're working two full-time jobs—because you are! But remember that it is only for a season. Once your business is strong enough to support you, you can quit your other job and that crazy season will be over. It may be a tough year or two, and it will likely require sacrifices in other areas of your life. Realistically, you probably won't have much (or any!) free time as you chase your dream and build your business. But remember, when you get there, it will all be worth it. You can leave your current job—that you may or may not like—and pursue your passion as much as you want to. Now, instead of needing your day job just to get by, your dream can pay the bills instead.

The biggest thing I want you to remember is that when your side thing becomes your main thing, it's no longer just an optional, fun, part-time side gig bringing in bonus cash. It's your real job with a real boss (you), and you can't afford to take your foot off the gas. If anything, since it's your only source of income, that's when you need to go for it like you never have before.

MAKING SOME MOVES

In addition to taking your side business full time, another way you might want to grow and expand is by moving locations. Here are some different ways you can move:

- Moving from Etsy to a full website
- Moving from online to a brick-and-mortar store
- Moving from having one location to opening multiple locations

Let's look at these examples and what each would involve.

Growing from Etsy to a Full Website

As I mentioned in chapter 10, if your business is booming and you want more flexibility and options for how your business is represented online, it might be time to create your own website. With your own site, you can choose exactly how you want your business to look and you have greater control over how the customer interacts with your business. You can also incorporate other marketing initiatives, such as email capture and paid advertising, enabling you to more easily interact with your customers.

If you're ready to have your own website, you'll want to do a few things.

Choose a URL That Is Easy to Say, Type, and Remember.
Your URL is the web address that you type into the bar at the top of your browser. It should be short, clear, and concise.

Choose a Hosting Platform That Is Easy to Use.

There are platforms that sell entire website packages. This is a (virtual) "website in a box," so to speak. It includes all the elements you need including the URL (web address), the hosting (where your website lives in the internet space), design templates (how your website looks, including layout, colors, and fonts), and email addresses (your custom email account where people can reach you).

A ton of these web platforms are out there to choose from, and each one brings something unique to the table. Take your time and shop around. Make sure you select one that you understand, though, so you don't add additional stress to your business and life.

Get Help.

Whether it's the customer service department at the hosting platform or a friend from church, see if someone can help you learn the language and features of managing your own site before you throw yourself in the deep end to figure it out alone. Someone familiar with that world can explain the basics pretty easily and then you can manage and maintain most of your day-to-day operations on your own.

Of course, you can always pay someone to set up and manage a website for you, but as we've said before, that can get pricey. If you're setting up your first website, your business probably isn't ready to support that kind of bill.

Growing from Online to a Brick-and-Mortar Store

Expanding your business from online only to a retail location is a big, exciting step! At a minimum, you need to consider and plan for the following:

Location

Your location is the largest factor in determining the amount of "foot traffic" that comes into your store. Your location also determines the amount you'll have to pay in rent. Keep in mind that you don't have to make the jump from online to a retail store all at once. There may be an area of your home that you could fix up and use as your retail "store" to make the transition more gradual. That's what Valerie Guess of Val's Boutique did. She built up her business by running it out of her home until she was ready to open a commercial retail storefront. Remember, we're looking for steps, not leaps!

Budget

Again, don't do assumptive math here and assume that opening a retail location will automatically cause your sales to skyrocket in order to pay for that space. Build up your revenues enough to be able to pay for the space before you move, and then, when you open a storefront, the business can support the bills.

Lease Commitment

If you rent commercial space, think through the lease commitment you are agreeing to. If your business is in the early stages, committing to a long-term lease is risky. Plan for the future, but don't jump into it before you're ready.

Inventory

Another cost associated with having a retail location is inventory. Right now, if you are online, you can keep your inventory low and make products on demand. No one can see how much product you have at any given time. However, if you open a storefront, your inventory is on display for everyone to see and you should have enough to not only keep up with the demand coming in your store, but also enough to justify having a store to begin with.

Growing from One Location to Multiple Locations

Once you've opened your first brick-and-mortar store, you can do it again. You just duplicate the process at that point. First and foremost, you need to make sure an additional location is justified and will bring you a return on your investment. Once you know that the demand is there, then you can look into which additional location will be best for expansion. The biggest risk that comes when you expand to multiple locations is your personal availability and your brand.

First is your availability. Let me state the obvious: you can only be in one place at a time. With one location, you can be present as much as you need to be, and you can be hands-on with everything all the time if you want to. With multiple locations, though, you have to expand beyond yourself, which is a great, but scary, thing. This is where great hiring and delegation comes into play, which we will talk about next.

The other risk comes with expanding your brand. When your customers interact with you, they expect a certain experience. Therefore, your job is not only to open another physical location, but also to create that same experience for your customers no matter which location they visit.

As you expand and grow your business, your name and brand needs to stay consistent regardless of how many locations you open. For example, if you go to any Starbucks location around the world, you will have an almost identical experience. They have the same menus, same design, and same process for ordering. You know what kind of experience you're getting every single time, no matter where you are.

HIRING TEAM MEMBERS

In addition to moving, it may be time to hire your first or additional team members in order to support your business's growth. Hiring your first team member is one of the scariest things you do in business. Hiring your second is the second scariest. And so on. The reality is that hiring someone brings with it another level of responsibility and risk. It brings fear and doubt to the surface. Questions may flood your mind: *When is the right time to hire someone? How do I know if I can afford someone? How can I find someone who cares as much as I do? What do I look for in hiring someone? How can I make sure they won't damage my business and my brand? Where do I find good people?* I've hired hundreds of people in my career, and I can tell you, it's one of the most exhausting but important things you will do in your business. To help relieve some of your fears, let's answer some common questions.

When Is the Right Time to Hire Someone?

The right time to hire someone is when you have maxed out your capacity, you want to grow, you have the cash flow to pay someone else, and you want the responsibility of employing another person. If any one of those things is not true of your situation, you are not ready.

Let's talk about the idea of wanting to hire someone else. The fact is, not everybody wants to have employees. Even if they're maxed out, some people choose to slow growth and keep their business at this level. They want to keep it small enough for them to manage on their own instead of hiring help. If that's you, that's fine! It's your business, remember? It can be as big or small as you want it to be. But if you are maxed out, ready to grow, and want to employ another person, then it might be time to hire help.

How Do I Know if I Can Afford Someone?

Before you hire someone, you need the margin in your business finances to be able to pay them and you need a plan for how they are going to give you a return on your investment (ROI). Once you start adding employees, payroll will likely become the largest expense in your entire business, so you want to make sure that your team members are making you more than they are costing you. Looking at the current profit margin and cash flow in your business can help you identify if you are able to afford another person. It may mean less take-home pay for you initially, but as the person begins to produce more than they cost you, your income should return to the previous amount and even higher. If it doesn't, that's probably a sign that you weren't ready for another team member or that you aren't using them enough.

You also need a plan for what that person is going to do in your business. I've talked to many business owners who complain about needing help, but when I ask what they want new potential team members to do, they realize they haven't thought that far ahead. They just know they need help. Creating a plan for what that person will do and produce will help that team member achieve those results for you. It will also help you manage them and give you metrics for evaluating them. Simply put, you and your team members need to know what winning looks like for that role. A simple job description, or as we call it at Ramsey Solutions, a Key Results Area (KRA) description, will do that for you. Simply list out expectations for what they will do for your business.

Never make a hire until you know you can afford to pay someone and you can clearly define exactly what they'll do for you.

How Can I Find Someone Who Cares as Much as I Do?

You can't. I hate to tell you this, but you will never find another person who cares as much about your business as you do. The possible exception is your spouse, if you're married and in business together. This business is your idea, your heart, and your baby. No one will ever care about it as much as you do. That's not to say that you can't find great people who are brought in, work hard, and care deeply. You can find people who get your vision and have your passion. Instead of having unrealistic expectations for candidates you interview, you can look for key qualities that will set them up to support you and help the business win.

What Do I Look for in Hiring Someone?

The best hiring advice I've ever received was, as Fast Company says, "Hire for attitude, train for skill."[85] You can teach skill, but you can't teach character qualities like integrity, passion, work ethic, and attitude if the person just doesn't have any to begin with. That's why you want to look for people who have the right character qualities first. These are the people who go above and beyond and do the right thing—not because you require it of them and not because they want to please you. You want to hire people who go above and beyond and do the right thing because that's who they are. They can't not do those things. It would go against their very core.

They Need to Care

I ran into someone like this just a few years ago. It was 4:40 a.m. and pouring down rain. I stood in the lobby of the Hampton Inn and tried to focus my mind on anything besides the stabbing hunger pangs as I waited for the airport shuttle. Since I had been speaking until late the night before, I hadn't eaten in almost twelve hours. That would be tough for anyone, but when you're in your second trimester of pregnancy like I was at the time, you're hungry all the time.

As I stood there in the lobby, waiting, I reminded myself that everything would be okay because I would get food as soon as I got to the airport. Then I got a text: "Your flight has been delayed from 6:00 a.m. to 7:45 a.m." I went back up to my room, crawled into bed, and set my alarm for the 6:00 a.m. airport shuttle. I lay there trying to sleep but the shooting pains in my stomach wouldn't let me relax. My body was demanding that I eat but I just kept telling myself, *When I get to the airport, I'll get food, and everything will be okay.* Finally, I drifted off.

I'm not sure how it happened, but the next thing I knew it was 6:55 a.m. I shot out of bed, my heart pounding out of my chest, and threw on my hat and shoes. I bolted downstairs to catch the 7:00 a.m. shuttle. When I got to the airport and through security, I arrived at my gate to find passengers already boarding. I had missed my boarding group, but that didn't matter because I made it. I got on the plane and sat down, trying to take a deep breath and calm my nerves. I prayed in that moment, *God, thank you for getting me on this plane.* And I felt God speak these words to me immediately: *I'm going to take care of you.* I fought back the tears and smiled at the truth in those words.

But as my nerves settled and my breathing slowed, another sensation took over: hunger. It was a deep, consuming, blinding, painful hunger. In my rush to the airport, I hadn't had time to grab food. And with a two-hour flight ahead of me, that meant sixteen hours without food! I grabbed the in-flight menu to see what I could purchase beyond the free peanuts and pretzels. There was nothing. My only hope was to beg the Southwest flight attendant to give me fifteen bags of pretzels.

I waited until everyone boarded. The pangs grew. I waited until we took off. Nausea had set in, and I started to feel dizzy. I waited until we got to 10,000 feet and then the flight attendant finally came by my row.

"I am so sorry to bother you, but I overslept, didn't get to eat, and I'm pregnant," I said. "Can I have as many pretzels as you can allow? I'm just starving." What she said next brings tears to my eyes even now. "I have a sausage-and-egg biscuit. Would you like that?" she asked. "Let me go get that for you." I nodded, unable to speak, as she walked to the front of the plane and returned with breakfast—her breakfast. It was a warm sausage-and-egg biscuit and a can of apple juice.

I knew the polite thing would have been to decline, but I couldn't. I was desperate. I ate her breakfast as tears streamed down my face and onto my tray table. God's words rang in my ears again: *I'm going to take care of you.* I will never forget that moment when God showed up in the form of a Southwest flight attendant— when a complete stranger cared.

There's no company policy that prepares someone for serving a ravenous pregnant woman on a plane. It's an act of service that can't be trained by a leader or taught in an employee handbook.

So regardless of what type of business you're in, the best thing that you can do is hire people who care. Of course, you want to hire competent, skilled team members who are high-performing individuals. But above all else, you want to hire people who care.

You Need to Like Them

They also need to have one other quality that's extremely important but few people talk about. You need to like them. Very few hiring evaluations include that measure of compatibility, but it's hugely important—especially in small business. If this is your first team member, this hire is going to make up 50 percent of your business. Make sure that you actually like the person, because you are going to be spending a lot of time together.

When you find someone you like who also cares deeply, works tirelessly, and goes above and beyond because that's who they are, then you have the most important qualities you need. From there, you can teach them the business.

How Can I Make Sure They Won't Damage My Business or My Brand?

Whether you're in a product-based or a service-based business, having someone else do the work for you can be terrifying, because we all know that no one can do the job better than we can, right?

If your business is making bows, who else could make a better bow than you? If you're a graphic designer, who else is going to design as well as you? If you have multiple employees, how can you be sure they will all do the job in a consistent way? After all, your product or service is a reflection of you, and it can be hard to trust your reputation to someone else. So, let me give you two specific things you need to look for in a potential hire before you hand them the responsibility of representing you to your customers:

First, they need to be competent. They need to be able to do the job—whether that's graphic design or sewing or packaging or answering customer-service calls. Whatever you've hired them to do, they need to be able to do it. They need to be competent.

Second, they need to have integrity. Without integrity, you can't trust them—regardless of how talented or skilled they may be. I don't care how good a salesperson is at selling, if they lie to me about something small, I know I can't trust them with something big. If there's an integrity breakdown, I can't work with them. Period.

But when you find a passionate team member you can trust who has the skills you need, you can delegate with confidence and know that they are going to do the best they can. They won't be perfect (like you're not!), and they will make mistakes (like you!). But with competency and integrity, you know you have a good, quality team member.

Where Do I Find Good People?

In chapter 14, we talked about your ideal customer. The same strategy works with hiring team members. Think of your ideal team member, what they like, and what's important to them. Think through what qualities they have and where they are, and then go get them.

If you have team members already, that should be the first place you start looking for referrals. Asking your current team members or even incentivizing referrals from them are great ways to find good people. As Dave Ramsey says, "Thoroughbreds run with thoroughbreds." If you have great people on your team, they probably know other great people who they can refer.

You Catch What You Go Fishing For

A coaching client of mine was struggling with hiring. While interviewing a candidate for an opening at his retail store, he had some concerns. The candidate wanted to talk about the hourly rate right off the bat, how few hours he "had" to work, and how often he could take vacation. This guy seemed to just want to do the minimum, collect a paycheck, and go home!

My client was right—this guy raised red flags in his interview. And this was definitely not the right guy for the job, but I wanted to know how my client got to the point of considering him to begin with. When I dug a little deeper, I discovered the cause of this disappointing interview. "How did you post the position?" I asked my client. "What specifically did you advertise?"

He responded, "I said it was a pretty easy cashier job with flexible hours and an opportunity to make more money quickly. I also listed the hourly rate and included that it offered paid vacation."

"Well, you got exactly what you advertised for," I said. Hiring the right people depends more on you as the business leader than it does on the people who walk through your door. You're in control of how you promote the position when looking for potential team members.

It's kind of like fishing. When you go fishing—which I never do because I can't be quiet that long—you use a certain kind of bait depending on what you want to catch. You also go fishing in the right body of water to get the fish you're after. In other words, don't go looking for swordfish in a lake in Alabama. You won't find it. Now apply that concept to business. Your strategy for hiring the perfect person shouldn't be to post a generic job description. You'll get anyone and everyone interested in those surface-level tasks. Instead, think of your ideal candidate. Who are they? What stage of life are they in? Why would they enjoy this particular position on your team? Where do they hang out? Then go to their lake and start fishing.

When you get there though, don't just use any old worm. Use the right lure to attract the right candidate. Sell your vision. Promote your purpose. Invite this person into a crusade and a calling. Invite them to do work that matters. Make your recruiting so targeted that anyone who doesn't think or act or work like you've described will immediately dismiss your post because it's not for them. This helps you weed out the ones who won't fit and, instead, find the best candidates for your interview process. So, if you've had some lousy interviews lately, the problem may not be the fish. The problem may be the lure you're using or the pond you're fishing in.

Hiring Best Practices

By the time you're ready to hire your first team member, you are probably just trying to keep your head above water. You need help, and you don't care where it comes from. I've been in your shoes, and it's a frustrating place to be. You want to hire any breathing human that walks through the door. Unfortunately, this leads to making bad decisions that we always end up regretting and paying for later. Instead, follow these best practices to ensure you're getting the right people.

Hire Slow

Take your time and get to know them. You need more than a single five-minute interview to do that. You need several thirty-minute or hour-long interviews. You need to get to know their personality. You need to learn their character and work ethic. You need to see their passion. You need to see them in different environments, for instance, how they interact with servers at a restaurant. You need to allow your intuition to pick up on red flags. Take your time and hire slow.

Don't Dismiss Red Flags

When I started my job with the YMCA, and we were a new location, I had to hire fifty people fast. I was as desperate as I possibly could have been. I had red flags about a couple of candidates, but because I let my desperation blind my judgment, I made excuses for the individuals and dismissed my concerns. As expected, they ended up causing me more trouble than they were worth, and one of them actually ended up stealing from the organization. Don't dismiss red flags. Even if you can't pinpoint what is off, something is. If you can't get to the bottom of it and feel a peace about the person, pass on that candidate. I promise you, it's not worth it in the end.

Date Before You Get Married

Give each new team member a ninety-day trial period to test things out before you offer them a permanent role. This gives you both a chance to see if they are a good fit for the position and your business. Be up front about the trial period in the interviews, and refer to "the first ninety days" often once they start working. Make sure they understand that you're still considering them for the role until they get past that milestone.

If you follow these basic guidelines, you'll have a leg up on most business leaders. You'll weed out the bad ones and end up with strong team members who help you take your business to the next level.

CHASE YOUR VERSION OF SUCCESS

"Women-owned businesses are trailing in size and revenue." [86] This *Fortune* article is just one of many articles I've read that paints a sad picture of the state of women-owned businesses lagging behind other businesses owned and operated by men.

But here's the problem with that perspective: the success metrics they use in these studies only reflect size, revenue, and team members. For example, research shows that 90 percent of women-owned businesses have no team members. Many business "experts" see that as one more indication of how they are lacking. But after years of my own research, as well as working with women at all levels of business, my perspective is entirely different. I believe that many women-owned businesses don't have team members, not because they can't have them, but because they don't want them.

What if the experts didn't measure business "success" by size, revenue, and team members? What if some women approach business differently and want something altogether different? What if her small home-based business that provides an income while giving her the freedom to be with her family is exactly what she wants? If she's reaching for and achieving her own goals, isn't that a huge success? It's working toward goals that you set for yourself, not achieving what someone else says you should have. And by that measure, many women-owned businesses are incredibly successful!

This isn't just my idea either. Research actually shows that women start businesses because they want more flexibility, freedom, and opportunity to grow in their strengths. *Forbes* reports, "With the cost of starting a business at an all-time low, women are saying 'no thank you' to spending years climbing and clawing their way up the corporate ladder, dealing with corporate politics, and working long days without feeling the overall fulfillment they crave."[87]

Maybe you're like Stephanie Parker of Zippadee-Zip, and you're ready to take this thing as far as it will go. Or maybe you're on the other end of the spectrum and you want to keep it small, like my friend Kelly.

Kelly Hancock is an example of someone who started a business, saw growth and success, and then brought it all to a halt.

Kelly and her husband had their first baby in 2008—smack-dab in the middle of the financial crisis. Even though they needed her income, both felt it was right for Kelly to be at home with the baby full time. Going to one income, however, meant that they had to make some drastic cuts to their budget. Finding ways to tighten up the budget became Kelly's new job.

Her family and friends were amazed at her thriftiness and wanted to know how she did it. She got so many requests for tips and ideas that she decided to start a blog called Faithful Provisions as an "easy" way of distributing the information. (She laughs when explaining that now, because anyone who runs a blog knows that it's quite time-consuming.)

Saving money was a hot topic at that time, and her little blog found a much larger audience. Before long she was invited to speak at local events—moms' groups, small businesses, etc.—and she found her sweet spot.

The next year, Kelly's husband lost his job. Because Kelly was seeing success in the blog and speaking at workshops, they decided to put her husband's brainpower behind her growing brand, and the business saw huge growth. When they worked together, Faithful Provisions made them more money than her husband had been making before. She even got a book deal that resulted in her book, *Saving Savvy*.

But eventually the business was pulling them away from the very reason she fell into it. She was working 5:00 a.m. to midnight to keep up and traveling all over the country for speaking engagements rather than spending time with their kids.

Kelly says, "It was beginning to consume us. We just rode that wave for a while, but eventually looked back and realized this isn't where we planned to be. My desire was never to be outside the home."[88] It was time to re-evaluate.

It was around that time, burning the candle at both ends, that she arrived at a fork in the road. She was offered a spot on a national speaking tour. Kelly and her husband knew this tour would mean a lot more publicity and opportunity—but it would require even more work and take more time away from the family. So they decided to decline and step back.

Her husband took a corporate job again (one he was more passionate about), and they hired employees to take the business load off Kelly. She's cut back from writing twenty blog posts every day (no, that's not a typo!) to writing four or five per month. The growth has tapered off, and she is spending more one-on-one time than ever with her children.

The reason I love Kelly's story is because it's a great example of how it's okay to stay small. Kelly knew her *why*. She valued staying home to spend time with her children, and once the business took her away from that, she knew she had to make a change. It doesn't matter if anyone else thinks she made the wrong choice by intentionally slowing the business down—she was successful on her own terms.

So whether you're like Stephanie, Kelly, or somewhere in between, I hope you feel empowered to do exactly what's right for you, your business, and your family. If you want to grow, expand, scale back, move, and hire, good for you! And if you don't want to do any of those things right now, good for you too! Either way, I'm proud of you for knowing what you want and having the courage to go for it. I've been around thousands of women like you representing all stages of life and all levels of business. And regardless of the background, industry, number of team members, or level of revenues, you are out there on the front lines making money doing what you love. That's why I know that many women-owned businesses aren't "trailing" at all. Instead, you are creating, pursuing, and achieving your own version of success, which is the only version of success any of us should want, anyway.

chapter 17 action items
LET'S APPLY WHAT YOU'VE LEARNED!

If you're just getting started, this chapter may not apply to you for a while, and that's okay. Keep it handy to reference as your business and goals grow, and when you're ready to expand, you can make sure you do it the right way.

Moving

Write out your goal for your next move and then reference this checklist to make sure you're ready.

The next move I will make in my business will be from _____ to _____. My goal is to make this move by _____(date).

___ My revenues are currently high enough to support this move.

___ The demand for my business justifies this expansion.

___ I have the help and support I need to make this expansion possible.

Hiring

Use this checklist to help you hire your team members the right way.

___ My business demand and revenues can support another team member.

___ I want to have the responsibility of leading and paying another person.

___ My job posting is designed to attract the right type of person.

___ I have a job description/plan for what this person will do.

___ Qualities to look for:

   ___ Right attitude

   ___ Good work ethic

   ___ Excellent character

___ Competency

___ Integrity

___ I like them

Reassessing Success

In chapters 5 and 6, you dreamed, cast a vision, and set goals for your business. But over time, those goals may grow or change. It's important to constantly reevaluate and reassess what you're working toward so that you're always chasing your own version of success. Review what you wrote as the action steps for those chapters and update those goals if necessary below.

THE BALANCING ACT

How to Build Your Business and Still Have a Life

My life looked a lot different in my early twenties than it does right now. I was working at the YMCA trying to build my career as a young professional. Because it was nonprofit and because we were opening a brand-new location, I was working crazy hours. I worked seventy, eighty, and ninety hours per week—every single week. My team joked that they thought I had a cot set up in the pump room behind the pool because they were sure I never actually went home.

At the same time, as I said earlier, I rented a farm. Don't ask me what was going through my head at the time. Everybody who works ninety hours a week wants to be a farmer in their free time, right? No? Just me, then? Great. But as I mentioned before, it had always been a dream of mine to live on a farm, so this was my chance and I went for it. I got my horse, a mini-donkey, fainting goats, and a real pair of overalls. I was doing this thing!

So, in the few hours I wasn't at my real job, I was just trying to survive on the farm. I remember in the winter, I had to put on my muck boots and trek down to the barn in the pitch-black dark at four in the morning and use a shovel to break up the ice in the trough for the horses to be able to drink water. I remember when the pipes burst from freezing, and I remember when the heat went out one night. I had to go out to this rickety old shed and try to figure out how to relight the pilot light on a gigantic propane tank and (hopefully) not blow myself up in the process. The farm life didn't turn out to be all butterflies and Bambi like I had imagined.

It also probably doesn't come as a huge shock that I wasn't dating anyone during this time. It turns out that most guys in their midtwenties are not interested in a girl who spends her weekends bushhogging the fields and shoveling manure. Who knew?

But something happened on my birthday that first summer that I'll never forget. You can probably tell that I'm a people person, and I love any reason to celebrate. I love all birthdays, especially my own birthday. As my birthday was approaching, I was eagerly anticipating how I would celebrate. But that year, no one reached out to me to make plans. When I made a few calls, no one was available to hang out. So that year, as I celebrated my birthday by having brunch with my boss from the YMCA, I had a rude wake-up call. I didn't have any friends. Of course, this would be sad for anyone, but for someone who thrives on being around people, this was a bad sign.

I didn't have any friends, I wasn't dating (and had no prospects), and I didn't even have an inch of margin in my life for anything else that I cared about. What I realized that summer was that my life was way out of balance.

That was then. Today my life looks a lot different. What is incredible to me looking back is that in a season when everything was overwhelming and out of balance, I was single, without children, and without even a fraction of the demands that I have on me currently.

Today, I am married with two young children. I have a job that involves heavy travel year-round. I lead a small group at my church, and I regularly spend time with my friends. I work out and do things I love, like take vacations and run marathons. I'm building a national brand and, of course, as I sit here, I am writing a book! I am doing more now than I have ever done in my life and yet, amazingly, I have never felt more balanced. I don't feel overwhelmed, and I love my life more than I ever have before.

There's one major difference between my life back then and my life now that led to me feeling "out of balance" then and "in balance" now. It's not the stage of life or how many things I have going on. It's not how much I work, and it's not how many responsibilities I have in either situation.

Everything about the balance in my life came down to what I spent my time on. And the same is true for you. When we say we need more balance in our lives, what we're really saying is that we want to change how we manage our time. That's why, in this chapter, I want to teach you what I've learned from personal experience and coaching others about creating balance. I want to help you unapologetically pursue your dreams and build your business while still having a life.

UNDERSTANDING LIFE BALANCE

The phrase "life balance" has gotten a lot of attention over the last several years. It seems that every generation feels more overworked, overwhelmed, overstressed than the previous one. This doesn't make sense when you consider that so many breakthroughs in technology were supposed to make our lives better. But it turns out, all that stuff just gives us even more to worry about. We all want balance in our lives but we have no idea what that even means, much less how to achieve it. If we want to truly take control of our lives, we need to figure out what life balance is—and what it's not.

What It's Not

I've been speaking on life balance for years, and I can tell you from experience that it's not what many people think it is. First of all, it's not about a picture-perfect life. It's not about creating a life that looks like your sister's, coworker's, neighbor's, or friend's lives. It's not about things being easy and clear-cut. Creating your own version of life balance doesn't mean that you won't have hard days or bad days or that you won't sometimes get tired, discouraged, and burned-out. There's no version of life balance that promises that because all of those things are just a part of life. Life balance is messy because life is messy.

Life balance is also not about an even split between "work" and "home." And when you work from home, you know this better than anyone. Balance makes us think of a scale that needs to be evenly weighted on both sides, but that's not realistic. A man came up to me after one of my speaking events and said, "Are you saying I need to spend 50 percent of my time at home and 50 percent of my time at work?"

No! That's not realistic, or even desirable, for many people. It's not about an even 50/50 split; it's about being 100 percent present wherever you are. We'll talk about what that means and how to accomplish it.

Finally, life balance is not about equality. People think that life balance must mean that you spend the exact same amount of time on every area of your life every day. That doesn't just sound unrealistic; it doesn't sound fun either. There will be seasons in your life when things are more heavily weighted in one area than in others, and that's okay. Life balance isn't about doing everything in your life for an equal amount of time. It's about doing the right things at the right time.

The goal is to create your own version of balance. It's about doing more of what you love and less of what you don't, while creating a life you're proud of in the process.

What Gets in the Way of Balance

When I lived on the farm, I didn't mean for my life to get out of balance. I didn't intentionally spend all of my time on only two things I cared about: work and my side business. I didn't intend to neglect every other aspect of my life that was also important to me. But that's what happened anyway. A few things can get in the way of us feeling a sense of balance in our lives. Let's look at what those are.

We Try to Keep Up

In business, we usually feel like we are trying to catch a tidal wave in a teacup, and our efforts are never enough. The work is never done. We are never finished. We are never "off." When I was working at the YMCA and on the farm, I always had this thought and maybe you've had it too. I thought, *If only* _____, *then* _____. If only I could get caught up on my emails . . . If only I could get through this week . . . If only I could fix this problem . . . then. Then I will hang out with my friends, read a good book, take a bubble bath, buy a new outfit, take a vacation, work out. Then I will . . . next week, next month . . . then.

The problem with this way of thinking is that the finish line always moves, doesn't it? You get there and it's something else. You fix one problem and a new one pops up. You get caught up on orders and twenty more hit your inbox. The truth is that if you're waiting until you have some time left over before you start spending time on what is important to you, it's never going to happen. Something else will always be more deserving of your time if you don't intentionally put your values and what you care about at the top of your priority list. When we live our lives with an "If only . . . then . . ." mind-set while trying to keep up with the never-ending demands around us, we find that "then" never comes.

We Try to Be Perfect

In addition to trying to keep up, we don't feel that sense of balance because we are trying to be perfect. Even if you're a confident person, the pressure to be perfect is everywhere. Every day, we are sucked into comparisons on social media as we scroll through what my friend Rachel Cruze calls everyone's "highlight reel." We've got Pinterest showing us everything we don't have. Not to mention the world full of mommy-wars, judgment, and shaming in our neighborhoods, schools, churches, and communities. The whole thing is exasperating and exhausting. We are tempted to believe that everyone else has it together and has it figured out. Everyone else feels balance in their lives while we want to pull our hair out. But the truth is that no one has it figured out. Perfect is an illusion. And as long as we chase this lie of perfectionism, we're going to be exhausted trying to achieve something that doesn't even exist. It keeps us from feeling peace and pride in our own messy, imperfect lives.

Perfectionism is a self-imposed prison, and we hold the key.

We Try to Be the Hero

I don't know about you, but I love to be the hero. I love saving the day and being needed. So when my family needs my help, I feel important. When my team needs my input, I feel valued. If I am honest with you, being needed makes me feel good about me! But this has gotten me into some trouble in my life because my decision-making paradigm used to be this:

Step 1: Do they need me?
Step 2: Can I do it?

That's it! I never asked myself, *Is this a good idea? Is this in line with my goals? How will this affect my family? Does this compete with a higher priority? Do I want to do it?* I just asked myself, *Do they need me?* (and the answer was always yes) and,

Can I cram or crowbar this into my schedule somehow? This has sucked me into more jobs and roles and responsibilities than I can even count. I have been president of clubs I didn't care about. I've gone to events I didn't want to go to. And I've taken on projects that someone else could have and probably should have done.

One time I even got sucked into being a volunteer puppet for a kids' ministry at church. I don't have a particular calling to be a puppeteer. To add insult to injury, that puppet was a rat! So there I am on Sunday mornings making rat voices behind a box thinking, *How did I get here?* But that's where we land when we try to be everyone else's hero—in places we don't want to be, doing things we don't want to do. And we end up missing our own lives.

I know you want to be helpful. I do too. But if we are honest—and I mean really honest—our need to be helpful is often more about us than it is about the other person. My pastor said something about this that cut straight to my heart: "There's a difference between doing something to be loving and doing it to be loved." Isn't that so true? When we stop trying to be the hero to everyone else, we can finally have the confidence to say no and create balance in our own lives.

What Happens as a Result

When we try to keep up, be perfect, and be the hero, we end up focusing our time in one area when what we actually care about is somewhere else. We say things like, "I like to work out, but my schedule is so full that I never get to." Or, "I love playing with my kids, but I am so tired by the time I get home that I have no energy." Or, "I value spending time alone with my husband, but we never seem to get our schedules to line up."

When you aren't able to spend time on things you care about, you are stressed, exhausted, and frustrated because you feel the inconsistency in your life between what you care about and what you're actually doing. Stress and anxiety are caused when there's a disconnect between your values and your behavior.

I experienced this myself early in my first pregnancy with my son, Carter. I was tired. First-trimester tired. Like having mono and the flu while running five marathons on no sleep. That's what it felt like. I was exhausted and couldn't do anything!

That hit me hard, because I'm generally a pretty active person. So when I was on the couch in the fetal position for weeks and weeks on end, it wasn't just a shock to my schedule, it was a shock to my whole sense of identity.

One day, I was at home in my usual spot on the couch with a blanket pulled over me, sipping on some ginger ale. I was having a pity party and feeling real sorry for myself when my husband came home. He commented on how beautiful the weather was outside—perfect temperature, perfect breeze, perfect sun—and he decided to go on out for a run. Well, isn't that nice?

He came downstairs wearing his dry wick shirt and bright running shoes. The sun was beaming in through our living room windows. It was a perfect day for a run. So he bebopped by me with a little extra pep in his step and grabbed his water bottle and headphones. He just looked sooooooo happy. And that's when I felt it happening. I felt the crazy creeping up inside of me. Now you probably know that there's crazy, and then there's pregnancy-crazy—and that's a whole other level. As I lay there, I felt both rage and tears boiling up inside of me, and I couldn't stop it. It was like a sneeze—if I tried to stop it, things would only have gotten uglier. I burst into tears on the couch, and of course, my husband was in the kitchen, totally oblivious to what was happening.

He slowly turned around and cautiously tiptoed toward me. He said nervously, in a half-whisper, "What's wrong, babe?" He was terrified of the answer, but he knew he had to ask. That's when the dam burst. I started crelling at him—crying and yelling at the same time. There I was, bawling my eyes out and too weak to get off the couch but still magically energetic enough to shout at the top of my lungs, "Well it would be nice to go for a run, wouldn't it, Matt! It would be sooooo nice to go for a run! You just get out there and live your life, Matt! Just LIVE YOUR LIFE!"

Yes, I am a real delight as a wife. He slowly backed out of the room and started to untie his shoes and he said, "You know, suddenly I'm not in the mood for a run today. I don't think I'll go for a run actually." My poor husband.

But what I was feeling in that moment and what I said later when I was a little less crazy was that I was jealous. I was jealous that he could do something that was important to him and I couldn't. I wasn't mad at him and he hadn't done anything wrong. But you know what? It doesn't change how frustrating it is when you can't spend time on things that are important to you.

Because your values, the things that are important to you, aren't just things. They are a part of you. When you give up what you care about, whether that's working out or spending time with friends or a hobby you enjoy or just having a moment alone, you aren't just giving up the thing. You are giving up a part of yourself.

LIVING YOUR VALUES

I've traveled all over the country speaking on life balance, and I've read a lot of books and articles that show you how to be more efficient and manage your schedule better, and those are great tools. But life balance is actually very simple. Life balance is living from your values. It's creating a life that reflects what's actually important to you.

Living from your values doesn't happen by accident. You have to align your time and schedule with your most important priorities on purpose or, as I said, it will never happen. There are three simple steps to creating your version of life balance: you need to figure out what matters to you, stop doing what doesn't matter, and then protect what does. Let's talk about how to do that.

Figure Out What Matters to You

If you want to create balance in your life, the first thing you need to know is what makes you feel in balance. Since life balance comes from living from your values, you need to know what your values are. And because every person's values are different, every person's version of life balance will be different. So, what things do you care about? What do you enjoy? What breathes life into you? What is important to you?

Your values can be as general as "alone time" or as specific as "Sunday night dinners around the dinner table with every family member present eating a home-cooked meal." There are no right or wrong answers. The right answer is simply your answer. So what is important to you? One of your action items at the end of this chapter is to write out your top values. Here are some of mine, for example:

1. **Time with my family**

    Time with my husband and my boys is extremely important to me. In fact, it's the most important thing to me.

2. **Exercising**

    We've seen what can happen when I don't get to exercise. Things can get ugly! I make exercising a priority in my life.

3. **Being outside**

    I love being outdoors, so I spend time doing something outside any chance I get.

4. **Time with friends**

    I am happy to report that, since that sad birthday brunch years ago, I actually have friends now! I definitely make them a priority in my life.

5. **Being creative**

    Whether it's writing for my blog or redecorating a room in my house for the fifteenth time, I love being creative.

What are your values? Once you know what they are, you can start aligning your time and schedule with those things. When you do that, then you can be crazy busy but still feel a sense of balance. That's the reason I felt overwhelmed and exhausted all the time in my early twenties even though I had a lot less to manage than I do now. I'm busier now than I've ever been, yet I feel more balanced than ever.

Add Yourself to the List

Years ago, I saw a magazine ad that stuck with me. It had a picture of a beautiful girl admiring herself in the mirror. I think it was an ad for jeans, but that's not why I remember it. I remember the ad because of the caption over the image: "You don't flirt when he looks good. You flirt when you look good." Isn't that so true?

You don't want to go out on the town when everyone else is excited. You want to go when you are excited. You don't want to be in a bunch of pictures when everyone else looks good. You want to when you look good. You don't want to have fun, laugh, get into an adventure, tell stories, or make memories when everyone else is in a good mood. You want to when you are in a good mood. It all starts with you.

I was thinking the other day about all of my many responsibilities. Most are the same as yours, I'm sure—financial, family, work, and so on. Then I realized something that caught me off guard. I regularly neglect one of my most important responsibilities: me. I saw working, taking care of my boys, being a supportive wife, showing up for my friends, helping others—as important responsibilities. And like many people, I saw taking care of myself as a luxury I indulged in—if I had some extra time left over.

But we shouldn't view taking care of ourselves (like working out, spending time on a hobby, or having cute clothes that make us feel good) as luxuries saved for guiltless times of the year such as birthdays and holidays. We should instead view it for what it truly is: our responsibility.

Because here is the reality: It's your responsibility to make yourself feel good. It's your responsibility to make yourself happy, confident, and proud. It's your responsibility to make yourself a person that your family wants to be around, a woman that your husband wants to take on a date, a mom that your kids want to play with, and a friend that people want to hang out with. No one can do that for you. For instance, no matter how many times my husband tells me I look pretty, if I don't feel pretty, I don't act like it.

And when you use the martyr syndrome of putting everyone else first as an excuse to live your life grumpy, rushed, and running ragged, everyone loses. You know that feeling, don't you? I sure do. It's spending that extra twenty minutes before you leave the house vacuuming the floors instead of putting on makeup, which then leads to shying away from pictures later at dinner with friends. It's being impatient with your kids, unhappy with your spouse, and easily frustrated at work because you haven't had even two free minutes for yourself to unwind, read a good book, or just take a nap.

When you don't take care of you, you feel bad. And when you feel bad about you, you feel bad about everything else too. I'm not saying you need to ignore your other responsibilities, and I am certainly not saying you need to obsess over how you look. If you've heard me speak or read my writing for any length of time, you know that I'm not about that. But I am about you taking care of yourself and doing things that make you happy. It's not selfish; it's self-preservation. And it's not a luxury; it's your responsibility.

So let's take our responsibilities seriously. Not just the responsibilities we have to others, but the responsibility we have to ourselves, as well. After all, we can't offer something we don't have, and we can't lead others where we haven't been. I love how Meg Meeker describes this. She says, "The most powerful way to teach a daughter how to enjoy life is to let her see her mother do the same." That is true in every area of our lives.

As you write down your values and plan your priorities, make sure you put yourself on the list. Make it a priority in your life to make yourself the best possible version of you. That might mean spending an extra fifteen minutes putting on makeup, going for a run, getting a pedicure, or buying a new outfit. Take time to do whatever makes you feel good, whatever makes you happy, whatever makes you want to flirt (figuratively speaking, of course).

Stop Doing What Doesn't Matter

A lot of the stress and feelings of being overwhelmed in our lives come not from doing too many things, but from doing the wrong things. We say yes when we mean no, and we commit to things that we end up resenting and regretting later. We stare at our phones and miss what's going on right in front of us. We do things out of guilt or obligation, then get mad about it. We end up grumpy and disappointed about how we are spending our lives. There are a lot of things that take up our time that aren't important and don't actually matter to us. And unfortunately, they are taking away precious time from things that we really do care about.

Let's be real here: we control what we spend our time on and what we don't. And we have the ability and responsibility to cut everything out of our lives that doesn't matter to us. So if we want to create more balance, we've got to intentionally take control of what we spend our time on.

For example, everywhere I go I see foreheads illuminated by screens. Did you know the average American checks their phone one hundred and fifty times a day?[89] Nonstop screen time is one of the biggest distractions from the important moments around us. In the grand scheme of things, what you're seeing on your screen doesn't really matter. If we don't figure out how to put our stupid phones down, we are going to know everything about everyone else's lives but totally miss out on the amazing people and experiences right in front of us. I struggle with this daily, just like you. That's why I've started asking myself one key question whenever I feel the urge to pick up my phone: Is it more important that I know what the outside world is doing right now, or is it more important that I experience what I am doing right now?

Posting photos and updating statuses isn't a bad thing, but sometimes I also find myself missing everyday moments because I'm so busy trying to document them. It's not just me, either. If you go to a concert, you'll see thousands of people who paid good money to see a live show, but they're watching it through their tiny phone screen. That's crazy!

But we don't just capture it. After we capture it, we have to write a clever caption. Then we have to post it. And the moment we upload that Instagram picture or Facebook post, we push over the first domino in a series. The next domino is a notification that our old high school friend Amber likes our post. How is Amber? I haven't thought of her in years. I heard she moved to California . . .

Then there's another notification. It's John. His comments are always so clever and witty! It'll just take a second to respond. What started as a moment with family or friends turned into a photo, then a post, then a notification—and the dominoes keep falling. And we get halfway through the concert or dinner only to realize the entire first half was spent staring at a screen and missing out on the moment that we're in.

A similar question works in these situations as well. Is it more important that the outside world knows what I am doing right now, or is it more important that I experience it myself? When I'm tempted to pick up my phone, it gives me some perspective. With a little less phone time and a little more perspective, we can all be more present for the most important people, moments, and memories happening right in front of us.

Think about what you might need to cut out. Do you need to put your phone down more often and simply look up? Do you need to replace TV time with going for a walk with your family or having some time alone? Do you need to quit a volunteer commitment that you've been doing for years but that your heart isn't really in anymore? Do you need to say no more often to the endless requests people have of you? Regardless of how you create margin in your life, it's up to you to stop doing things that don't matter to you to make time for more things that do. That way, you can do more of what you love, less of what you don't, and create your own version of balance.

Protect What Matters

If you don't decide what's important to you and protect it, everyone else will decide for you. The whole world will push you around if you let them. In order to create balance in your life, you have to say no to things that come up that compete with your most important priorities. You may find this hard to believe, but the word *no* is not a cussword. In fact, the most successful people in life and business attribute their success to their ability to say no and say it often. I love how Warren Buffet puts it: "The difference between successful people and very successful people is that very successful people say no to almost everything."

And "no" is a complete sentence. You don't need a reason or excuse. You don't have to qualify it, apologize for it, justify it, or explain it. Not only do you have the right to say no, you have the responsibility to say no. If someone has the nerve to ask you for something, you need to have the nerve to say no if it isn't a fit for you. And remember, an honest no is always better than a dishonest yes.

Here's the best part: you can say it without ever saying the word! My husband does this to me all the time when I've got a new brilliant idea to redecorate another section of our house. It's similar to the criticism sandwich. You start with an affirmation, politely decline, and then end with an affirmation. It looks something like this. "What an interesting idea! I don't think we need to take on any more projects right now but that is very creative." He never said the word, but the answer is still the same: "No!" This is such a difficult skill for most people that I actually have a free download on BusinessBoutique.com to help you with it. It's called "25 Ways to Protect Your Time" and it's a script of twenty-five ways to say no without ever saying the word. It will help you develop this often-neglected skill.

Turning things down is hard, but it gets easier the more you do it. Being able to say no is a muscle. If you never use it, then when you try to, it feels difficult and awkward. But the more you use that muscle, the stronger it becomes and saying the word becomes easier. Eventually, once you get the hang of it, it actually feels good. You feel more powerful—like you actually have a say in your own life. Imagine that!

Besides, life balance isn't really about saying no, anyway. It's about giving an enthusiastic yes to what is most important to you. But you have to be the one to do it. You have be the one willing to draw the line in the sand, turn your phone off, and shut it all down. Because I promise you this, if you don't protect what matters to you, no one else will.

When you figure out what matters to you and make those things a priority, when you cut everything that does not matter to you out of your life to make more room for things that do, and when you protect those things that matter the most, then you will finally feel that sense of balance. It still won't be perfect, and it may not look like anyone else around you, but that's okay. Your version of balance can and should be exactly what you want it to be. Because at the end of the day, the only one living your life is you.

REMEMBER WHAT'S IMPORTANT

My husband and I welcomed our first baby boy, Carter, into the world on January 31, 2015. As you can imagine, we were filled with a flood of emotions: excitement and anxiety, gratitude and uncertainty, relief and fear. But there is one stressful emotion that I started experiencing the day my first child was born, and unfortunately, I believe I'll battle it the rest of my life—guilt.

Dealing with Guilt

You know that feeling, don't you? I'd been a mom all of five minutes and I already knew it all too well. It's that feeling in the back of your mind that you've done something wrong, you're not doing enough, and you could have done it better. It's the feeling that all of the thousands of choices you have to make that affect these little lives that God has entrusted you with are probably wrong. It's feeling that everyone else has this life balance thing figured out and you don't.

I don't think anyone is immune to it, and I don't think you ever fully graduate out of it. I'll be honest: Most days, I don't even feel like a mom. I feel like a poser.

I feel like maybe I am the babysitter, and I just keep waiting for the real mom to swoop in and take over with confidence and all of the right answers.

Many things make that guilt flare up, but the one that seems to do it the most for moms is around how or where we work. And the mom guilt gets you regardless of the path you choose. If you work outside the home, you feel guilty for not staying with your kids. If you stay home with your kids, you feel guilty for not working outside the home.

I felt God remind me of something recently that has helped me shake off the mom guilt a little bit. When I was feeling discouraged about leaving my son at daycare one day, I felt God say, *Remember that what you're doing is important.* I felt immediate relief as I rested in that.

It's true. What I am doing is important. The work that I do, the messages I share, and the lives I get to impact are important. It would be really difficult to leave my sons for something I didn't believe in. But I practice in my daily life what I teach others: I only spend my time on things that are important to me. So when I focus on the importance of what I am doing, I keep the mom guilt from distracting me from living out the life I've been called to.

But focusing on the importance of what you do goes the other way too. When I don't answer emails at night because I am being present with my family, leave the office on time to go for a run, or take time off to go on vacation and rest, I choose not to feel guilty. When everyone in our culture is working seventy to eighty hours a week, I remind myself again: What I am doing is important. My family, my exercise, my rest, my hobbies, my values—those things are important.

I love how my friend Tony explains it. He says, "I'm always driving to somewhere I love. When I'm driving to work, I'm driving to a place that I love. When I'm driving home, I am driving to a place that I love." It's the difference between looking through the front windshield to see where you're going instead of looking in the rearview mirror to see what you're momentarily leaving behind.

That's how I'm able to be fully present and guilt-free at work, and again fully present and guilt-free at home. Don't look at what you're leaving behind. Focus on the importance of what you're going to. Wherever you are, be there. The next time you've got guilt nagging at you no matter what choice you make, remind yourself that what you're doing is important.

CREATING YOUR VERSION OF BALANCE

Creating a sense of balance in our lives is messy and imperfect. And unfortunately, as we each navigate this messy and imperfect journey of building our businesses, raising our families, and living our lives, it's easy to let the decisions we face as women—intimate, vulnerable, and personal decisions—become what define and divide us.

I see this all of the time, and it's something we've all been wounded by at one time or another. It's not always obvious, of course. It's the scowl on another woman's face when she hears you are taking time off from work for a weeklong vacation. It's the tone in another woman's voice when she asks where your baby's hat is "in this weather." Yet it's something that every one of us is guilty of. It's the faces we make and the tones we take. It's the eye rolls and the passive-aggressive comments. It's the disapproval and judgment that oozes out of every pore of our bodies. And really, why do we care?

Why do we care if another mother chooses natural childbirth or modern medicine? Why do we feel so compelled to turn up our noses at how she spends her money or what she wears? Why are we so appalled when a woman works full time just weeks after giving birth or stays home full time when her children are in school all day? Why is another woman's work life and personal life and family's life and child's life any of our business? But most of all, why are we so consumed with the things that divide us instead of the ties that bind us?

Often, the reason we're so quick to judge other women with decisions different from our own is that we aren't completely comfortable with our own choices. The woman with a full-time office job looks down on the stay-at-home mom while battling her own guilt about not attending every class party and field trip. The stay-at-home mom judges the woman working long hours while at the same time struggling with her own sense of identity and purpose. We're all starving for grace, and at the same time, withholding that same grace from each other. And my friend, it's doing damage.

It's damaging our relationships, and it's destroying our trust. It's fueling the fire of perfectionism and planting seeds of self-doubt. It's tearing down and dividing us when we should be building each other up and coming together. And really, at our core, all the women I've ever met want the same things. We want a purpose that we can be proud of. We want a family that is healthy and happy. We want a body that we can feel comfortable in. We want a life that we love. These are the ties that bind us together as women.

How different would our lives be—and how different would our relationships be—if we focused on that instead? How different would our conversations be if we focused on how all the women around us are doing exactly what we are, the very best they can? Her methods may be her way and not my way, but that's okay, because it's her life. We don't need more standards to meet; we need support. We don't need more advice; we need affirmation. We don't need more guidance; we need grace.

I love how Ann Voskamp captures this picture when she says:

I won't judge you for dishes in your sink and shoes over your floor and laundry on your couch. I won't judge you for choosing not to spend your one life weeding the garden or washing the windows or working on organizing the pantry. I won't judge you for the size of your waist, the flatness, bigness, cut or color of your hair, the hipness or the matronliness of your clothes, and I won't judge whether you work at a stove, a screen, a store, a steering wheel, a sink or a stage. I won't judge you for where you are on your road, won't belittle your offering, your creativity, your battle, your work.[90]

Amen to that.

Let's save our well-meaning advice, suggestions, and opinions and instead focus on loving the woman in front of us. Let's deliberately dissolve the judgment between us and realize that each of us is on a uniquely and perfectly messy journey of our own. When we focus on that, we can sit next to a woman with a life entirely different from our own and appreciate everything she is and everything she offers without feeling envious or superior. When we stop focusing on what divides us, we can champion each other in a way that allows the women in our lives to feel supported and accepted exactly as they are, and most importantly, we can feel the freedom to accept ourselves and our own choices as well. We can unapologetically create our own version of balance, and we can finally rest in the paradox of finding comfort in our own uncomfortable choices.

chapter 18 action items
LET'S APPLY WHAT YOU'VE LEARNED!

Step 1: Figure Out What Matters to You
Write out your values below.

1.

2.

3.

4.

5.

Step 2: Stop Doing What Doesn't Matter
What are some commitments, responsibilities, or areas of your life that you need to spend less time on in order to make time for your most important priorities?

1.

2.

3.

4.

5.

Step 3: Protect What Matters

Let's practice flexing your "no" muscle. Write out responses to the following theoretical requests. Decline the request in a way that feels authentic to you.

Coworker: Hey! Can you help me with a project I'm late on?

Friend: Can you come over with your SUV and help me move on Saturday?

Mother-in-law: We're so excited for Christmas this year! Will you all be coming to spend time with us?

Neighbor: We need more volunteers Wednesday night for the neighborhood fall festival. Can you help out?

Spouse: My favorite documentary on Led Zeppelin is playing at a theater across town. Do you want to go with me?

chapter 19

YOU'VE GOT THIS!

Congratulations! By this point, if you've done the action steps in each chapter, you have a customized plan for your business to give you what you need to make your dream a reality. Remember, you can download a full pdf of the action items at www.businessboutique.com. You may have breezed through some chapters and topics while others may have been a grind. Don't worry, it was no different for me in writing it. Business is like that. Some parts will be a blast and others will be a challenge. And let's be honest, we've covered a lot. We've gone through four tiers, twenty-four elements, and covered important topics such as selling, business technicalities, money management, and life balance. But you've made it this far so don't stop now.

You have the tools and now you just need to put them to work. You don't have to do it all at once and you shouldn't. Just start at the beginning, take a deep breath, and take it one step at a time. As you work your plan, a little at a time, your plan will begin to work for you. And even though you have everything you need to win (I hope you know that by now), it still won't be easy or perfect and that's okay. I love how Dave Ramsey says, "Success isn't a gleaming, shiny mountain. It's a pile of mistakes that you're standing on instead of under." Even if you work your plan, you'll still make mistakes and you'll still struggle along the way. My mom did,

I do, and every other person out there making a difference does as well. But the struggle isn't going to break you. In fact, it may be the very thing that makes you.

Don't Be Sorry for the Struggle

From the time I was a young child, my friends and family warned my mom that her parenting would ruin me. They said I would grow up selfish—that I would expect everything handed to me on a silver platter. It's true that I didn't suffer many consequences when I misbehaved. They were right that my mom rarely told me no when I wanted a new toy or outfit.

That's because my mom, like many single mothers, often operated out of a sense of guilt that my dad wasn't in the picture for me. This led to more freedom and fewer consequences. But all of those well-meaning family members and friends didn't consider this: I watched my mother struggle every day, and I was in the struggle with her.

I was with her at 2:00 a.m. when she arrived at her small cake shop to start the day's baking. I was with her when we arrived at the shop one day to find it had been broken into the night before. I was by her side when the pipes froze in the winter, when we got locked out of the house, and when we had a flat tire on the side of the road. I was with her in every challenge we faced—and overcame—together.

Many parents try to insulate their kids from any type of struggle, and if their kids happen to see it, they feel guilty. Maybe it's because we want to protect our children, or maybe it's because we live in a world where the standard is to be Pinterest-perfect. This pressure to keep our kids from any type of struggle, imperfection, or inconvenience is all around us. But I can tell you from experience—it's the struggle that made me.

I watched my mom struggle and overcome. I watched her work hard, and I saw her hard work pay off. I watched her hope when situations seemed hopeless. I watched her persevere with an absurd level of persistence. I watched her do the right thing, even when it cost her. I watched the way she treated every single person with kindness. I watched how she went above and beyond for her customers. I watched how she always paused and talked to homeless people—even in the middle of the night when we were downtown unloading bags of powdered sugar and flour. I watched her and I was with her. She worked harder than anyone I'd ever seen, gave generously of her time and money, and loved every person without limits.

And that's what I learned growing up. I learned values, integrity, and character. I developed resilience, persistence, and self-esteem. Having a mother who worked hard didn't harm me; it helped me. I am who I am today because of everything my mom and I overcame together. So what if she gave in every time I wanted a new coloring book at the grocery store checkout line? Watching her—in the celebrations and in the struggles—is what created the best parts of me. So don't be sorry for the struggle. Don't be sorry for stepping into your gifts. Don't be sorry when it's messy and imperfect and sometimes altogether crazy. Don't be sorry for pursuing your passion and doing what you love. I can tell you from the experience of watching my mother chase her dream, who you are will always be more than enough.

You Are Called to Go and Win

I love cheering women on to chase their dreams. That's what my mom did, that's what I am doing, and that's what I've gotten to watch thousands of other women across the country do as well. But this idea of taking what we have been given—talents, ideas, money, or resources—and growing them isn't a new idea. In fact, one of the best illustrations of this concept dates all the way back to the first century. You may have heard it before, but when you think of it in the context of your own life and business, it takes on a new significance.

Once there was a wealthy man who was about to head out on a long journey. Before he left, he decided to entrust his wealth to his servants, who were instructed to manage it while he was away. He gave a certain sum of money to three different servants. In today's currency, let's say he gave one servant a few million dollars. To another, he gave a few hundred thousand. And to the third, he gave tens of thousands. And then he left on his journey.

The servant who received millions invested the money and used it for trade, and he doubled his money. The servant who received hundreds of thousands did the same thing. But the third servant, the one who had the least money, freaked out. He couldn't take the pressure, he was scared to fail, and he didn't even try to do anything with his money. So, he simply buried it in the ground and didn't increase it at all.

After a long time, the wealthy man came back to settle his accounts. Each of the servants presented him with the money they were entrusted to manage. The servant with millions showed the man how he doubled it, and the man responded, "Well done! You've been faithful with a few things, so I will put you in charge of many things! Let's celebrate!" The servant who received hundreds of thousands showed the man how he also doubled his money, and the man responded the same way. "Way to go! You've been faithful with what I've given you so I will give you more! Let's celebrate!"

Then there was the servant who buried the money he was given. As he gave the original sum of money back, he hung his head and said, "Master, I know you have high standards and hate careless ways, that you demand the best and make no allowances for error. I was afraid I might disappoint you, so I found a good hiding place and secured your money. Here it is, safe and sound down to the last cent."

While he thought he was playing it safe to avoid disappointing his master, the servant actually did the exact opposite. The man was furious with him. He said, "That's a terrible way to live! If you knew I was after the best, why did you do less than the least?"[91] Look at what was lost because he was afraid to try.

I don't want that to be you. When we're born, we are created with unique gifts and they have a purpose. Our skills, passions, interests, and abilities are all resources to be managed and grown over time. I don't want to be the servant who buried his treasure in the backyard because he was too scared to step out and try something new. I want to be a servant who doubles or triples or quadruples everything that I can! And I want you to as well.

You've got these gifts and passions for a reason, and I want you to use them. What you're good at, what you're interested in, what you're passionate about are all gifts that have been put into your hands, but it's up to you to decide what you're going to do with them.

You Can Do This

Making your way on this journey of chasing your dream, pursuing your passion, and building your business can be overwhelming. You will have times when making the right decision seems impossible. Times when you can't help but feel pulled in multiple competing directions at the same time. Times when your daughter wants you to braid her hair and you're right in the middle of taking care of a customer. Times when you are trying to finish a project and you realize you forgot about the dinner in the oven that's now burnt to a crisp. (That seriously happened to me just last night!) Some days just taking a shower will seem like too big of a task. I know because I've been there, too, and I still have those days. I know the guilt of dropping my kids off at daycare while I do my work. The fear of putting something out there that people may not need or want. The frustration of boring business stuff and paperwork and taxes. And in those moments, you will want to throw your hands up and surrender because you just can't do it all. I get it.

But I also want you to know that, while you can't do everything, you can do this. You can build your business and not be consumed by it. You can take care of yourself without being selfish. And you can be the woman you were created to be instead of everyone else's version of what you should be. It may not feel like it at times, but I promise you, you can do this.

You may have times when you feel scared. You might feel intimidated or overwhelmed.

But none of that stopped my mom.

It's not going to stop me.

And, my friend, when you dig in your heels, put the things we've talked about into practice, and take on this adventure with everything you've got, I promise . . . it won't stop you, either.

I know you've got this, and I'm cheering you on every step of the way.

So get out there and start making money doing what you love!

notes

Introduction

1. Kate Taylor, "The Difference Between a Solopreneur and a Side-Gigger (Infographic)," *Entrepreneur*, November 9, 2014, https://www.entrepreneur.com/article/239522.
2. Ibid.
3. Jeremiah 29:11, NIV.

Chapter One

4. Amanda Macias, "15 Pieces of Advice from Maya Angelou," *Business Insider*, May 28, 2014, http://www.businessinsider.com/maya-angelou-quotes-2014-5.
5. Author paraphrase of Esther 4:14.

Chapter Two

6. Everything we teach is about reducing your risk and increasing your power. Can you do what that guy suggested? Yes. But you will have significantly greater risk and less power. Let's look at two scenarios:

   Scenario #1: You take out a three-year loan for $18,000 with 0% interest. You know you can make the monthly payments of $500 (which is right around the actual average car payment in North America today) so you think this is a great deal.

   Scenario #2: You save that same amount for three years and buy the $18,000 car in cash.

   Here's where the risk/power comes into play. Let's say six months in, you lose your job. Or have a medical emergency. Or have a family member out of state who is diagnosed with cancer and you want to move to be with them. In Scenario #2, you can redirect that money in savings wherever you want. Your priorities have changed, and you have complete power and control to put that money toward taking time off, medical bills, or anything you want. You have no risk and all of the power.

In Scenario #1, the bank doesn't care about your job or family or health. You will owe them that car payment no matter how much your priorities have changed. You have zero power and all of the risk. The bills and payments due will not stop pouring in.

Can you technically invest over paying off debt because of the "time value of money?" Yes. But think about the other cost of your power and control. I'd rather be in complete control than "slave to the lender" any day. *"The borrower is slave to the lender."* Proverbs 22:7

7. Beth Jones, "New Levels, New Devils," iDisciple, https://www.idisciple.org/post/new -levels-new-devils.
8. Kirsten Weir, "Feel Like a Fraud?" American Psychological Association, http://www.apa .org/gradpsych/2013/11/fraud.aspx.
9. Margie Warrell, "Afraid of Being 'Found Out?' How to Overcome Imposter Syndrome," *Forbes*, April 3, 2014, http://www.forbes.com/sites/margiewarrell/2014/04/03/ impostor-syndrome/#22ac68dfeb9d.
10. Ibid.
11. Ibid.
12. Maya Angelou Quote, Goodreads, http://www.goodreads.com/quotes/220406-each -time-i-write-a-book-every-time-i-face.
13. Michael Jordan "Failure" Commercial, https://www.youtube.com/watch?v=JA7G7AV-LT8.
14. Taylor Swift, Twitter: @taylorswift13, Posted August 20, 2015, https://twitter.com/ taylorswift13/status/634535703616049152.
15. Zig Ziglar, *Staying Up, Up, Up in a Down, Down World: Daily Hope for the Daily Grind* (Nashville, TN: Thomas Nelson, 2000).
16. Jon Gordon, *The Carpenter: A Story About the Greatest Success Strategies of All* (Hoboken, NJ: Wiley, 2014).

Chapter Three

17. John C. Maxwell, *The 21 Irrefutable Laws of Leadership: Follow Them and People Will Follow You* (Nashville, TN: Thomas Nelson, 2007).
18. Craig Groeschel, Twitter: @craiggroeschel, Posted January 5, 2014, https://twitter.com /craiggroeschel/status/419883397763182594.

Chapter Four

19. *Fast Company*, "25 Top Women Business Builders," May 1, 2005, https://www .fastcompany.com/52566/25-top-women-business-builders.
20. Author interview with Megan Hardwick.
21. Viktor E. Frankl, *Man's Search for Meaning* (Boston: Beacon Press, 2006).
22. Author interview with Cordia Harrington.
23. Simon Sinek, "How Great Leaders Inspire Action," TEDxPuget Sound, Filmed September 2009, https://www.ted.com/talks/simon_sinek_how_great_leaders _inspire_action?language=en.

24. Ibid.
25. Ibid.

Chapter Five

26. Psalm 37:4, ESV.
27. Seth Godin, "On Owning It," October 30, 2013, http://sethgodin.typepad.com/seths _blog/2013/10/on-owning-it.html
28. Michael Hyatt, "5 Reasons Why You Should Commit Your Goals to Writing," January 3, 2014, http://michaelhyatt.com/5-reasons-why-you-should-commit-your-goals-to-writing.html.
29. Proverbs 29:18, KJV.
30. "Mission Statements with Dan Miller," EntreLeadership Podcast, December 2011.

Chapter Six

31. Jordan E. Rosenfeld, "How Anticipation Can Be Beneficial," *Rewire Me*, December 24, 2015, http://www.rewireme.com/wellness/anticipation-can-be-beneficial/.
32. Brené Brown, *Daring Greatly* (New York: Avery, 2012).
33. Earl Nightingale, *The Strangest Secret* (Merchant Books, 2013). Emphasis added.

Chapter Seven

34. Tom Rath, *StrengthsFinder 2.0* (Gallup Press, 2007).
35. Austin Kleon, *Steal Like an Artist: 10 Things Nobody Told You About Being Creative* (New York: Workman Publishing, 2012).

Chapter Eight

36. Rabbi Daniel Lapin, *Thou Shall Prosper: Ten Commandments for Making Money* (Hoboken, NJ: Wiley, 2009).
37. Dessislava Yankova, "Jeremy Cowart Named Web's Most Influential Photographer," *The Tennessean*, July 10, 2014, http://www.tennessean.com/story/news/local/ hendersonville/2014/07/10/hhs-grad-named-webs-influential-photographer/12490437/.

Chapter Nine

38. Author interview with Melissa Hinnant.
39. Peter F. Drucker, *The Effective Executive: The Definitive Guide to Getting the Right Things Done* (New York: HarperBusiness, 2006).
40. "Benefits of Dressing Professionally When You Work or Study from Home," Ashford University, September 30, 2016, http://forwardthinking.ashford.edu /benefits-dressing-professionally-work-study-home/.

Chapter Ten

41. Hayley Peterson, "The Worst Starbucks Product Flops of All Time, *Business Insider*, November 11, 2013, http://www.businessinsider.com/failed-starbucks-products-2013-11?op=1.

42. Craig Smith, "By the Numbers: 40 Amazing Etsy Statistics (May 2016)," *DMR*, July 14, 2016, http://expandedramblings.com/index.php/etsy-statistics/.
43. Internet Users, *Internet Live Stats*, http://www.internetlivestats.com/internet-users/.
44. Author interview with Crystal Paine.
45. Ibid.
46. Ibid.
47. Author interview with Shane Gibson.
48. Jim Nantz, "My Shot: Jim Nantz," *Golf Digest*, "March 25, 2016, http://www.golfdigest.com/story/my-shot-jim-nantz.

Chapter Eleven

49. Austin Kleon, *Steal Like an Artist: 10 Things Nobody Told You About Being Creative* (New York: Workman Publishing, 2012).
50. Tony A. Gaskins, Jr., Twitter: @TonyGaskins, Posted on January 16, 2013, https://twitter.com/tonygaskins/status/291748201919295488.
51. Jesse David Fox, "The History of Tina Fey and Amy Poehler's Best Friendship," *Vulture*, December 15, 2015, http://www.vulture.com/2013/01/history-of-tina-and-amys-best-friendship.html.

Chapter Twelve

52. Bill Carmody, "Why 96 Percent of Businesses Fail Within 10 Years," *Inc.*, August 12, 2015, http://www.inc.com/bill-carmody/why-96-of-businesses-fail-within-10-years.html.
53. If you need help creating your family budget, check out my favorite budgeting tool, EveryDollar. You can find it in your phone's app store and online at www.everydollar.com.
54. Research conducted by Ramsey Solutions.
55. Simon Sinek, *Start with Why* (New York: Portfolio, 2009).
56. Ali Brown, http://alibrown.com.
57. Nicholas Confessore and Jason Horowitz, "Hillary Clinton's Paid Speeches to Wall Street Animate Her Opponents," *New York Times*, January 21, 2016, http://www.nytimes.com/2016/01/22/us/politics/in-race-defined-by-income-gap-hillary-clintons-wall-street-ties-incite-rivals.html.
58. Harry Beckwith, *Selling the Invisible* (New York: Grand Central Publishing, 2012).

Chapter Thirteen

59. "Estimated Taxes," IRS, Last updated: September 12, 2016, https://www.irs.gov/businesses/small-businesses-self-employed/estimated-taxes.
60. "What Kind of Records Should I Keep?," "IRS, Last updated: June 22, 2016, https://www.irs.gov/businesses/small-businesses-self-employed/what-kind-of-records-should-i-keep.
61. "Women-Owned Businesses: The Numbers Are In and They're Better than We Could Have Imagined!" National Women's Business Council, https://www.nwbc.gov/content/women-owned-businesses-numbers-are-and-theyre-better-we-could-have-imagined.

62. "Business Structures," IRS, Last updated: September 6, 2016, https://www.irs.gov /businesses/small-businesses-self-employed/business-structures.

63. "Business Entity Types," Incorporate.com, https://www.incorporate.com/business _structures.html.

64. "Business Structures," IRS, Last updated: September 6, 2016, https://www.irs.gov /businesses/small-businesses-self-employed/business-structures.

65. For help finding a great insurance pro in your area that I recommend, visit www .daveramsey.com/elp.

66. "Trademark, Patent, or Copyright?" United States Patent and Trademark Office, http://www.uspto.gov/trademarks-getting-started/trademark-basics/ trademark-patent-or-copyright.

Chapter Fourteen

67. Maeve McDermott, "Justin Timberlake and Chris Stapleton Stole the CMA Awards," *USA Today*, November 5, 2015, http://www.usatoday.com/story/life/entertainthis/2015/11/04/ justin-timberlake-chris-stapleton-cma-awards/75189476/.

68. Marissa R. Moss, "See Chris Stapleton and Justin Timberlake's Stunning CMA Awards Duet," *Rolling Stone*, November 4, 2015, http://www.rollingstone.com/music/news/ see-chris-stapleton-and-justin-timberlakes-stunning-cma-awards-duet-20151104.

69. Chris Willman, "Chris Stapleton Talks Justin Timberlake Friendship, His Star-Is-Born Performance, and What's Next," *Billboard*, November 8, 2015, http://www.billboard.com/articles/columns/country/6754068/ chris-stapleton-justin-timberlake-traveller-cma-performance.

Chapter Fifteen

70. Dan Antonelli, "5 Reasons Your Small Business Needs Content Marketing," *Entrepreneur*, November 24, 2015, https://www.entrepreneur.com/article/250163.

71. Mike Wood, "7 Content Marketing Tips for New Entrepreneurs," *Entrepreneur*, July 27, 2016, https://www.entrepreneur.com/article/279230.

72. TED, "Bryan Stevenson: We Need to Talk About an Injustice," *Vialogue*, March 5, 2012, https://vialogue.wordpress.com/2012/03/05/ted-bryan-stevenson-we-need-to-talk -about-an-injustice/.

73. Carmine Gallo, *Talk Like TED* (New York: St. Martin's Press, 2014).

74. Ibid.

75. Carmine Gallo, "The 5 Storytellers You'll Meet in Business," *Forbes*, March 18, 2016, http://www.forbes.com/sites/carminegallo/2016/03/18/the-5-storytellers -youll-meet-in-business/#49c848fe7b60.

76. Gary Vaynerchuk, *Jab, Jab, Jab, Right Hook* (New York: Harper Business, 2013).

77. Seth Godin, *Permission Marketing* (New York: Simon and Schuster, 1999).

78. You can build your email list with a variety of providers such as MailChimp or MyEmma. Many of them are surprisingly user-friendly and affordable.

79. Nora Aufreiter, Julien Boudet, and Vivien Weng, "Why Marketers Should Keep Sending You E-mails," McKinsey & Company, January 2014, http://www.mckinsey .com/business-functions/marketing-and-sales/our-insights/why-marketers-should -keep-sending-you-emails.

80. Author interview with Amy Porterfield.

Chapter Sixteen

81. "How to Close More Sales: The Law of 4 Interactions," *The Lighthouse Principles*, March 11, 2015, http://thelighthouseprinciples.com/category/sales/.

Chapter Seventeen

82. Elizabeth MacBride, "How a Texas Couple Started with $500 and Built a $1M Shark Tank Winner," *Forbes*, September 30, 2014, http://www.forbes.com/sites/elizabethmacbride /2014/09/30/how-a-texas-couple-started-with-500-and-built-a-1m-shark-tank-winner /#480b4dc86146.

83. Elizabeth MacBride, "How a Texas Couple Turned Down 'Shark Tank' Money and Still Took Their Babywear Firm to $4M Revenue," *Forbes*, August 30, 2015, http://www.forbes .com/sites/elizabethmacbride/2015/08/30/a-texas-couple-turned-down-shark-tank-money -and-took-their-babywear-company-to-3m-revenue/2/#3f2836052aa4.

84. Jay Goltz, "Top 10 Reasons Small Businesses Fail," New York Times, January 5, 2011, http://boss.blogs.nytimes.com/2011/01/05/top-10-reasons-small-businesses-fail/?_r=0.

85. Peter Carbonara, "Hire for Attitude; Train for Skill," *Fast Company*, August 31, 1996, http://www.fastcompany.com/26996/hire-attitude-train-skill.

86. Valentina Zarya, "Women-owned Businesses Are Trailing in Size and Revenue," *Fortune*, September 2, 2015, http://fortune.com/2015/09/02/women-business-size-revenue.

87. Natalie MacNeil, "Entrepreneurship Is the New Women's Movement," Forbes, June 8, 2012, http://www.forbes.com/sites/work-in-progress/2012/06/08/ entrepreneurship-is-the-new-womens-movement/#52c49bdb5339.

88. Author interview with Kelly Hancock.

Chapter Eighteen

89. Joanna Stern, "Cellphone Users Check Phones 150x/Day and Other Internet Fun Facts," ABC News, May 29, 2013, http://abcnews.go.com/blogs/technology/2013/05/ cellphone-users-check-phones-150xday-and-other-internet-fun-facts.

90. Ann Voskamp, "How Women Can Stop Judging Each Other: A Movement of Key Women," July 30, 2014, http://www.aholyexperience.com/2014/07 /how-women-can-stop-judging-each-other-a-movement-of-key-women.

Chapter Nineteen

91. Matthew 25:14–30, MSG.

PUT YOUR PLAN INTO ACTION

by joining the Business Boutique Academy

Get the videos, tools and resources you need to build your business and connect with women just like you in our online community!

Sign up today at
BusinessBoutique.com/Academy

DISCOVER HOW MUCH MONEY YOUR BUSINESS CAN MAKE

with the **FREE** Profit Potential app!

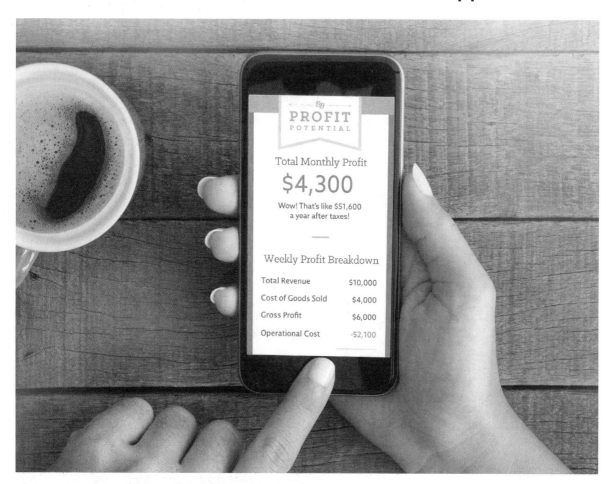

The Profit Potential app calculates the most important numbers in your business for you. Answer a few simple questions and adjust your numbers to see how your profit increases!

Try the Profit Potential app at
BusinessBoutique.com

The only person standing between you and the work you're capable of is you. In this inspiring book, Christy Wright doesn't only teach you what she knows, she inspires you to go faster, further, and with more heart than you thought possible.

—Seth Godin, author of *Linchpin*

Nothing is more fulfilling than making a living out of something you love. If you have an entrepreneurial dream that's been laying dormant in your heart, *Business Boutique* is the resource you need to give it new life!

—Lysa TerKeurst, *New York Times* bestselling author
and president of Proverbs 21 Ministries

Most marketing books tell you what to do, but they leave out the important details of how to implement the strategies they teach. Christy's step-by-step approach leaves readers feeling like she's there holding their hand as they build the kind of business they've always dreamed of.

—Amy Porterfield, online marketing trainer and strategist

This is an excellent recipe book for building a small business—one part practical advice, two parts encouragement, and a whole lot of love. If you're looking for a guide to help you get started as an entrepreneur, you've found it.

—Donald Miller, founder, StoryBrand

Business Boutique is inspiring, encouraging, and well-written. Most importantly, it helps every woman who dreams of owning her own business or making money by turning her passions into a business—a reality. Thank you, Christy!

—Meg Meeker, MD, bestselling author of
Strong Fathers, Strong Daughters

The best way to break through the glass ceiling is to build a business without one. Christy Wright shows women how the process works, all the way from dreaming to payroll. Her tier system is like Dave Ramsey's baby-steps system for business builders.

—Michael Hyatt, CEO, Michael Hyatt & Company;
New York Times bestselling author

When you're building a business and having to do everything yourself, the thing you need more than anything is a plan. You just need to know what to do—and what to do *next*. Whether you're just starting out or have been in the game for years, *Business Boutique* delivers a plan that can help you win.

—John C. Maxwell, author, speaker, and leadership expert

Christy Wright has the unique ability to give specific details of encouragement to help ignite the powerful spirit within us. God made each of us unique, with our own dreams and desires. His plan is that we LIVE our DREAMS. *Business Boutique: A Woman's Guide for Making Money Doing What She Loves* specifically addresses the steps necessary to turn your passions into income! The tough subjects about money, marketing and planning, and making the most of your resources are addressed like a friendly conversation! Woven in every word and every example is hope and sincere encouragement! You will be so inspired you will shout, "I got this!"

—Cordia Harrington, CEO, The Bakery Cos.

Christy's enthusiasm is contagious and it jumps off of these pages as she provides you with practical wisdom that will encourage you to move from being a dreamer to a doer! Christy provides the perfect step-by-step guide to turn your passions into profits.

—Stephanie Parker, owner, Sleeping Baby

As a father to four daughters, I couldn't be more excited about Christy Wright's book, *Business Boutique: A Women's Guide for Making Money Doing What She Loves.* Christy's writing is warm and accessible, practical and useful, challenging and inspiring. With an abundance of wisdom and experience, Christy gently guides the reader through a step-by-step, achievable process to turn a burning passion into a profitable and difference-making business.

—Craig Groeschel, pastor of Life.Church and author of
Divine Direction—7 Decisions That Will Change Your Life

Business Boutique has changed not only how I think about the business I run, but how I dream, plan, employ, and inspire. Christy Wright has painstakingly researched and listened to what women need to know and want to hear about running their own company, big or small, and has put that information together in an easy-to-read way. With a generous voice and heart, Christy's writing, instruction, and tips will make any woman feel capable and prepared for success.

—Annie F. Downs, bestselling author of *Looking
For Lovely* and *Let's All Be Brave*

I'm more convinced than ever that entrepreneurship holds the key to creating the life you truly desire. *Business Boutique* shows you how to build a profitable business that will give you the freedom to do exactly that.

—Andy Andrews, *New York Times* bestselling author
of *The Noticer* and *The Traveler's Gift*

I love Christy Wright and know that *Business Boutique* will empower you and draw out the greatness in you. She lives this message with passion and equips us all to do the same.

—Christine Caine, founder, Propel Women and A21

Business Boutique is a much-needed fire-starter for women who dream of giving life to their passions, pursuing their entrepreneurial callings, and living their best lives. Throughout its pages, Christy reminds us that we each possess unique strengths and incredible stories that, woven together, can provide livelihood, fulfill dreams, and impact the world in beautiful and specific ways. I highly recommend *Business Boutique* for women in any stage—whether you are a seasoned businesswoman or a gal with a desire to step into your calling. *Business Boutique* is a wonderful road map for putting your dreams into action.

—Emily Ley, author of *Grace, Not Perfection*
and creator of the Simplified Planner®

Wishing you could figure out how to turn your passion and gifts into a part-time or full-time income? In *Business Boutique*, Christy provides a practical and proven game plan to help you start a successful business from the ground up!

—Crystal Paine, *New York Times* bestselling author
and founder of MoneySavingMom.com

Smart and inspiring, *Business Boutique* is a must-read for every woman who dreams of turning her passion into profit. Christy Wright's advice is both savvy and approachable, making it an ideal nuts-and-bolts guide for women starting a business or growing an existing one.

—Susan Spencer, Editor-in-Chief *Woman's Day*

All women starting a business need to read this book! I've never seen so much practical information in one place, combined with the heartfelt inspiration Christy provides from having helped thousands of women step up to change their lives and go for their dreams. *Business Boutique* is a must-read.

—Ali Brown, entrepreneur mentor, Angel Investor,
CEO featured on ABC's *Secret Millionaire*

All entrepreneurs and would-be entrepreneurs face obstacles, but those who are women confront different and, in many cases, additional challenges. They have long needed a guide designed especially for them. With her enormous experience and the vast network of information upon which she draws, Christy Wright has finally produced the definitive road map for women in business. It makes no sense to go into business without this volume.

—Rabbi Daniel Lapin, author *Thou Shall Prosper* and TV host

If you want to do what you love but aren't sure where to start, then *Business Boutique* is the perfect guide for turning your dreams into reality. Christy Wright will not only help you get your new business up and running, but she'll also help you develop a plan for long-term success.

—Laura Vanderkam, author, *I Know How She Does It, 168 Hours,* and *What the Most Successful People Do Before Breakfast*

Christy Wright taps into years of wisdom with this page-turning primer for anyone considering entrepreneurship, while seeking to maintain what matters most—life balance. Read this book, and take notes. It's a game changer.

—Nicole Walters, founder & CEO, The Monetized Life

Christy Wright's *Business Boutique* is a best-in-class, step-by-step guide for any entrepreneur. Her conversational tone and engaging stories make difficult business concepts and planning seem simple. Even the most cynical individual will believe that they too can live out their dream! This is a must-read!

—Chanda Bell, founder and co-CEO, Creatively Classic Activities and Books; co-author of *The Elf on the Shelf*®

I love small business and seeing people take their passion and turn it into a business. *Business Boutique* will be a welcome companion to any woman who wants to take her dream from being a dream to being a profitable reality.

—Dr. Henry Cloud, PhD, author of *Boundaries: When to Say Yes, How to Say No to Take Control of Your Life*